HEALTHY
Country Cooking

Grandma's
Secret Recipes

By Sharon Broer

Healthy Country Cooking by Sharon Broer
Published by B & A Publications
100 Ariana Blvd
Auburndale, Florida 33823

Library of Congress Catalog Card Number:
ISBN 0-9716215-3-5

This book is not intended to provide medical advice or to take the place of medical advice and treatment from your personal physician. Readers are advised to consult their own doctors or other qualified health professional regarding the treatment of their medical problems. Neither the publisher nor the author takes any responsibility for any possible consequences from any treatment, action or application of medicine, supplement, herb or preparation to any person reading or following the information in this book. If readers are taking prescription medications, they should consult with their physicians and not take themselves off medicines to start supplementation without the proper supervision of a physician.

Cover –
    Photography: Tim Kelly – Orlando, FL
    Hair: Vickie Davis – Lake Wales, FL
    Stove: Wolf – Westye Group
    Mantel: Busby Cabinets – Orlando, FL
    Counter Tops: Lakeland Granite & Marble, Inc.

Printed in the United States of America

DEDICATION

I am dedicating this cookbook to Shirley Bennett,
my wonderful mother who taught me to cook at a very young age.
Thanks for the memories Mom.

FORWARD

I was privileged to start my Health and Fitness company in 1980, the same year I graduated from Graduate School at Florida State University. However, it was not until 1984, after Sharon and I were married, that I felt my life and business were complete. We have now been married for twenty-one years and have four incredibly healthy children. By the Grace of God, we have been able to work together, helping millions around the world to realize the importance of proper health choices.

If it had not been for Sharon's first cookbook, *The Maximum Energy Cookbook*, I would not have had a way to actually provide people with healthy, great-tasting recipes. Since the publication of the first cookbook, we have been besieged by requests to write a healthy "normal food,""easy to find ingredients," and "simple to understand" new cookbook.

Keeping all the requests in mind from over the years, Sharon and two of her friends, Brenda Browning and Kathleen Harris, have worked together to compile the wonderful recipes in this cookbook. Generational favorite recipes have been taken and made as healthy as possible. The recipes in the cookbook do not contain pork, shellfish, hydrogenated oils, trans-fat, artificial flavors or coloring. The recipes are, however, delicious.

Sharon, Kathleen, Brenda, and I hope that you enjoy these wonderful, kitchen-tested favorites.

TABLE OF CONTENTS

Dedication iv
Forward vi
Introduction x

1
Why Organic? 1
Growing a Healthy Family

2
The Pampered Pantry 5
Stock It Right

3
The Breakfast Bar 13
Eggs, Pancakes, Casseroles & More

4
The Appetizer Plate 33
Spreads, Salsas, Dips & More

5
The Soup Bowl 49
Soup, Chili, Stew & Gumbo

6
The Bread Basket 61
Bread, Biscuits, Muffins & Rolls

7 The Salad Cart 77
Fruit, Veggies, Rice, Chicken & Tuna

8 The Dinner Table 97
Main Entrees: Fish, Chicken, Turkey

9 The Vegetable Platter 147
Side Dishes: Veggies, Rice & Casseroles

10 The Dessert Tray 179
Cakes, Pies & Puddings

11 The Cookie Cutter 213
Cookies, Bars & Tarts

12 The Herb Garden 243
Tea, Broth, Salad & More

In My Kitchen 146
Appendix A 244
    Weights & Measures
Appendix B 245
    Roasting Chart
Appendix C 246
    Fun Cooking Hints
Appendix D 247
    Tips for Creating a Warm, Workable Kitchen
More Books and CD's by Ted & Sharon Broer 248-253

INTRODUCTION

What do you visualize when someone mentions, "country cooking"? Most of us think of grandma's country kitchen filled with aromas of her freshly baked cakes and breads. Others may recall memories of your mom baking your favorite meal on Sunday afternoon. Country cooking makes me think of sitting in my grandmother's kitchen, helping her dip the chicken in the batter to fry up crispy artery blockers. I remember watching her take her famous pound cake out of the oven while I revved up the electric mixer, attempting to beat the potatoes into the perfect consistency the way my mother did so successfully every time (and still does). Every Christmas day, while we are preparing our Christmas dinner, she still reminds me, "Make sure you beat the potatoes with the butter and don't add the milk until all the lumps are gone, or you'll have lumpy mashed potatoes." I thought lumpy mashed potatoes were in.

There is a famous restaurant chain that displays interstate billboards, drawing hungry customers to their locations with their "country cooking" motto. The food is great and you can shop while you wait. Unfortunately, we no longer eat there because they use margarine instead of butter in all of their food. If enough people would voice their concerns about the use of hydrogenated oil (or trans-fats, margarine), we could make a difference and good restaurants like this one would be "butter friendly."

When we decided to create *Healthy Country Cooking*, we wanted to offer a cookbook that contained recipes that you and I grew up with, but consisted of good, wholesome ingredients.

Country cooking isn't just southern cooking. It's northern, eastern and western as well. It's cooking passed down from generation to generation. It's families spending special times together-cooking together, eating together and fellow-shipping together.

Just recently, I met someone who had a major impact on my life in just the four hours I had the privilege of meeting her and spending time in her company. Ted and I were recently in Canada where Ted was a guest on 100 Huntley Street for three days. One of the days, Cheryl McGuinness was a guest being interviewed on the same show. Cheryl McGuinness is the wife of Tom McGuinness, the co-pilot of American Airlines Flight 11, the first airplane to crash into the World Trade Center on September 11th. That afternoon the three of us toured a castle in Toronto together. Cheryl was so kind to give me one of her books, *Beauty Beyond the Ashes*.

The time I spent with Cheryl and then reading her book on our return trip home caused me to do some deep introspective thinking. I thought of things I had known before, but had never seen them through someone else's eyes who had experienced such a tragic loss. She exemplified the importance of leaving a legacy in the lives of our children.

We do not realize how important it is today to "get back to the basics," to spend more time with our family, and to "make memories" our children and grandchildren will always remember and pass on to their children. In times gone by, the kitchen was the focus of the home and was a gathering place while meals were being cooked. I try to involve every one of our children in helping me in the kitchen in some way. Sometimes it gets a little crowded in there, and I suddenly realize everyone in the family is in the kitchen at the same time. Times such as these in the kitchen make me know that Ted and I have been and still are, making memories in the lives of our children.

I encourage you to stop and "smell the muffins." If you are eating out consistently, try to slow down and make some memories in the kitchen with your family. Try to spend some quality time together other than loading up the car and hurriedly driving to the fast food restaurant.

In this cookbook I have tried to convey the importance of time spent together, especially in the kitchen. Cheryl was instrumental in my decision to include photographs in the cookbook. Years from now our children, and hopefully yours, will remember the aroma of a special recipe which was made together in the kitchen. Perhaps you will also take a picture to capture the moment when "the memory was made."

Today it is frustrating in trying to make wise choices when it comes to eating. We are on a roller coaster of fad diets: low carb, high protein, low fat, no fat, and many others. Ted and I have been teaching healthy dietary life styles for twenty years. We encourage you to follow Ted's "Top Ten Foods Never to Eat" list and enjoy the healthy recipes in the cookbook. If you stay with smaller portions and maintain a reasonable calorie level for your size, along with exercise, you will be able to maintain your ideal body weight.

We have so many programs and materials to help you stay trim and feel great. If you are not sure where to start I suggest you listen to our "Eat, Drink, and be Healthy" CD teaching series. Then next, read Ted's book, *Maximum Energy*. For those of you over 20, 30, or 40 and beyond, our DVD of the same title, "20, 30, 40, and Beyond" is excellent. Also, my *Maximum Energy* cookbook is a good companion cookbook to *Healthy Country Cooking*, and is excellent to help you get started on a healthy eating life style.

I've compiled some of your old favorite recipes, but replaced the bad ingredients with good ones. The recipes in this cookbook contain no artificial colors, artificial flavors, canola oil, chemical additives, chlorine, fluoride, MSG, Nutra Sweet, pork, shellfish, soy, Splenda or tofu. Isn't that refreshing?

Have fun using this book, and thank you for the priviledge of allowing us to be instrumental in helping you and your family enjoy a healthier lifestyle.

NOTES

Why Organic

Growing a
Healthy
Family

1

All of the ingredients I use when cooking at home are organic. Why use organic food, you may ask? There are three main reasons I use organics: nutrition, quality and taste. Organic foods are grown without synthetic fertilizers, pesticides or herbicides.

Organic refers not to the food itself, but to how it is processed. Organic food production is based on a system of farming that maintains and replenishes the fertility of the soil, producing fresh foods that contain the highest possible vitamin and mineral content.

For a processed product like soup, juice, cereal, etc. to be labeled organic, 95% of the ingredients must be organically produced. If the phrase "made with organic ingredients" appears on the front of a package, that means the primary ingredients are organic and make up more than 50% of the total ingredients by weight. Organic ingredients must be specifically listed in the ingredient listing panel, such as "organic onions, garlic, organic rice, cilantro."

Organic farms must undergo a three-year transitional period. During this time, no synthetic pesticides or herbicides may be used. This allows the soil time to build its mineral stores like zinc, potassium and iron. When the soil is ready for production, these minerals will be readily available in their natural state.

Organic Dairy Food

Certified organic dairy products are processed from the milk of cows or goats that are fed organically grown feed. These animals are not given growth hormones or antibiotics. The grazing pastures are pesticide free and abide by organic farming land standards.

No Homogenization

When buying organic dairy products, make sure they are not homogenized. When milk is homogenized, it becomes a type of slow poison for the circulatory system. Homogenization was introduced in this country in 1932. It is a mechanical process in which the milk is passed through pipes and fine filters at a pressure of 2500 psi and a speed of 600 feet per second. Thus, the fat portion of the milk is broken up into very small globules. Almost all of the milk in the United States is homogenized. Milk is homogenized primarily to extend its shelf life. Homogenization does nothing to make the milk a better product from a nutritional standpoint. In the textbook of dietary chemistry, homogenized milk is classified as "denatured."

Milk fat contains a substance called xanthine oxidase. When non-homogenized milk is consumed, both the fat and the xanthine oxidase are digested. Homogenized milk allows some of the xanthine oxidase to pass undigested, which when entering the bloodstream, creates havoc within the artery walls.

Raw milk and other dairy products are becoming more available. We drink raw milk and our kids love it. It is legal in many states to sell raw dairy products. When milk is obtained from disease-free cows or goats and regular testing is administered for high sanitary standards, raw dairy products are my first choice. These unpasteurized and unhomogenized dairy products can be purchased in some grocery stores and in most whole food markets. One brand I like is Alta-Dena. They make delicious raw butter.

NOTES

The Pampered Pantry

2

Stock It Right

One of the most irritating moments in the kitchen is when I'm right in the middle of throwing together a new recipe and realize I am missing one particular ingredient. My personality is more on the sanguine side when I'm in the kitchen. I love throwing things together and not planning. This has led to some incredible recipes in the past, but it has also led to a frustrated cook....me. What would I do without my pantry?

Webster defines a pantry as "a room or closet used for storing (as provisions) or from which food is brought to the table." Your pantry may be one or two cabinets in your kitchen. It may be a closet in your hall. Whatever your pantry is, big or small, short or tall, you need a space in or by your kitchen to organize your food and recipe ingredients. I love organization. I love to walk in my pantry and find exactly what I need instantly, admiring the organized shelves that I spent hours laboring on, and in the meantime, thinking to myself, "I surely do wish it would stay this way." Three weeks later, I find myself in the pantry putting things back where they belong in some organized fashion. If you can keep your pantry area organized, time spent in the kitchen will be more efficient and enjoyable.

I find it so humorous when my husband Ted is on a live radio broadcast and I hear him saying, "Hey, if you're in the Orlando area, come by and look in our pantry. You'll realize that we really do practice what we preach." Thankfully, we have not had anyone knock on our front door asking to look in our pantry. But when we do have dinner guests, the pantry seems to always be visited.

I've said in the past, you can know the state of someone's health by looking in their medicine chest. The same can be true about one's pantry.

Keeping A Well-Stocked Pantry

By keeping a well-stocked pantry, you will be able to enjoy putting your grocery list together more efficiently. When cooking or baking, you will be able to flow more easily with your recipes.

I would like to take you through my pantry and share with you ingredients and brand names that can be used in place of those you may already be using. Many of these items can be purchased in the health food section of your local grocery store or at a whole foods market. Ninety-nine percent of the items in my pantry are organic. Hopefully after reading the "Why Organic" section of this book, you will slowly begin to replace your food items. If you have any problems finding some of these ingredients, many of them can be ordered through our office. For information on these products, call our office at 1-800-726-1834.

Your pantry should include the following items:

Almond Butter: Much better for you than peanut butter.

Angel Hair Pasta: Artichoke or tomato basil are my favorites. I use DeBoles.

Cornbread Mix: Good, quick for a cornbread base. I use Arrowhead Mills.

Baking Mix: Great for pie crust, biscuits, etc. I use Arrowhead Mills.

Beans-Canned or Dried: (a good variety-you decide)

- Organic black beans

- Organic refried beans

- Organic black-eyed peas

Brown Rice: There are many types of organic rice. I use several of these in the recipes in this book. My favorite brand is Lundberg.

- Arborio Rice: A creamy, chewy texture, Arborio is used in the Italian rice dish called risotto.
- Basmati Rice: Drier texture with exotic aroma. Use in stir-fry, salads, stuffing, pilaf and desserts.
- Brown long-grain rice: After cooking, the grains remain fluffy and separate. Suitable in stuffing, pilafs, salads, casseroles and stir-fry.
- Brown short-grain rice: One of the most full flavored rices. After cooking, grains are soft and cling together. Especially suitable for puddings, rice balls, croquettes and risotto.
- Japonica Rice: Juicy, textured rice with a nutty mushroom-like flavor and sweet spiciness; originated in Japan.
- Jasmine Rice: Considered the premium rice of choice in Thailand, with a floral aroma and flavor. It contains 10% rice bran that gives it a light tan color and an oat-like flavor; great for pilaf, soup and salads.

- Sushi Rice: Japanese short-grain rice that is superb in traditional sushi rolls, salads and other Asian dishes.
- Wehani Rice: Long-grain rice that separates beautifully. Has a deep red color and nutty flavor which takes average recipes to new dimensions.

Cake Mixes: I use only organic mixes. I like Simple Organic brand.

Cereal: I use high fiber, low sugar organic brands.

Chicken Broth: I like Pacific or Imagine brands. The organic comes in 16 ounce and 32 ounce cartons.

Chocolate Chips: I like Rapunzel organic; Ghirardelli is good too, but it's not organic.

Coffee Substitutes:

- Caffix: All natural, instant beverage; 100% caffeine free, made with malted barley and chicory; a product of Switzerland.
- Green Tea: I use only organic green tea; I like Long Life organic with ginseng.
- Roma: Roasted malt barley and chicory beverage.

Condiments:

- Mayonnaise: I use Hains safflower mayonnaise. I don't care for the low-fat because it is too watery. Use ½ low-fat sour cream in recipes for less calories.
- Catsup: I use Hains brand.
- Mustard: Any organic brand is fine.
- Peanut Butter: Fresh ground is my first choice.
- Preserves & Marmalades: Any organic brand is fine. I love apricot, orange and raspberry.

Crackers: There are many good organic brands.

Cream of Mushroom Soup: I like Amy's but there are a lot of other good organic brands.

Flour:

- Unbleached wheat flour-sometimes, but not very often, I may need to use unbleached white flour
- Whole wheat flour-good for a grainier texture
- Whole wheat pastry flour-good for cakes and fluffier items

Milks:

- Condensed Milk: Organic sweetened contains only milk and organic sugar. I use Bantine brand.
- Coconut Milk: I use organic lite by Thai Kitchen.
- Evaporated Milk: I use Santini brand.
- Goat's Milk: Used for children 2 and under
  (see my book *Train Up Your Children in the Way They Should Eat* and *The Maximum Energy Cookbook* for more information)
- Raw Cow's Milk: My first choice see page 3

Oils:

- Grape Seed Oil: Good oil for light frying.
- Macadamia Nut Oil: High in linoleic acid.
- Olive Oil: Use premium select, extra virgin, cold pressed, green in color. My favorite brand is Lucini from Italy.

Ramen Noodles: Use in recipes for a flavorful twist.

Rolled Oats: Organic whole grain oats, high in protein and fiber.

Spices: Keep at least one each of these organic spices. I like to use fresh cilantro, parsley and basil whenever possible.

- Basil
- Chili powder
- Cilantro
- Cinnamon
- Cumin
- Garlic powder
- Onion flakes
- Parsley
- Sage

Sweeteners:

- Fructose: The predominant sweetener found in honey, fruit and berries. Use ⅓ less fructose in your recipes instead of sugar. 1 cup of sugar is equal to ⅔ cup fructose.
- Stevia: A natural, herbal sweetener from Brazil. Great for sweetening fresh lemonade.
- Brown rice syrup: Allergen-free alternative to other sweeteners; a good replacement for honey. Use 1¼ cup brown rice syrup for 1 cup of sugar, using ¼ cup less liquid in your recipes. I like Lundberg.
- Molasses: Use high quality brands; they contain iron.
- Brown sugar: True brown sugar contains the natural molasses of the sugar cane. Others are white sugar with caramel coloring added. I use Billington's dark brown molasses sugar, a product of England.
- Rapadura: Whole organic sugar from unrefined, evaporated sugar cane juice.
- Agave nectar: Extracted from the core of the agave, a cactus-like plant native to Mexico. 90% fruit sugar content helps it to absorb slowly into the body, decreasing highs and lows associated with hypoglycemia. This is my favorite sweetener.

Tomato Products: (any organic brand)

- Diced tomatoes

- Tomato paste

- Tomato soup (carton)

- Dried tomatoes

Tortilla Chips: I use organic brands that contain no canola oil.

*Sharon's well-stocked pantry makes
cooking easier and more efficient.*

NOTES

The Breakfast Bar

Eggs,
Pancakes,
Casseroles
and More

3

TURKEY SAUSAGE PATTIES

1 pound ground turkey breast

1 tablespoon crushed red pepper

2 tablespoon paprika

1 tablespoon ground sage

1 teaspoon sea salt

Mix all of the above ingredients together. Form into patties. Cook on medium heat in an iron skillet until brown. These may also be frozen. **Serves 4-6**

FANCY FRENCH TOAST

8 slices whole wheat bread

Butter

1 teaspoon cinnamon

¼ cup milk

Maple syrup

4 large eggs

¼ teaspoon sea salt

With a whisk or fork, mix the eggs, milk, salt and cinnamon together. Slice the bread in half. Heat an iron skillet on medium heat. Spray skillet with olive oil or use a teaspoon of organic butter. Place bread slices in egg mixture for 30 seconds. Place in hot skillet until brown on each side. Serve with warm maple syrup. **Serves 4-6**

GRANNY'S GRITS

1⅓ cup grits

½ teaspoon sea salt

1 cup shredded low fat cheese

1 tablespoon butter

5⅓ cups boiling water

Bring water, salt, and butter to a full boil. Add grits and stir until it comes back to a full boil. Add shredded cheese and stir until boiling. Cover, reduce heat to low. Stir occasionally. Cook 10 minutes or until desired doneness. For thinner grits, add more water. For thicker, creamier grits, cook longer. **Serves 6**

COUNTRY SAUSAGE GRAVY

1 pound ground turkey sausage
3 tablespoons butter
1 teaspoon sea salt
2-3 cups milk

½ cup whole wheat flour
¼ cup olive oil
¼ teaspoon pepper

Brown sausage in butter over medium heat. Add olive oil, salt, pepper, and flour. Stir constantly until flour mixture is medium to dark brown. Add milk to mixture until it reaches desired thickness. Serve over biscuits or grits. **Serves 4**

EGGS OVER EASY

8 large eggs
Sea salt (to taste)

2 tablespoons butter
Pepper (to taste)

In a large iron skillet, heat butter. Break one egg into hot skillet and wait until white is partially cooked. Carefully slide spatula under the middle of the egg and turn over quickly and gently. Cook until white appears to be solid. Slide spatula under egg, lift gently and place on plate. **Serves 4-6**

SOUTHERN SCRAMBLED EGGS

1 cup shredded low fat cheese
8 eggs
½ teaspoon sea salt

¼ cup diced bell pepper
2 tablespoons butter
¼ cup milk

Place butter in iron skillet. Heat skillet over medium heat. Mix all remaining items and pour into hot skillet. Stir constantly until desired doneness. **Serves 4**

Amazing Oatmeal Casserole

⅓ cup melted butter

1½ teaspoon aluminum free baking powder

¼ teaspoon sea salt

½ teaspoon ground cinnamon

1 large egg, beaten

¾ cup milk

1½ cups rolled oats

½ teaspoon vanilla

Preheat oven to 350°. Mix together the butter, eggs and vanilla. Add remaining ingredients. Pour into greased 9-by-5-inch pan. Bake for 45 minutes. **Serves 4**

Rice Breakfast Burrito

¼ cup diced celery

½ cup green and/or red bell peppers, diced

½ cup shredded carrots

¼ cup fat free milk

1-2 cups natural shredded cheddar

¼ teaspoon black pepper

3 cups cooked short grain brown rice

Salsa, if desired

½ cup diced mushrooms

½ cup diced onions

1 tablespoon butter

½ cup sliced olives

8 eggs

¼ teaspoon sea salt

6 warm tortillas

Heat large skillet over medium-high heat. Add butter. When butter bubbles, add vegetables and cook for 5 minutes. In a separate bowl, whisk together the eggs, milk, salt and pepper. Reduce heat to low-medium and pour eggs over vegetables. Continue to cook and add rice. Heat for 2 minutes and then serve immediately or spoon into warmed tortillas. Top with cheese and salsa, if desired. **Serves 6**

PECAN PANCAKES

3 eggs, separated
1¼ cups whole grain flour
¼ cup bran or cornmeal

1½ cups milk
Chopped pecans
Grape seed oil

Place the yolks in a large bowl and whip them with a fork. Beat the whites separately in a grease-free bowl until they hold stiff peaks. Stir milk into the yolks, followed by the flour and bran or cornmeal. Fold in the beaten egg whites gently with a fork using light whipping motion until well mixed. Heat and oil a griddle. Spoon the batter onto the griddle to form pancakes not more than 3 inches in diameter so they will cook evenly. Sprinkle pecans on top of the pancakes. As the pancakes puff up and begin to bubble on the top, turn them over. Watch them closely until the bottoms become dark. **Serves 4**

APPLE FRENCH TOAST

3 large green apples, cut in thin wedges
12 slices firm whole grain bread
¼ cup brown sugar
12 oz cream cheese
Cinnamon

1 stick butter
8 eggs
1 quart milk
2 tablespoons vanilla

Set rack in lower third of oven and preheat oven to 350°. Butter a 13-by-9-inch baking pan. In a skillet, melt the butter with the brown sugar and 1 tablespoon water. Add the apples and cook, stirring for 2 to 3 minutes. Transfer to the baking dish and let cool. Cut cream cheese into cubes and arrange evenly over the apples. Cut the slices of bread in half diagonally and layer over the apples to cover the whole dish. In a large mixing bowl, beat together eggs, milk and vanilla. Pour the egg mixture over the bread, taking care to dampen all the bread. Sprinkle with cinnamon. Bake for 40 to 50 minutes, until golden and puffed. Cool 10 minutes before serving. **Serves 6-8**

Yummy Waffles

1 cup milk

½ cup brown rice flour

2 teaspoons aluminum free baking powder

1 egg

Chocolate chips (optional)

¼ cup grape seed oil

1 teaspoon vanilla

½ cup millet flour

1 teaspoon fructose

Natural peanut butter (optional)

Plug in a waffle iron and set timer for 6 minutes. In a mixing bowl, combine milk, oil, egg and vanilla. Blend all with an egg beater. Add both flours, baking powder and fructose. Add chocolate chips or peanut butter, if desired. After 6 minutes of heating, wipe inside of waffle iron with a pastry brush dipped in oil, then pour the waffle batter onto the grid, close the lid and let cook for 3 minutes. When done, take waffles out and lay on a cake rack to cool. **Serves 4-6**

Cheesy Poached Eggs

2 whole grain english muffins, split

¾ cup shredded cheddar cheese

3 ounces cream cheese with chives, cut up

½ cup milk

4 eggs

⅛ teaspoon pepper

Toast muffins. In a medium skillet combine cheeses, milk and pepper. Cook and stir over medium heat until cheeses melt. Break 1 egg into a cup. Carefully slide the egg into the cheese mixture. Repeat with remaining eggs. Cover and cook over medium-low heat for 3 to 5 minutes or to desired doneness. Top each muffin half with an egg. Stir cheese mixture with a wire whisk and spoon over eggs. **Serves 4**

ASPARAGUS CASSEROLE

10 ounce package frozen asparagus

¼ cup chopped onion

¼ cup chopped green pepper

2 tablespoons butter

2 tablespoons unbleached flour

½ teaspoon dry mustard

¼ teaspoon sea salt

¼ teaspoon pepper

½ cup shredded cheddar cheese

¾ cup milk

3 hard cooked eggs, chopped

2 teaspoons melted butter

¼ cup crushed whole wheat crackers

Cook asparagus according to package directions; drain. For sauce, in a medium saucepan cook onion and green pepper in the 2 tablespoons butter until tender. Stir in flour, dry mustard, salt and pepper. Add milk. Cook and stir until thickened and bubbly. Add cheese; stir until melted. Reserve ¼ cup asparagus. Stir remaining asparagus and chopped eggs into sauce. Pour into a 1-quart casserole. Bake, covered, in a 375° oven for 10 minutes. Arrange reserved asparagus on top. Combine crushed crackers with the melted butter and sprinkle on top of casserole. Bake, uncovered, for 10 minutes more. **Serves 6**

SCRAMBLED EGG CASSEROLE

¼ cup chopped green pepper

3 tablespoons butter

1 tablespoon unbleached flour

6 beaten eggs

¼ cup seasoned fine dry bread crumbs

2 tablespoons diced pimento

¾ cup shredded American cheese

⅔ cup milk

In a large skillet, cook green pepper in 1 tablespoon butter until tender. Add eggs; cook over medium heat without stirring until mixture begins to set on bottom and around edges. Lift and fold partially cooked eggs so uncooked portion flows underneath. Continue cooking until just set. Transfer to a 1-quart casserole dish. In a small saucepan melt 1 tablespoon butter. Stir in the flour and ⅛ teaspoon pepper. Add milk all at once. Cook and stir until thickened and bubbly. Stir in cheese until melted. Stir in pimento. Fold cheese mixture into cooked eggs. Melt remaining butter and toss with breadcrumbs. Sprinkle over egg mixture. Bake at 350° for 15 to 20 minutes or until hot. **Serves 4-6**

VEGGIE FRENCH OMELET

2 eggs

⅛ teaspoon sea salt

⅓ cup sliced zucchini

¼ cup shredded cheddar cheese

1 tablespoon water

2 tablespoons butter

⅛ teaspoon dried basil

Dash of pepper

In a bowl combine eggs, water, salt and pepper. Using a fork, beat until combined but not frothy. In a skillet with flared sides, heat 1 tablespoon of the butter until a drop of water sizzles. Lift and tilt the pan to coat the sides. Add the egg mixture to the skillet and cook over medium heat. As eggs set, run a spatula around the edge of the skillet, lifting eggs and letting uncooked portion flow underneath. In a separate saucepan, add the zucchini and the remaining 1 tablespoon butter. Add basil and sauté until zucchini is tender. When the eggs are set but still shiny, spoon the zucchini and cheddar cheese down the center of the omelet. Remove from heat and fold omelet in half. **Serves 1**

CHEESY ROLL-UPS

2 cups sliced mushrooms

½ cup sliced green onion

½ cup chopped green pepper

8 (7-inch) flour tortillas

1 tablespoon unbleached flour

2 cups shredded cheddar cheese

2 tablespoons butter

4 beaten eggs

2 cups milk

¼ teaspoon garlic powder

Hot pepper sauce

In a saucepan, cook mushrooms, onion and green pepper in butter until tender; drain. Dividing mushroom mixture evenly, spoon along center of each tortilla. Divide 1½ cups of the cheese among the tortillas. Roll up the tortillas and place seam side down in a greased baking dish. In a bowl stir together eggs, milk, flour, garlic powder and pepper sauce. Pour over rolled tortillas. Bake at 350° for 35 to 40 minutes or until set. Sprinkle the remaining cheese over the top. Let stand for 10 minutes. Cut into 6 squares. **Serves 4-6**

HUEVOS RANCHEROS

½ cup chopped onion

1 (16 ounce) can tomatoes, chopped

2 tablespoons diced green chili peppers

3 (6-inch) corn tortillas

¾ cup shredded Monterey jack cheese

1 tablespoon olive oil

1 teaspoon chili powder

⅛ teaspoon garlic powder

1 teaspoon olive oil

6 eggs

In a large skillet cook chopped onion in the 1 tablespoon olive oil until tender. Stir in undrained tomatoes, chili peppers, chili powder and garlic powder. Simmer, uncovered, for 5 to 10 minutes or until slightly thickened. Meanwhile, place tortillas on a baking sheet and brush lightly with the 1 teaspoon olive oil. Bake at 350° for about 10 minutes or until crisp. Break 1 egg into a measuring cup. Carefully slide egg into simmering tomato mixture. Repeat with remaining eggs. Simmer gently, covered, for 3 to 5 minutes or to desired doneness. To serve, place tortillas on 3 plates. Top each tortilla with 2 eggs; spoon tomato mixture over eggs. Sprinkle with cheese and hot pepper sauce, if desired. **Serves 4**

BREAKFAST PUFFS

⅛ cup fructose

1½ cups unbleached flour

1½ teaspoons aluminum free baking powder

⅛ teaspoon sea salt

½ cup milk

½ teaspoon ground cinnamon

¼ cup fructose

¼ teaspoon ground nutmeg

1 egg, beaten

⅓ cup butter, melted

Combine the ⅛ cup fructose and the cinnamon in a small bowl; set aside. In a separate bowl, stir together the flour, ¼ cup fructose, baking powder, nutmeg and salt. In another bowl, combine the egg, milk and melted butter; add to flour mixture, stirring just until moistened. Lightly grease muffin cups or line with paper baking cups; fill ⅔ full. Bake at 350° for 20 to 25 minutes or until golden. Immediately dip tops into 3 tablespoons melted butter, then into the fructose-cinnamon mixture. Serve warm. **Serves 8**

FRUIT COFFEE CAKE

1½ cups raspberries

2 tablespoons cornstarch

1½ cups unbleached flour

½ teaspoon aluminum free baking powder

¼ teaspoon aluminum free baking soda

¼ cup unbleached flour

½ cup fructose

6 tablespoons butter

1 beaten egg

½ cup buttermilk

½ teaspoon vanilla

¼ cup water

In a saucepan combine the fruit and water. Bring to boiling; reduce heat. Cover and simmer about 5 minutes or until tender. Combine ¼ cup of the fructose and the cornstarch. Stir into fruit mixture. Cook and stir until thickened and bubbly. Cook and stir 2 minutes more. Set aside. In a mixing bowl stir together ½ cup of the fructose, flour, baking powder and soda. Cut in 4 tablespoons of the butter until mixture resembles fine crumbs. Combine egg, buttermilk and vanilla. Add to flour mixture. Stir until just moistened. Spread half of the batter into an 8-by-8-by-2-inch baking pan. Spread fruit mixture over batter. Drop remaining batter in small mounds atop filling. Combine the remaining fructose and the ¼ cup flour. Cut in remaining butter until mixture resembles fine crumbs. Sprinkle over batter. Bake in a 350° oven for 40 to 45 minutes or until golden brown. Serve warm. **Serves 6-8**

BUCKWHEAT PANCAKES

½ cup whole wheat flour

1 tablespoon brown sugar

2 teaspoons aluminum free baking powder

2 tablespoons macadamia nut oil

½ cup buckwheat flour

¼ teaspoon sea salt

1 beaten egg

1 cup milk

In a mixing bowl stir together both flours, brown sugar, baking powder and salt. In another mixing bowl combine egg, milk and oil. Add to flour mixture all at once. Stir mixture just until blended but still slightly lumpy. Pour about ¼ cup batter onto a hot, lightly greased griddle or heavy skillet for each standard size pancake or about 1 tablespoon batter for each dollar size pancake. Cook until pancakes are golden brown, turning to cook second sides when pancakes have bubbly surfaces and slightly dry edges. **Serves 4**

Peanut Butter Coffee Cake

½ cup packed brown sugar

½ cup unbleached flour

¼ cup natural peanut butter

¾ cup packed brown sugar

2 teaspoons aluminum free baking powder

½ teaspoon aluminum free baking soda

½ cup natural peanut butter

3 tablespoons butter

¼ teaspoon sea salt

2 cups unbleached flour

1 cup milk

2 eggs

¼ cup butter

For topping, in a bowl stir together the ½ cup brown sugar and ½ cup unbleached flour; cut in ¼ cup peanut butter and 3 tablespoons butter until crumbly. Set aside. In a bowl stir together the 2 cups flour, 1 cup brown sugar, baking powder, baking soda and salt. Add milk, ½ cup peanut butter, eggs and ¼ cup butter. Beat with an electric mixer on low speed until blended. Beat at high speed for 3 minutes, scraping the sides of the bowl frequently. Pour batter into a greased 13-by-9-by-2-inch baking pan, spreading evenly. Sprinkle with topping mixture. Bake in a 375° oven for about 30 minutes or until a toothpick inserted in the center comes out clean. **Serves 8-10**

Baked Oatmeal

2½ cups regular oats

¼ cup steel-cut oats

2 teaspoons aluminum free baking powder

2 cups milk

⅓ cup applesauce

2 cups fresh chopped apples & pears

⅛ cup packed brown sugar

¼ cup oat bran

½ teaspoon sea salt

½ teaspoon ground cinnamon

1 egg, beaten

¼ cup grape seed oil

⅛ cup fructose

Preheat oven to 400°. In a large mixing bowl stir together rolled oats, oat bran, steel-cut oats, baking powder, salt and cinnamon; set aside. In a medium bowl stir together milk, egg, applesauce, oil, fructose and brown sugar; add to oat mixture, stirring until combined. Turn into a lightly buttered 2-quart casserole dish. Bake, uncovered, for 20 minutes. Stir mixture. Gently fold in fruit. Bake, uncovered, for 20 minutes more or until top is lightly browned. **Serves 4-6**

NUTTY STICKY BUNS

½ cup maple syrup

2 tablespoons butter

⅓ cup chopped pecans

2 cups unbleached flour

2 teaspoons aluminum free baking powder

⅛ cup fructose

¼ cup brown sugar

1 tablespoon water

¼ teaspoon sea salt

¾ cup milk

⅓ cup butter

½ teaspoon ground cinnamon

In a small saucepan combine syrup, brown sugar, the 2 tablespoons butter and the water. Cook and stir over low heat just until butter melts. *Do not boil!* Spread onto the bottom of a 9-by-9-by-2-inch baking pan. Sprinkle nuts over syrup mixture. In a mixing bowl stir together flour, baking powder and salt. Cut in the ⅓ cup butter until mixture resembles coarse crumbs. Make a well in the center. Add milk all at once, stirring just until dough clings together. On a lightly floured surface, knead dough gently for 15 to 20 strokes. Roll dough into a 12-by-10-inch rectangle. Combine the fructose and cinnamon; sprinkle over dough. Roll up from one of the long sides. Slice into 1-inch pieces. Place, cut side down, atop nuts in the baking pan. Bake in a 425° oven for about 25 minutes or until golden. Immediately loosen sides and invert onto a serving plate. Spoon any topping in pan over rolls. Serve warm. **Serves 8-10**

SOUTH OF THE BORDER EGGS

8 eggs

¼ cup chopped onion

¼ cup chopped cilantro

1 corn tortilla, torn in small pieces
  or 1 cup broken tortilla chips

2 tablespoons butter

⅛ cup diced tomato

Sea salt & pepper to taste

In a large skillet melt butter on medium heat. Add onions and sauté for 2 minutes. In a mixing bowl, stir together eggs, salt and pepper. Add to onions in skillet. Add remaining ingredients. Stir and cook eggs until they are done, not runny, but not overcooked. **Serves 4-6**

PECAN BISCUIT SWIRLS

2 cups unbleached wheat flour

1 tablespoon aluminum free baking powder

1 beaten egg

1 tablespoon butter

¼ cup finely chopped pecans

1 tablespoon fructose

½ cup butter

½ cup milk

3 tablespoons brown sugar

¼ teaspoon sea salt

In a mixing bowl combine flour, fructose, baking powder and salt. Cut in the ½ cup butter until mixture resembles coarse crumbs. Make a well in the center. Combine egg and milk; add all at once to flour mixture. Stir just until dough clings together. On a floured surface, knead gently for 15 strokes. Roll dough into a 15-by-8-inch rectangle. Melt 1 tablespoon butter; brush on dough. Combine nuts and brown sugar; sprinkle over dough. Fold dough in half lengthwise. Cut into fifteen 1-inch wide strips. Holding a strip at both ends, carefully twist in opposite directions twice. Place on a lightly greased baking sheet, pressing both ends down. Repeat. Bake at 450° for 8 to 10 minutes or until golden. Serve warm. **Serves 8**

STUFFED APPLES

⅓ cup chopped dates

2 tablespoons chopped walnuts

5 tablespoons orange juice

¼ cup water

1 teaspoon grated orange peel

4 large apples

2 tablespoons granola

2 tablespoons brown sugar

4 teaspoons butter, melted

2 teaspoons lemon juice

⅛ teaspoon cinnamon

In a small bowl, combine dates, granola, walnuts, brown sugar, 1 tablespoon of orange juice, butter, lemon juice, orange peel and cinnamon; set aside. Core apples; set in 9-inch round baking dish. Fill cavities with date mixture, dividing equally. Combine remaining ¼ cup orange juice with water, pour around apples in dish. Cover and bake at 350° for 30 minutes. Uncover and continue baking 15 minutes longer, or until apples are tender when pierced with a fork. Serve warm or cold, drizzled with maple syrup. **Serves 4**

CHEESE GRITS

2 cups water
½ cup white or yellow grits
¼ cup shredded cheddar cheese

1 tablespoon butter
1 teaspoon sea salt

Cook grits on medium heat. Bring to a boil; reduce heat and simmer for 20 minutes or until creamy. Remove from heat. Add salt and stir in cheese until melted. **Serves 4-6**

PEPPER OMELET

1 teaspoon olive oil
2 teaspoons grated parmesan cheese, divided
1 sweet red pepper, thinly sliced
1 yellow pepper, thinly sliced

4 egg whites
½ teaspoon dried basil
¼ teaspoon black pepper

In a large non-stick frying pan over medium heat, warm oil; add the red and yellow peppers; cook, stirring frequently for 4 to 5 minutes. Keep warm over low heat. In a small bowl, lightly whisk together the egg whites, basil and black pepper. Coat a small non-stick frying pan with butter. Warm over medium-high heat for 1 minute. Add half of the egg mixture, swirling the pan to evenly coat the bottom. Cook for 30 seconds or until the eggs are set. Carefully loosen and flip; cook for 1 minute, or until firm. Sprinkle half of the peppers over the eggs. Fold to enclose the filling. **Serves 2**

BREAKFAST BANANA SPLITS

6 cups whole strawberries
6 cups vanilla yogurt

12 bananas
¾ cup chopped almonds

For individual servings, peel and split 1 banana. Place banana halves in serving bowl. Top with 1 cup strawberries, ½ cup yogurt and 1 tablespoon chopped, toasted almonds. **Serves 6-8**

APPLE & TURKEY SAUSAGE COFFEECAKE

4 nitrate free turkey sausage patties

2 tart apples, peeled, cored and sliced

1½ cups pancake batter

2 tablespoons brown sugar

1 teaspoon cinnamon

1 tablespoon butter

Preheat oven to 450°. In a large skillet, sauté sausage until browned. Pour off any fat from skillet, add apple slices, sprinkle with brown sugar and cinnamon. Sauté 1 to 2 minutes until apples just lose their crispness. Set aside. Place the butter in a well seasoned 9-inch iron skillet and heat in preheated oven until bubbly and hot. Arrange the sausage in the pan, cover with apples, distributing evenly. Pour the batter over the apples and bake until nicely browned, about 8 to 10 minutes. Cut into pie-shaped wedges and serve immediately. **Serves 4**

ORANGE COMPOTE AND GRANOLA

2 oranges, peeled, segmented & halved

½ cup seedless red grapes, halved

½ cup low-fat granola cereal

1 apple, diced

1 banana, sliced

2 tablespoons fresh orange juice

In a medium bowl toss together orange half segments, apple, grapes, banana and orange juice. Sprinkle granola over mixture; toss lightly. Serve immediately topped with yogurt. **Serves 4-6**

BREAKFAST PARFAIT

1⅓ cups unsweetened applesauce

1½ cups natural wheat & barley cereal

4 pitted prunes, for garnish

1 cup pitted prunes

1 pint plain yogurt

Combine applesauce and 1 cup of prunes. For each serving, in a 9 to 10 oz stemmed goblet, layer ¼ cup cereal, ¼ cup yogurt, ½ cup applesauce-prune mixture and another ½ cup yogurt. Top with 2 tablespoon cereal and garnish with a prune. Serve immediately or refrigerate up to 4 hours before serving. **Serves 2**

SWEET POTATO PANCAKES

2 tablespoons butter, melted

½ cup cooked, mashed sweet potatoes

½ teaspoon aluminum free baking powder

Sour cream

⅓ cup unbleached flour

¼ cup milk

1 egg

Maple syrup

Place sweet potatoes in a mixing bowl, add egg and mix well. Stir in the flour and add the baking powder. Add milk and stir. Stir in 1 tablespoon butter. The mixture should have the consistency of thick, lumpy sauce and be able to coat a wooden spoon. Place a non-stick or heavy iron skillet over medium heat and add ½ teaspoon butter. Spoon 3 tablespoons of batter per pancake into the skillet and cook until bubbles rise to the surface of the pancakes and break, about 1 to 2 minutes. Using a spatula, flip the pancakes and cook another 2 minutes. Remove pancakes from the skillet and keep warm on a covered plate in the oven. After the first batch is cooked, add as little butter as possible to keep the pancakes from sticking to the bottom of the pan. Repeat the procedure until all the pancakes are cooked. Serve with sour cream or maple syrup. **Serves 2**

ORANGE MARMALADE MUFFINS

1¾ cups unbleached flour

½ cup orange marmalade

2 teaspoons aluminum free baking powder

¾ cup milk

⅛ cup fructose

2 eggs

¾ teaspoon sea salt

4 tablespoons butter, melted

Icing:

⅓ cup orange marmalade

¼ cup fructose

1 tablespoon soft butter

Preheat oven to 400°. In a medium bowl, combine flour, salt, fructose and baking powder. In a separate bowl beat eggs; add butter, marmalade and milk. Add all at once to the dry ingredients. Stir quickly and lightly until just mixed. Mixture will be lumpy. Fill greased muffin tins ⅔ full. Bake 20 to 25 minutes. For icing, blend all ingredients in a small bowl until smooth. Frost muffins when cool. **Serves 8**

COCONUT FRENCH TOAST

3 eggs

¼ teaspoon vanilla

8 to 10 slices whole wheat bread

Maple syrup

3 cups milk

1 to 2 tablespoons butter

1 cup shredded coconut

Whisk eggs, milk and vanilla in a shallow dish or pie plate. Spread coconut on a pie plate. Melt 1 tablespoon butter on griddle or in large skillet over medium heat. Dip bread slices, one at a time, into egg mixture, turning once to allow egg mixture to soak into bread. Lay bread in coconut and press down. Coat each side. Place dipped slices on hot griddle. Cook, turning once, until lightly browned on both sides. Add more butter to griddle as needed. Serve with maple syrup. **Serves 6-8**

TEX-MEX SOFT SCRAMBLED EGGS

Remember in the movie *Runaway Bride*, Julia Roberts didn't know which way she liked her eggs cooked? However the boyfriend liked his eggs cooked, she would say those were her favorite. At the end of the movie, she made poached, over easy and scrambled and tasted them all, finally deciding on her own. My favorite kind of eggs are tex-mex eggs. Try these flavorful eggs and you never know, they may be your favorite.

4 to 6 large corn tortilla chips

¼ cup chopped tomatoes

¼ cup chopped cilantro

1 tablespoon butter

¼ cup chopped onions

4 eggs

In skillet, melt butter. Whisk eggs in bowl with a pinch of sea salt. Pour in skillet. Cook on medium heat, scraping bottom of pan so that eggs do not stick. Before eggs are fully scrambled, stir in onions, tomatoes and cilantro. Turn off heat to prevent eggs from drying out. Crumble chips in eggs and mix. Serve with grated cheese and salsa. **Serves 2**

STRAWBERRY BUTTERMILK PANCAKES

(Prepare syrup and butter before making pancakes; recipes are below)

1 cup whole wheat flour	¼ teaspoon sea salt
1 teaspoon aluminum free baking powder	1 large egg, beaten
½ teaspoon aluminum free baking soda	¾ cup buttermilk
¼ cup sweetened condensed milk	

Stir together flour, baking powder, baking soda and salt in a medium bowl. Add egg, milk and buttermilk. Stir until well blended. Pour ¼ cup of batter onto a hot griddle. Cook 1 to 2 minutes or until tops bubble. Flip and cook the other side 1 more minute. Repeat with remaining batter. Top with pecan agave butter and strawberry syrup.

PECAN BUTTER

½ cup softened butter	⅓ cup chopped pecans
¼ teaspoon ground cinnamon	

Mix together all ingredients until well blended. Chill and store in refrigerator.

STRAWBERRY SYRUP

1 quart fresh strawberries, sliced	½ cup maple syrup
⅛ cup fresh orange juice	

Combine all ingredients in blender. Quickly mix for no more than 20 seconds. Pour into saucepan and cook over medium heat until it starts to boil. Immediately remove from heat. Serve hot over pancakes. Store leftover syrup in refrigerator.

COCONUT PECAN OATMEAL

3 cups water

1 cup sweetened coconut milk

$\frac{1}{2}$ cup shredded coconut

1 tablespoon butter

$\frac{1}{4}$ teaspoon vanilla extract

1 cup coconut milk

2 cups whole oats

$\frac{1}{2}$ teaspoon sea salt

$\frac{1}{4}$ teaspoon ground cinnamon

Bring water, milk, oats, shredded coconut and salt to a boil. Reduce heat and simmer for 20 minutes, stirring occasionally. Remove from heat. Stir in remaining ingredients. Sweeten to taste with brown sugar. Top with pecans and a little milk.

NOTES

The Appetizer
Plate

Spreads,
Salsas,
Dips and
More

4

FIESTA BLACK BEAN AND CHEESE SPREAD

1 can black beans, rinsed & drained

½ cup cucumber, peeled, seeded, & chopped

¼ cup fresh chopped chives

1 tablespoon fresh lime juice

8 ounces goat cheese or cream cheese, softened

⅓ cup roasted tomato

½ cup sliced olives (optional)

½ teaspoon minced garlic

Dash of hot sauce

¼ cup light olive oil

Mix beans, tomato, cucumber, olives, and chives together, being careful not to mash completely. Beat the remaining ingredients until well blended. Add to bean mixture and stir well. Cover tightly and chill thoroughly.

NOTE: Additional olive oil may be added if needed. 1 teaspoon of your favorite dried herb may be added to the cheese mixture before stirring in the bean mixture.

CORN & BLACK BEAN CHEDDAR SALSA

2 cups cooked corn kernels

3 cups plum tomatoes, chopped

2 (15 ounce). cans black beans, rinsed & drained

⅓ cup lime juice

½ cup chopped cilantro

½ teaspoon black pepper

1 cup sliced black olives

1 teaspoon sea salt

½ cup diced onion

¼ cup light olive oil

2 cloves garlic, minced

1 jalapeno, seeded & minced

2½ cups shredded
   cheddar cheese

Combine all ingredients. Stir the mixture until well blended. Cover tightly and refrigerate at least 4 hours before serving. This salsa is very good served as a dip for fresh vegetables or tortilla chips. Serve over slices of fresh avocado and you have a wonderfully different salad.

DELUXE STUFFED MUSHROOMS

36 large fresh mushroom caps
1 pound nitrate-free smoked turkey sausage
1 tablespoon. chopped fresh chives

10 ounces feta cheese, soft
$\frac{1}{2}$ teaspoon fresh minced garlic

Preheat oven to 350°. Wipe mushroom caps inside and out with a damp paper towel and set aside. Place sausage, garlic, and chives in a skillet and cook over medium heat until sausage is brown and crumbly. Drain off all grease and place sausage mixture in bowl. Add goat cheese and stir well. Fill mushrooms with sausage mixture and place in a very shallow pan. Bake on middle oven rack for 10 minutes. Just before serving, place on top rack under a hot broiler for 3 to 5 minutes, watching very carefully.

STUFFED FIGS

36 figs, pitted
6 ounces goat cheese, softened
$\frac{1}{2}$ tablespoon. pure honey
$\frac{1}{2}$ cup toasted almonds

$\frac{1}{4}$ teaspoon sea salt
2 teaspoons chopped rosemary
$\frac{1}{2}$ teaspoon ground cinnamon

Mix cheese, salt, honey, almonds, rosemary, and cinnamon. Make a cut lengthwise in the side of each fig. Do not cut all the way in half. Stuff figs with cheese mixture and wrap tightly. Refrigerate until ready to serve.

STUFFED CELERY

Celery, cleaned and cut in 2 inch pieces
6 ounces goat cheese, softened
$\frac{1}{2}$ cup golden raisins soaked in hot apple juice
$\frac{1}{2}$ cup fresh chopped pineapple

$\frac{1}{8}$ teaspoon sea salt
1 tablespoon chopped parsley
$\frac{1}{2}$ cup toasted walnuts

Combine all ingredients except celery in a bowl and mix by hand until well blended. Stuff celery with the cheese mixture, wrap well, and refrigerate until ready to serve.

CHEESY PECAN BITES

8 ounces shredded gouda

1 cup unsalted butter, softened

1 tablespoon stone ground mustard

¼ teaspoon ground red pepper

1 tablespoon chopped fresh parsley

4 ounces shredded cheddar

1 teaspoon minced garlic

3 cups whole grain flour

¼ teaspoon sea salt

4 cups pecan halves

Preheat oven to 375°. In large bowl, combine gouda, cheddar, butter, mustard, and garlic. Beat with electric mixer until well blended. Stir flour, salt, red pepper, and parsley together in separate bowl. Add flour mixture to cheese mixture. Beat until it isn't crumbly. Using your hands, shape pieces of the dough into 1-inch balls. Place balls on baking sheets lined with parchment paper. Very carefully push a pecan half into the top of each ball. Bake on the middle oven rack for 15 minutes or until light golden brown. Cool on racks before storing in an airtight container in the refrigerator.

NOTE: Best if eaten within 3 days

CREAMY SALMON DIP

12 ounces canned pink salmon, drained & flaked

8 ounces low fat cream cheese, softened

¼ cup minced purple onion

½ teaspoon celery seed

½ cup low fat sour cream

¼ cup minced celery

1 teaspoon garlic powder

½ teaspoon minced dried dill

In a bowl, combine all ingredients except the salmon until well blended. Stir the salmon into the cream cheese mixture until completely blended. Cover well and keep refrigerated until ready to serve. This is very good served with raw vegetables of your favorite crackers.

GOAT CHEESE, DRIED FRUIT, & NUT LOGS

½ cup chopped toasted pecans

2 tablespoons fresh chopped parsley

½ teaspoon fresh ground black pepper

12 ounces goat cheese

1 tablespoon pure honey

Combine all of the above ingredients in a bowl and beat on medium speed with an electric mixer until well blended. Place the cheese mixture on wax paper and shape by hand into an 8-inch log. Wrap the cheese log in the wax paper, close tightly and refrigerate for 1 hour.

Mix the following ingredients together while the cheese log is chilling:

1 cup chopped toasted pecans

½ cup candied red cherries

½ cup candied pineapple

½ cup shredded coconut

Remove the cheese log from the refrigerator, unwrap and roll in the fruit/nut mixture. Make sure the cheese log is completely covered in the fruit/nut mixture. Wrap the log tightly in doubled wax paper and place back in the refrigerator until ready to serve.

Note: Will keep in the refrigerator for one week. If wrapped tightly and securely, will keep in the freezer for one month.

Wonderful when sliced and served alone, with crackers, or with your favorite thinly sliced sweet bread.

GARLIC, CHIVE & CHEESE SPREAD

6 ounces goat cheese, softened	$\frac{1}{2}$ teaspoon dried basil
2 ounces fresh shredded cheddar	1 teaspoon dried minced garlic
$\frac{1}{3}$ cup sliced black olives	$\frac{1}{8}$ teaspoon hot sauce
1 tablespoon olive oil	$\frac{1}{2}$ tablespoon red wine vinegar

Mix all ingredients until well blended. Put cheese mixture in an airtight container and place in refrigerator overnight. Allow to soften at room temperature before serving.

CHICKEN DESTINY

36 chicken drumettes	1 cup water
1 cup low sodium soy sauce	$\frac{1}{3}$ cup pineapple juice
$\frac{1}{3}$ cup olive oil	1 teaspoon minced fresh garlic
1 teaspoon minced fresh ginger	2 tablespoons pure honey

Place chicken in a single layer in a large container. Whisk the rest of the ingredients together and pour over chicken. Cover tightly and place in refrigerator overnight, turning chicken 2 or 3 times.

Preheat oven to 350°. Remove chicken from refrigerator and place on large baking sheet. Bake in preheated oven for 30 to 40 minutes or until tender and brown. Remove from oven and allow to set 20 minutes before serving.

Note: 1-inch wide strips of chicken breast may be substituted. Adjust cooking time as needed.

Spicy Cheese Wafers

1¼ cups whole grain flour

½ teaspoon ground black pepper

½ teaspoon crushed dried rosemary

4 ounces goat cheese, softened

½ cup unsalted butter, softened

¼ teaspoon sea salt

¼ teaspoon ground red pepper

½ teaspoon garlic powder

⅓ cup chopped pecans

Mix all ingredients except the pecans until well blended. Stir pecans into the dough. Cover and place in the refrigerator for 15 minutes. Remove dough from refrigerator and divide in half. Shape each half into a 7-inch log, wrap tightly in wax paper and place in refrigerator overnight.

Preheat oven to 350°. Remove dough from refrigerator, slice into ¼ inch slices and put on baking sheet. Place on middle rack in oven for 10 minutes or until light brown. Remove from baking sheet and cool on wire racks. When wafers are completely cooled, remove from racks and store in an airtight container. Wafers will keep for about a week.

Spicy Mixed Nuts

½ cup (1 stick) butter

½ teaspoon cayenne pepper

1½ cups walnut halves

1½ cups almonds

¼ cup fructose

1 tablespoon ground cumin

1½ cups pecan halves

1½ cups cashews

2 teaspoons sea salt

Preheat oven to 300°. Lightly butter 2 large baking sheets.

In a large skillet, melt the butter. Add cumin and cayenne pepper and cook for 1 minute stirring constantly. Remove skillet from heat and stir in all of the nuts, fructose and salt. Stir until the nuts are well coated with the butter mixture. Spread nuts in a single layer in the buttered pans. Place pans of nuts in oven for 25 minutes or until lightly browned. Be sure to stir the nuts occasionally while they are baking. Cool nuts completely and store in an airtight container.

Guacamole Dip

6 to 8 avocados, mashed smooth
6 to 7 diced green onions
Juice of two limes

2 medium diced red onions
2 tomatoes, diced
Sea salt, to taste

Mix all of the above ingredients until smooth and well blended. Store in refrigerator in airtight container.

Chicken Fingers

4 skinless, boneless chicken breasts
1 cup unbleached flour
$\frac{3}{4}$ cup milk

$\frac{1}{2}$ teaspoon sea salt
$\frac{1}{4}$ teaspoon pepper
1 cup grape seed oil

Honey Mustard Sauce:

$\frac{1}{2}$ cup honey

$\frac{1}{4}$ cup Dijon mustard

Cut chicken into $\frac{1}{2}$-by-2-inch strips. For honey mustard sauce, blend honey and mustard in a small bowl. Set aside. Mix flour, salt and pepper in a shallow bowl. Dip chicken in milk. Roll in flour mixture to coat well. Place chicken on waxed paper. Pour $\frac{1}{4}$ inch of oil into a large heavy skillet. Heat over medium-high heat to 350° or until a cube of white bread dropped in oil browns evenly in 1 minute. Divide chicken into batches. Place chicken in an even layer in hot oil. Fry, turning once, for about 3 minutes on each side or until golden brown and crisp. Drain on paper towels. Serve with sauce.

ARTICHOKE DIP

1 (12 ounce) jar marinated artichoke hearts	2 tablespoons green salsa
1/3 cup sliced green onion	1/4 cup sour cream
1/2 cup shredded white cheddar cheese	1/4 cup fresh cilantro

Drain artichoke hearts, discarding marinade. Coarsely chop artichoke hearts. In a small saucepan combine chopped artichoke hearts, green onion and salsa. Cook over medium heat until heated through, stirring frequently. Remove from heat. Stir in cheese, sour cream and cilantro. Serve immediately.

CHILI NUTS

2 tablespoons butter	1 teaspoon chili powder
2 tablespoons Worcestershire sauce	1/4 teaspoon onion salt
2 cups walnut or pecan halves or pieces	1/4 teaspoon ground red pepper

In a saucepan combine butter, Worcestershire sauce, chili powder, onion salt and red pepper. Heat and stir until butter melts. Spread nuts in a 9-by-9-by-2-inch baking pan. Toss with butter mixture. Bake in a 350° oven for 12 to 15 minutes or until toasted, stirring occasionally. Spread on foil and cool. Store in airtight containers.

CHEESE DIP

1/4 cup finely chopped green onion	1 clove garlic, minced
1/2 teaspoon dried tarragon, crushed	1 tablespoon butter
1 teaspoon cornstarch	3/4 cup milk
2 cups shredded American cheese	3 ouncs cream cheese, cut up
French bread cubes or tortilla chips	

In a saucepan cook onion, garlic and tarragon in butter. Stir in cornstarch. Add milk all at once. Cook and stir until thickened and bubbly. Gradually add cheeses, stirring until melted. Serve with bread or chips.

AVOCADO PITAS

3 small whole wheat pita bread rounds	1 medium avocado
⅓ cup organic mayonnaise	½ small tomato, chopped
¼ cup shredded mozzarella cheese	2 tablespoons shredded carrot
¼ cup alfalfa sprouts	

Cut each pita bread round into quarters. Spread the inside of each with mayonnaise. Peel and seed avocado. Cut half of the avocado into 6 slices. (Reserve the remaining avocado for another use.) Cut each slice in half crosswise. Toss together cheese, tomato and carrot. Spoon into each pita quarter. Place an avocado piece in each. Top with alfalfa sprouts. Secure with toothpicks, if necessary.

SPINACH TRIANGLES

10 ounces chopped spinach	½ cup chopped onion
6 ounces feta cheese, finely crumbled	1 clove garlic, minced
½ teaspoon dried oregano, crushed	½ cup butter
12 sheets phyllo dough	

For filling, cook spinach, onion and garlic until spinach is slightly wilted and heated through. Drain well in colander. Press the back of a spoon against mixture to force out excess moisture. Combine spinach mixture, feta cheese and oregano. Lightly brush 1 sheet of phyllo dough with some of the melted butter. Place another phyllo sheet on top and brush with some of the butter. Repeat with a third sheet of phyllo and butter. Cut the stack of phyllo lengthwise into 6 strips. For each triangle, spoon about 1 tablespoon of the filling about 1 inch from one end of each strip. Fold the end over the filling at a 45° angle. Continue folding to form a triangle that encloses filling. Repeat with remaining phyllo, butter and filling. Place triangles on a baking sheet. Brush with butter. Bake in a 375° oven for 18 to 20 minutes or until golden brown.

STUFFED TOMATOES

24 cherry tomatoes
8 ounces cream cheese, softened
¼ teaspoon dried basil, crushed
⅛ teaspoon garlic powder

1 tablespoon fresh chives
1 tablespoon milk
¼ teaspoon black pepper

Slice a thin layer off top of each tomato. Using a small spoon, carefully scoop out and discard pulp. Invert tomatoes and drain on paper towels. For filling, in a small bowl combine cream cheese, chives, milk, basil, pepper and garlic powder. Beat until smooth. Spoon or pipe the filling into the tomatoes. Serve immediately or chill up to 8 hours.

CHICKEN SPREAD

3 tablespoons organic mayonnaise
2 tablespoons finely chopped green onion
2 tablespoons finely chopped nuts
½ cup finely chopped cooked chicken
12 slices party rye or pumpernickel bread

2 tablespoons sour cream
¼ teaspoon curry powder
⅛ teaspoon sea salt
Snipped parsley

In a medium mixing bowl, combine mayonnaise, sour cream, green onion, nuts, curry powder and salt. Stir in chicken. Spread chicken mixture over bread. Sprinkle with parsley, if desired.

FESTIVE CHEESE BALL

16 ounces cream cheese, softened
10 ounces shredded sharp cheddar cheese
1 (8 ounce) can crushed pineapple, drained

2 cups chopped walnuts
2 teaspoons Worcestershire
2 tablespoons green onion

Thoroughly blend cream cheese, sharp cheddar cheese, Worcestershire and onion. Fold in pineapple. Chill for several hours. Shape into a ball; roll in nuts and chill. Serve with crackers.

8 LAYER DIP

8 ounces refried beans

1 cup shredded lettuce

2 avocados, mashed

1 cup shredded cheddar cheese

2 medium tomatoes, chopped

¼ cup salsa

8 ounces sour cream

2 tablespoons sliced olives

¼ cup sliced green onion

Stir together beans and salsa. Arrange lettuce on a 12-inch platter, leaving a 2-inch open rim at edge of platter. Spread bean mixture over lettuce, making a layer about ¼ inch thick. Then layer sour cream and avocado dip. Top with cheese, onion and olives. Cover and chill up to 24 hours. Before serving, arrange tomatoes on top. Arrange tortilla chips on the platter around the spread.

CHEESY TWISTS

1 cup all-purpose flour

⅛ teaspoon ground red pepper

1 cup finely shredded cheddar cheese

3 to 5 tablespoons cold water

2 tablespoons toasted sesame seeds

¼ teaspoon garlic powder

⅛ teaspoon sea salt

¼ cup butter

1 beaten egg

In a large mixing bowl combine flour, garlic powder, salt and pepper. Cut in cheese and butter until pieces are the size of small peas. Sprinkle 1 tablespoon of the water over part of the mixture. Gently toss with a fork. Push to side of bowl. Repeat until all of the flour mixture is moistened. Shape dough into a ball. On a lightly floured surface, flatten dough with hands. Roll out dough from center to edges, forming a 10-inch square. Brush with egg. Sprinkle with sesame seeds. Cut dough into 5-by-½-inch strips. Twist each strip. Place on a lightly greased baking sheet. Bake in a 400° oven for 10 to 12 minutes or until golden brown.

TANGY MEATBALLS

¼ cup fine dry bread crumbs
¼ cup milk
1 teaspoon dry mustard
1 pound ground beef

1 beaten egg
2 tablespoons snipped parsley
¼ teaspoon sea salt
dash of pepper

In a bowl, combine egg, bread crumbs, milk, parsley, mustard, salt and pepper. Add beef. Mix well. Shape into 1-inch meatballs. Place in a 15-by-10-by-1-inch baking pan. Bake in a 350° oven for 15 to 20 minutes, or until done. Drain.

TANGY CRANBERRY SAUCE

In a saucepan, combine one can jellied cranberry sauce, 2 tablespoons steak sauce and 1 tablespoon brown sugar. Heat, stirring occasionally. Add cooked meatballs to sauce and heat through, stirring occasionally.

ORANGE BALLS

1 can frozen orange juice
12 ounces crushed vanilla wafers
1 cup chopped nuts

1 cup fructose
1 cup melted butter

Mix all ingredients together until well blended. Shape into 1-inch balls. Roll in coconut if desired.

PECAN CHEESE CRACKERS

1 pound sharp cheddar cheese
2 cups unbleached flour
2 cups finely chopped pecans

2 sticks butter
4 dashes cayenne pepper

Mix all ingredients together until well blended. Shape into 1-by-8-inch rolls; roll in wax paper and chill. Slice in thin slices. Bake on cookie sheet at 350° for 8 to 10 minutes or until lightly browned. May be frozen or cooked as needed.

BAKED POTATO SKINS

12 medium baking potatoes
2 cups shredded cheddar cheese
Salsa

½ cup butter, melted
Garlic salt
Sliced green onion

Prick potatoes with a fork. Bake at 425° for 40 to 50 minutes or until tender. Cut into quarters. Scoop out the insides, leaving ½-inch thick shells. Brush both sides of potato skins with butter. Place, cut side up, on a large baking sheet. Bake at 425° for 10 to 15 minutes or until crisp. Sprinkle with cheese and garlic salt. Bake about 2 more minutes or until cheese melts. Serve with salsa and green onion.

CHICKEN CUCUMBER SPREAD

3 ounces cream cheese, softened
2 tablespoons organic mayonnaise
4½ ounces cooked, shredded chicken breast
¼ cup chopped seeded cucumber

1 tablespoon catsup
1 teaspoon Dijon mustard
Dash of garlic powder
1 tablespoon chopped onion

In a mixing bowl stir together cream cheese, mayonnaise, catsup, mustard and garlic powder. Stir in chicken, cucumber and onion. Spread mixture on melba toast or crackers.

ITALIAN POPCORN

¼ cup butter

½ teaspoon dried Italian seasoning

⅓ cup grated parmesan cheese

¼ teaspoon garlic powder

10 cups popped popcorn

In a saucepan cook and stir butter, Italian seasoning and garlic powder until butter melts. Toss with popcorn, coating evenly. Toss with cheese.

BARBECUE CHICKEN WINGS

1½ pound chicken wings

¼ cup finely chopped onion

1 tablespoon vinegar

½ cup catsup

1 tablespoon honey

1 clove garlic, minced

Rinse chicken and pat dry. Cut off and discard wing tips. Cut each wing at joint to make 2 sections. Place the wing pieces in a single layer in a shallow baking pan. Bake at 375° for 20 minutes. Drain fat from baking pan. For sauce, combine remaining ingredients. Brush wings with sauce. Bake for 10 minutes. Turn wings over, brush again with sauce. Bake for 5 to 10 minutes more or until chicken is tender.

SOUR CREAM FRUIT DIP

8 ounces sour cream

¼ cup peach preserves

⅛ teaspoon cinnamon

Apple or peach slices

Stir together sour cream, preserves and cinnamon. Chill up to 24 hours. Serve with fruit.

GRILLED CHICKEN & APPLE KEBABS

½ cup peach jam

1 tablespoon tomato paste

1½ pounds skinned, de-boned chicken

1 granny smith apple, in 8 wedges

2 tablespoons cider vinegar

2 tablespoons olive oil

Sea salt & pepper

1 red onion, in 8 wedges

Heat grill to medium-high. Make the sauce: in a large bowl combine jam, vinegar, tomato paste and 1 tablespoon oil. Season with salt and pepper. Set aside. Assemble 4 long skewers, alternating 4 chicken pieces with 2 onion wedges and 2 apple wedges on each (begin with chicken and end with apple). Roll skewers in remaining oil. Season with salt and pepper. Lightly oil grates of grill. Place skewers on grill; cover grill and cook, turning occasionally, until grill marks are visible, 6 to 8 minutes. Open grill; baste skewers with some sauce, and cook, turning skewers and basting occasionally with more sauce, until chicken is no longer pink in the center and is nicely glazed, about 4 to 8 minutes more.

LEMON GARLIC SALMON KEBABS

1½ pounds wild salmon, cut into cubes

¼ cup olive oil

4 garlic cloves, minced

8 thin lemon wedges

2 tablespoons fresh lemon juice

Sea salt and pepper

Heat grill to high. Assemble 4 long skewers, alternating 5 salmon cubes with 2 lemon wedges on each. Place on a large dish. In a small bowl, whisk together oil, lemon juice and garlic. Pour marinade over skewers; turn to coat. Let stand at least 5 minutes (or cover and refrigerate overnight, turning occasionally). Season with salt and pepper. Lightly oil grates. Place skewers on grill, turning occasionally, until grill marks are visible and salmon is cooked to desired doneness, 5 to 8 minutes per side. Serve with sauce.

The Soup Bowl

Soup,
Chili,
Stew and
Gumbo

5

HOMEMADE CHICKEN BROTH

2 pounds skinless chicken breast
2 stalks celery, cut in ½ inch pieces
2 whole peppercorns
¼ cup chopped parsley
¼ teaspoon dried thyme
10 cups water

1 small sliced onion
1 cup diced carrots
2 teaspoons sea salt
¼ teaspoon dried marjoram
¼ teaspoon minced garlic

Combine all ingredients in a large pot and bring to a full boil. Reduce heat, cover, and allow to simmer for 1 hour and 15 minutes. Remove cooked chicken and save to use in chicken salad or in other recipes. Strain and discard vegetables if desired. Save broth for use in recipes when needed. Rice, pasta, and potatoes are very good when cooked in this broth in place of water. Broth will keep in the refrigerator for 3 days or in the freezer for 2 months.

TRULY VEGETABLE SOUP

8 small red potatoes, quartered
2 cups baby carrots, cut in half
½ red pepper, chopped
2 cups green beans, cut in half
2 cups mushrooms, sliced
5 cups low sodium vegetable broth
4 cups plum tomatoes, chopped
½ teaspoon dried oregano
2 tablespoons low sodium soy sauce

1 large chopped onion
3 stalks celery, chopped
½ green pepper, chopped
1 cup cabbage, chopped
3 cloves garlic, minced
1 teaspoon dried thyme
2 teaspoons dried basil
2 tablespoons light olive oil
2 teaspoons dried bay leaves, crushed

Combine olive oil, garlic, and onion in a large pot and sauté for 8 to 10 minutes, stirring often. Add all of the other ingredients except the mushrooms and stir until well combined. Bring the soup to a low slow boil, stirring often. Turn the heat down until soup is just simmering. Cover the pot and allow to simmer for 30 minutes, stirring 2 or 3 times. Remove the lid and stir in the mushrooms. Re-cover and simmer about 15 more minutes or until vegetables are tender.

SMOKED TURKEY SAUSAGE & POTATO SOUP

1 pound nitrate-free smoked turkey sausage

6 large potatoes, cut into 1-inch pieces

3 stalks celery with leaves, chopped

¼ cup chopped chives

½ teaspoon dried rosemary

1 teaspoon dried oregano

1 teaspoon fresh ground black pepper

3½ quarts low sodium chicken broth

2 tablespoons light olive oil

2 tablespoons flour

1 large diced onion

1 cup diced carrots

¼ cup chopped parsley

1 teaspoon minced garlic

½ teaspoon dried marjoram

1 teaspoon sea salt

¼ cup butter

1 cup chopped basil

1 cup milk

In a large pot, cook the sausage until it is almost brown and in big crumbles, stirring often. Add the rest of the ingredients except the basil, butter, and olive oil. Stir well and bring to a low boil. Cover the pot and allow the soup to simmer for 2 hours, stirring often. Add the basil, butter, and olive oil and stir well. Cover and simmer for 30 minutes. In a small bowl, stir 1 cup milk and 2 tablespoons. flour until smooth and well blended. Slowly stir milk/flour mixture into simmering soup. Cover and simmer 20 minutes, stirring often. Watch soup carefully and do not allow to scorch or stick. Sprinkle with fresh diced tomato, sliced black olives, or freshly grated romano cheese.

BEEF STEW

1¼ pounds lean beef chuck, cut in cubes

2 medium onions, thinly sliced

1 clove garlic, minced

1 can tomato paste

1 envelope onion-mushroom soup mix

1 cup sour cream

1 pound carrots, sliced

3 cups sliced cabbage

2 cups water

1 tablespoon paprika

1 teaspoon caraway seeds

Mix all ingredients except sour cream in a 3½-quart or larger slow cooker. Cover and cook on low 8 to 10 hours until tender. Turn off cooker and stir in sour cream until well blended. Serve with pasta or rice.

LAZY DAY SPICY BEAN SOUP

1 (15 ounce) can navy beans, drained & rinsed	1 large chopped onion
1 (15 ounce) can pinto beans, drained & rinsed	1 cup diced carrots
1 (15 ounce) can kidney beans, drained & rinsed	1 cup diced celery
1 (15 ounce) can black beans, drained & rinsed	3 cloves garlic, minced
1 large can diced tomatoes, undrained	1½ tablespoons chili powder
4 cans low sodium chicken broth	¼ teaspoon red pepper
1 cup sweet green pepper, diced	½ cup minced cilantro

In a large pot, combine all of the ingredients, stirring until well mixed. Bring soup to a boil, lower heat, cover, and simmer for 3 hours, stirring often. 1½ cups fresh corn niblets may be added during the last 30 minutes of cooking.

DADDY'S HAMBURGER SOUP

3 cups peeled, cubed potatoes	2 pounds. ground chuck
6 cups low sodium beef broth	1½ cups chopped onion
2 cups low sodium tomato juice	1 cup chopped celery
2 cups chopped plum tomatoes	2 cups fresh lima beans
½ cup diced sweet red pepper	2 cups chopped cabbage
2 cups fresh green beans, cut in ½ inch pieces	2 cloves garlic, minced
1 teaspoon dried thyme	1 teaspoon dried oregano
2 teaspoons hot sauce (adjust to taste)	1 tablespoon paprika
1 teaspoon sea salt	½ teaspoon black pepper
2 bay leaves (remove before serving soup)	

In a large deep pot, cook the ground chuck until brown, stirring to break into small pieces. Add the rest of the ingredients to the meat and drippings. Stir well after adding each ingredient and bring to a boil over medium heat. Cover pot and lower heat so soup is just simmering. Simmer for 2 hours, stirring often.

Note: This soup is better the next day and freezes well.

EASY BEANY MAC VEGETABLE SOUP

4 cups canned navy beans, drained & rinsed

5 cups low sodium chicken broth

1 (28 ounce) can tomatoes, chop but do not drain

1 teaspoon dried crushed bay leaf

1½ teaspoons dried thyme, crushed

1 cup chopped purple onion

½ cup sweet chopped red bell pepper

1 cup small size macaroni, any shape

1 teaspoon fructose

1 teaspoon sea salt

½ teaspoon black pepper

1 teaspoon minced garlic

1 cup chopped carrots

1 cup chopped celery

1 cup chopped cabbage

¼ cup light olive oil

Stir all of the ingredients together in a large pot. Bring to a full boil, stirring often. Lower heat until the soup is just simmering. Allow soup to simmer 30 to 45 minutes or until all vegetables are cooked and soup has thickened slightly. Remember to stir soup often while cooking. This soup is very good served with your favorite cornbread.

CREAM OF BROCCOLI SOUP

1 bunch fresh broccoli, trim & cut in ½ slices

1½ cups diced onion

2 cloves garlic, diced

4 cups fresh milk

4 cups low sodium chicken broth

½ teaspoon ground black pepper

¼ cup butter

2 cups sliced celery

½ cup whole grain flour

½ teaspoon dried marjoram

½ teaspoon dried thyme

1 teaspoon sea salt

Steam the broccoli until tender and set aside. Melt butter in large saucepan and sauté the onion, celery, and garlic until they are a light golden brown. Add the flour gradually, stirring constantly. Combine the milk, broth, marjoram, thyme, salt, and pepper. Slowly stir the milk mixture into the flour mixture. Over low heat and stirring constantly, allow the soup to thicken and come to a boil. Add the broccoli and cook 5 more minutes, stirring constantly. Garnish with fresh diced plum tomatoes just before serving.

ROASTED CHICKEN MUSHROOM SOUP

1 roasted, skinless chicken breast, diced

1/4 cup extra light olive oil

2 cloves garlic, minced

4 cups low sodium chicken broth

1/2 cup chopped parsley

3 large egg yolks (do not use egg whites)

2 ounces grated romano cheese

1/4 cup butter

1 1/2 cups diced onion

1 pound sliced mushrooms

2 tablespoons tomato paste

1 teaspoon sea salt

1/2 teaspoon black pepper

Sauté the onion and garlic in the butter and olive oil. Add the mushrooms, cover and cook until they are less than 1/2 of their original size. Add the broth, tomato paste, salt and pepper. Bring soup to a boil, lower to a simmer and cook for 10 minutes. Lightly beat the egg yolks and add to the soup, stirring constantly. Stir in the chicken, cheese and parsley and simmer for 5 minutes.

NELLIE'S POTATO SOUP

3 cups potatoes, peeled & diced

1/2 cup diced celery

1 (11 ounce) can evaporated milk

1 teaspoon ground black pepper

2 tablespoons whole grain flour

1/4 cup fresh chopped parsley

1/2 cup diced onion

4 cups fresh milk

1/4 cup butter

1 teaspoon sea salt

1/4 cup water

Place potatoes, onions and celery in large pot and cover with water. Bring to a boil, reduce heat to medium and simmer until vegetables are done. **Do not drain off the liquid!!!** Add the milk, evaporated milk and butter, stirring constantly until mixture is very hot. Combine the flour and water and stir until well blended and smooth. Add the flour mixture to the potato mixture, stirring constantly until mixture thickens. Add salt, pepper and parsley. Stir until well blended and serve.

BOBBY'S CHILI WITH CREAMY VEGETABLE SAUCE

1 pound nitrate-free turkey sausage

2 teaspoons fructose

1 large chopped green bell pepper

2 (14½ ounce) cans diced tomatoes, do not drain

15 ounce can red kidney beans

15 ounce can black-eyed peas

¼ teaspoon ground red pepper

1 pound ground beef

1 large chopped onion

15 ounce can tomato sauce

15 ounce can black beans

½ teaspoon ground cinnamon

2 cloves garlic, minced

¼ teaspoon ground allspice

In a large pot, cook the ground beef and turkey sausage over high heat. When the beef and sausage crumbles and is no longer pink, drain off the grease. Stir in the onions, green pepper and tomatoes and cook over medium heat for 15 minutes. Add the tomato sauce, kidney beans, black beans, black-eyed peas, cinnamon, garlic, red pepper, allspice and fructose. Stir until well mixed. Cook over medium heat for 30 minutes, stirring often. Top bowls of chili with creamy vegetable sauce.

Creamy Vegetable Sauce

½ cup organic mayonnaise

½ cup diced black olives

¼ cup diced green bell pepper

¼ teaspoon garlic powder

½ cup low fat sour cream

¼ cup diced green onion

½ teaspoon sea salt

⅛ teaspoon hot sauce

Stir together all of the ingredients until well blended. Place in the refrigerator to chill for at least 2 hours before using.

BROWN RICE & MUSHROOM SOUP

2 cups sliced fresh mushrooms	1 cup sliced green onions
1 cup chopped fresh mushrooms	2 tablespoons olive oil
6 cups natural chicken broth	1 cup water
2 jars (7 ounces each) straw mushrooms	¾ teaspoon black pepper
3 cups cooked short grain brown rice	¾ teaspoon dried thyme leaves

Cook sliced and chopped mushrooms and onion in oil in Dutch oven over medium heat until tender and crisp. Add broth, straw mushrooms, water, pepper and thyme. Simmer uncovered for 5 to 7 minutes. Stir in rice and simmer for 2 minutes.

CHICKEN & RICE SOUP

10 cups natural chicken broth	1 large onion, chopped
1 cup sliced celery	1 cup sliced carrots
¼ cup snipped parsley	½ teaspoon black pepper
½ teaspoon dried thyme leaves	1 bay leaf
1½ cups cubed chicken	2 tablespoons fresh lime juice
2 cups cooked long grain brown rice	Lime slices for garnish

Combine broth, onion, celery, carrots, parsley, pepper, thyme and bay leaf in Dutch oven. Bring to a boil, stirring once or twice. Reduce heat and simmer uncovered for 10 to 15 minutes. Add chicken. Simmer uncovered for 5 to 10 minutes or until chicken is cooked. Remove and discard bay leaf. Stir in rice and lime juice just before serving. Garnish with lime slices, if desired.

SPLIT PEA SOUP

1 cup dry split peas

¼ teaspoon dried marjoram, crushed

½ cup chopped carrot

½ cup chopped celery

4 cups chicken broth

1 bay leaf

½ cup chopped onion

dash of pepper

Rinse peas. In a large saucepan combine peas, broth, marjoram, bay leaf and pepper. Bring to a boil; reduce heat. Cover, simmer for 1 hour. Stir occasionally. Stir in carrot, onion and celery. Return to boiling; reduce heat. Cover; simmer for 20 to 30 minutes or until vegetables are crisp-tender. Discard bay leaf.

TORTELLINI VEGETABLE SOUP

2 tablespoons snipped basil

4 cups chicken broth

½ cup cheese tortellini

1 cup chopped, peeled tomatoes

1 cup frozen cut green beans

Grated parmesan cheese

2 cloves garlic, minced

2 teaspoons olive oil

¼ teaspoon sea salt

⅛ teaspoon pepper

½ cup sliced carrot

In a medium saucepan cook basil and garlic in hot oil about 1 minute. Add broth, tortellini, salt and pepper. Bring to a boil; reduce heat. Cover and simmer for 10 minutes. Add tomatoes, green beans and carrot. Return to boiling; reduce heat. Cover and simmer 10 to 15 minutes more or until tortellini is done and vegetables are tender. If desired, sprinkle each serving with parmesan cheese.

CHEESE SOUP

1¾ cups chicken broth

½ cup finely shredded carrot

¼ cup minced onion

1 cup shredded American cheese

1¾ cups milk

¼ cup minced celery

Dash of pepper

¼ cup unbleached flour

In a medium saucepan combine chicken broth, carrot, celery and onion. Bring to boiling; reduce heat. Cover and simmer for 6 to 8 minutes or until vegetables are tender. Combine milk, flour and pepper. Stir into broth mixture. Cook and stir until thickened and bubbly. Cook and stir 1 minute more. Add cheese; stir until melted.

CORN CHOWDER

4 medium fresh ears of corn

½ cup cubed, peeled potato

2 teaspoons chicken bouillon granules

1¾ cups milk

2 tablespoons unbleached flour

⅓ cup water

½ cup chopped onion

¼ teaspoon pepper

1 tablespoon butter

Use a sharp knife to cut off just the kernel tips from the ears of corn, then scrape the cobs with the dull edge of the knife. In a large saucepan combine corn, potato, onion, water, bouillon granules and pepper. Bring to boiling; reduce heat. Cover and simmer for about 10 minutes or until corn and potatoes are tender, stirring occasionally. Stir in 1 ½ cups of the milk and the butter. Combine the remaining milk and flour. Stir milk-flour mixture into corn mixture. Cook and stir until thickened and bubbly. Cook and stir 1 minute more. If desired, garnish with snipped chives or parsley.

TOMATO HERB SOUP

½ cup sliced onion	2 tablespoons butter
2 cups chopped, peeled tomatoes	1½ cups chicken broth
8 ounces tomato sauce	½ teaspoon dried basil
¼ teaspoon dried thyme	Dash of pepper

In a large saucepan cook onion in butter until tender but not brown. Add fresh tomatoes, broth, tomato sauce, basil, thyme and pepper. Bring to boiling; reduce heat. Cover and simmer for 30 minutes. Cool slightly. Press mixture through a food mill. (Or, place mixture, half at a time, in a blender container or food processor bowl. Cover and blend or process until smooth.) Return mixture to saucepan; heat through. If desired, garnish with lemon slices.

FRENCH ONION SOUP

2 tablespoons butter	4 cups beef broth
2 cups thinly sliced onion	1 teaspoon Worcestershire
4 to 6 slices french bread, toasted	1 cup shredded swiss

In a large saucepan melt butter. Stir in onions. Cook, covered, over medium-low heat for 8 to 10 minutes or until tender and golden, stirring occasionally. Add beef broth. Bring to a boil; reduce heat. Cover and simmer for 10 minutes. Sprinkle toasted bread with cheese. Place bread under broiler until cheese melts and turns light golden brown. To serve, ladle soup into bowls and float bread on top.

CHICKEN GUMBO

1 pound boneless, skinless chicken thighs	2 tomatoes, diced
6 ounces nitrate free turkey sausage,	1 tablespoon olive oil
cut in cubes	1 medium onion, diced
Sea salt and pepper	1 medium green pepper, diced
2 stalks celery, diced	1 tablespoon tomato paste
2 tablespoons unbleached flour	1 package frozen okra, thawed
2 teaspoons dried thyme	2 quarts water

In a 5-quart saucepan, warm oil over high heat. Season chicken with salt and pepper; brown both sided, 8 to 10 minutes. Transfer to a plate to cool; slice into thin strips. Reduce heat to medium. Cook turkey sausage until browned, 1 to 2 minutes. Add onion, pepper and celery; cook until onion is translucent, 4 to 6 minutes. Stir in flour; cook until light brown, stirring constantly, until toasted, 30 seconds to 1 minute. Stir in tomato paste, thyme, half the okra, tomatoes and 2 quarts water. Bring to a boil; reduce heat to a simmer. Stir in chicken and any accumulated juices. Cover and cook until thickened, about 30 minutes. Stir in remaining okra; simmer, uncovered, until chicken is starting to fall apart, about 30 minutes. Season with salt and pepper.

BLACK BEAN SOUP

16 ounces dried black beans, rinsed	2 tablespoons olive oil
3 (1-quart) containers chicken broth	4 cloves garlic, minced
2 large onions, chopped	1 teaspoon oregano
1 cup cilantro, finely chopped	1 teaspoon cumin
2 tablespoons honey or agave nectar	1 teaspoon sea salt
$1/4$ teaspoon pepper	

Remove any foreign particles and debris from beans. Soak beans for 8 hours in a 6-quart pot with water one inch above beans. Rinse and drain beans. Place beans in the chicken broth and bring to a boil. Reduce heat and simmer for 5 hours. After 4 hours, add remaining ingredients, reserving one chopped onion. Serve alone or over rice. Top with sour cream and chopped onions. **Serves 8**

The Bread Basket

Bread,
Biscuits,
Muffins
and Rolls

6

SIMPLY DELICIOUS BISCUITS

4 cups unbleached, sifted twice

1 cup very cold butter, cut in small pieces

2 tablespoons aluminum free baking powder

$1\frac{1}{2}$ teaspoon sea salt

1 cup buttermilk

1 cup baked potato

Preheat oven to 425°. Stir flour, baking powder, and salt until well blended. Drop the butter pieces evenly on top of the flour mixture. Cut butter into flour mixture until crumbly. Stir the buttermilk and the mashed baked potato together until well blended. Slowly pour the milk mixture into the flour/butter mixture, stirring gently until all the ingredients are moistened. Turn the dough out on a lightly floured surface and knead 5 or 6 times. Gently pat the dough till it is about $\frac{1}{2}$ inch thick. Cut the dough with a 2-inch biscuit cutter. Place biscuits on a lightly greased baking sheet and bake for 12 minutes or until golden brown. Brush lightly with unsalted butter before serving.

EASY BISCOTTI

3 cups unbleached flour, sifted

1 teaspoon salt, coarse

1 teaspoon aluminum free baking powder

$\frac{1}{8}$ teaspoon fresh ground pepper

$\frac{1}{2}$ cup cold water

$\frac{1}{2}$ teaspoon dried garlic

$\frac{1}{2}$ cup sun-dried tomato

2 teaspoons fresh chives

3 large eggs

2 tablespoons olive oil

Preheat oven to 375°. Mix flour, baking powder, salt, tomato, garlic, chives and pepper together until well blended. Put eggs, water and oil in a separate bowl and stir well. Add egg mixture to the flour mixture and stir just until the dry ingredients are moistened. Place dough on a lightly floured surface and cut in half. Shape each half into a log about 3-inches wide. Place logs on a lightly greased baking sheet and bake for 40 minutes. Remove from oven and allow to cool. Being very careful and using a sharp knife, cut logs into $\frac{1}{4}$-inch slices. Place slices back in oven and bake for an additional 17 to 20 minutes. Cool completely on a rack before storing in an airtight container.

ALMOST A MEAL BREAD

2 cups milk, add 2 tablespoons white vinegar	1 cup regular oats
½ cup tart apples, peeled & chopped	½ cup golden raisins
3 cups unbleached flour	1 teaspoon caraway seeds
1 teaspoon celery seed	½ teaspoon sea salt
1½ teaspoons aluminum free baking soda	½ cup diced onion
6 slices nitrate-free turkey bacon, cut in 8 pieces	¼ cup diced celery

Preheat oven to 400°. Sprinkle 2 tablespoons stone ground corn meal on un-greased baking sheet. Mix the oats, raisins and 1 cup milk in a bowl and stir well. Let stand for 15 to 20 minutes. In a large bowl, mix the flour, seeds, salt and baking soda, stirring well. Put the chopped bacon in a skillet and cook over medium heat until crispy. Remove bacon and place on paper towels to drain. Add onions to the drippings in the pan and sauté for 3 minutes, add apples and sauté for 3 minutes. Remove skillet from heat and mix contents with the oat/raisin mixture, bacon and remaining milk. Stir until well blended. Dump dough onto a lightly floured surface and knead 2 to 3 times. Shape dough into a round loaf and place on baking sheet. Using scissors, cut criss crosses in top of loaf. Bake for 35 minutes.

RAISIN BREAD

2 cups unbleached flour	1 cup buttermilk
1 teaspoon aluminum free baking soda	1 teaspoon sea salt
½ teaspoon aluminum free baking powder	1 cup raisins

Preheat oven to 350°. Stir together the flour, baking powder, baking soda and salt in a large bowl and set aside. Combine the buttermilk and raisins and add to the flour mixture, stirring until all ingredients are moistened. Turn the dough out onto a floured surface and gently knead until elastic and smooth. Place the dough on a buttered baking sheet. Flatten and shape dough into a circle about 1½-inches thick. Bake for 30 to 35 minutes.

FRUITY HONEY NUT BREAD

1 large egg

2 tablespoons butter, softened

1½ cups unbleached flour

½ teaspoon aluminum free baking powder

1 teaspoon aluminum free baking soda

¾ cup raw old-fashioned oatmeal

¼ cup raisins, soaked in ½ cup hot apple juice

1 cup milk, add 1 tablespoon orange juice

⅓ cup pure honey

¼ teaspoon ground cinnamon

¼ teaspoon ground nutmeg

½ teaspoon sea salt

½ cup chopped figs

½ cup fructose

¼ cup chopped nuts

Preheat oven to 375°. Beat egg, add honey and butter and beat until well mixed. Stir the flour, baking powder, baking soda, salt, cinnamon, nutmeg, oatmeal and fructose until well mixed. Add the flour mixture and the milk/orange juice mixture to the egg mixture. Stir the raisins, figs and nuts into the batter and put in prepared loaf pan. Bake for 50 to 60 minutes or until tests done. Remove from oven and cool in the pan for 15 minutes. Cool completely before slicing.

SWEET PEPPER & ONION SPOON BREAD

4½ cups fresh milk

1¼ cup egg substitute

1½ cups stone ground cornmeal

¼ cup chopped red pepper

4 teaspoons aluminum free baking powder

5 tablespoons butter

1 teaspoon sea salt

1 teaspoon celery seed

½ cup diced onion

Preheat oven to 450°. Combine 3 cups of milk and all of the butter in a saucepan just to the boiling point. Slowly add the cornmeal and whisk constantly until mixture thickens and returns to a boil. Beat egg substitute,

1½ cups milk and salt in a bowl until well blended. Stir in the baking powder, red pepper, onion and celery seed. Pour the mixture into a shallow buttered 3-quart glass baking dish. Bake for 35 to 40 minutes or until slightly puffy and forming a crust on the top.

MOLASSES RYE ROUND BREAD LOAVES

2 cups unsweetened apple juice

2½ cups medium rye flour

½ ounce active dry yeast

3½ to 4 cups unbleached flour

¼ cup molasses

¼ cup butter

1 tablespoon sea salt

⅓ cup fructose

Preheat oven to 375°. Simmer the apple juice, molasses and butter in a small saucepan until butter melts. Combine the rye flour, yeast, fructose and salt in a bowl. Slowly add the molasses mixture while beating at low speed. Beat for 3 minutes at medium speed. Slowly stir in enough of the all purpose flour to make a soft dough. Put dough on well floured surface and knead until smooth and elastic. Place dough in a well buttered bowl, turning to butter top of dough. Cover and allow to rise in a warm draft free place until doubled in bulk. Punch the dough down and cut in half. Shape each half into a round loaf and place in buttered round cake pans. Cover each loaf and allow to rise in a warm draft free place until almost doubled in size. Bake the loaves of bread for about 30 minutes or until the bread sounds hollow when tapped with your finger. Remove bread from pans immediately and allow to cool on wire racks.

POPEYE'S BREAD

1 cup unbleached flour, sifted

1 teaspoon aluminum free baking powder

½ teaspoon ground red pepper

3 large eggs, lightly beaten

4 cups fresh spinach, trimmed & chopped

½ cup butter

1 teaspoon sea salt

1 cup milk

1 pound shredded cheddar

Preheat oven to 375°. Put the butter in a 13-by-9-by-2-inch pan and place in oven until the butter melts. Mix the eggs, flour, milk, baking powder and salt together. Beat the mixture with a large wooden spoon until well mixed and fairly smooth. Stir in the spinach and cheese until blended. Pour the mixture on top of melted butter and bake for 35 to 40 minutes.

GRANDMA'S CORNBREAD

1 cup cornmeal	2 tablespoons unbleached flour
1/4 teaspoon aluminum free baking soda	1/2 teaspoon garlic powder
1 cup fresh milk	1/4 teaspoon sea salt
1 large egg, lightly beaten	1 teaspoon fresh lemon juice
1 1/4 teaspoon aluminum free baking powder	1/4 cup minced onion
1 tablespoon fructose	6 tablespoons melted butter

Preheat oven to 450°. Put 2 tablespoons of the butter in an 8-inch cast iron skillet and place in oven while making the batter. In a medium bowl, combine the cornmeal, flour, baking powder, baking soda, salt, garlic powder and fructose and stir until well blended. In a small bowl, whisk together the milk, lemon juice, egg, onion and the remaining melted butter until well blended. Make a well in the center of the cornmeal mixture. Pour in the egg mixture and stir just until all the dry ingredients are moistened. Pour the batter on top of the melted butter in the hot skillet. Bake for 20 to 25 minutes or until golden brown and crispy around the edge. Serve right from the skillet while hot.

GOLDEN RAISIN BREAKFAST BREAD

3/4 cup golden raisins, soaked in hot apple juice	2 cups unbleached flour
2 teaspoons aluminum free baking powder	3 tablespoons fructose
1/2 teaspoon aluminum free baking soda	1 teaspoon sea salt
1/3 cup cold butter, cut in pieces	1 teaspoon sesame seeds
1 cup milk, add 2 teaspoons lemon juice	1 egg, lightly beaten
2 teaspoons fresh honey, add 1 tablespoon soft butter	

Preheat oven to 400°. Butter a 9-inch round cake pan. Drain the raisins and set aside. Sift flour, fructose, baking soda, baking powder and salt. Cut in the cold butter until mixture is crumbly. Add the raisins and sesame seeds and stir. Mix the milk/lemon juice and egg together. Add milk mixture to flour mixture and stir just until moistened. Put dough in prepared pan and bake for 25 minutes. Remove bread from pan and cool on wire rack. Allow to cool 15 minutes and then spread the honey over the top.

CHEDDAR GARLIC PARSLEY BISCUITS

4 cups unbleached flour

1/2 teaspoon cayenne pepper

3/4 teaspoon aluminum free baking soda

2 teaspoons aluminum free baking powder

1 cup shredded cheddar cheese

1 teaspoon garlic powder

2 teaspoons sea salt

1/2 cup cold butter

1 tablespoon chopped parsley

1 1/2 cups fresh milk with
   2 teaspoons vinegar added

Preheat oven to 400°.

Sift the flour, garlic powder, cayenne pepper, salt, baking powder and baking soda together in a large bowl. Cut the butter into small pieces and drop evenly over the flour mixture. Using a pastry blender, cut the butter into the flour mixture until it looks like coarse crumbs. Stir the cheese and parsley into the flour/butter mixture. Add the milk/vinegar and stir until mixture comes together. Put the dough on a lightly floured surface and gently knead 3 or 4 times. Do not overwork!!! Pat dough out to a 1/2-inch thick round and allow to set about 10 minutes. Cut biscuits out with a 2 1/2-inch round serrated cutter. Keep rolling and cutting to use up most of the dough. Place cut biscuits about 2-inches apart on baking sheet that has been sprayed with non-stick spray. Bake for 15 to 20 minutes or until golden brown. Remove from baking sheet and place on a wire rack. Brush the tops of biscuits with melted butter. Wrap any leftovers tightly and refrigerate for up to 2 days. Re-heat in a 350° oven for about 5 minutes.

CHEESY BISCUITS

2 cups unbleached flour

4 teaspoons aluminum free baking powder

1 cup shredded sharp cheddar cheese

1 teaspoon sea salt

1/2 cup butter

2/3 cup buttermilk

Combine flour, baking powder and salt; cut in butter. Add cheese; gradually stir in buttermilk. Turn out onto a lightly floured surface and roll thin. Cut into small biscuits; place on greased baking sheets and bake at 400° for 8 to 10 minutes.

TRIPLE FRUIT ALMOND SCONES

2¼ cups unbleached flour, sifted twice

½ teaspoon aluminum free baking soda

¼ cup fructose

1 tablespoon aluminum free baking powder

6 tablespoons cold butter, cut in pieces

½ cup chopped dried pineapple

½ cup chopped dried cherries

½ cup chopped dried peaches

1 teaspoon vanilla extract

½ teaspoon sea salt

1 egg, lightly beaten

1 teaspoon almond extract

½ cup buttermilk

¼ cup chopped almonds

1½ teaspoon lemon peel

Preheat oven to 400°

Sift the flour, baking powder, baking soda and salt into a large bowl. Using a pastry blender, cut the cold butter into the flour mixture until it looks like coarse crumbs. In a smaller bowl, whisk the buttermilk, fructose, egg, vanilla extract and almond extract until well blended. Using a large fork, stir all of the dried fruit and almonds into the flour/butter mixture. Add the lemon peel to the buttermilk mixture. Pour the buttermilk mixture into the flour/fruit mixture and stir just until a sticky dough forms. Turn the dough out on a lightly floured surface and gently knead for about 1 minute or until the dough is no longer sticky. Place dough on baking sheet and form a round mound shape, patting to about 1-inch thick. Cut the round into 8 wedges. ***Do not separate wedges!*** Brush the wedges with buttermilk and sprinkle lightly with brown sugar. Be sure to wipe off any milk or sugar that gets on the pan before placing it in the oven. Bake for 17 to 20 minutes or until golden brown.

QUICK ROLLS

2 cups self-rising unbleached flour

4 tablespoons mayonnaise

1 cup milk

½ teaspoon fructose

Mix all ingredients in a bowl and blend for about 2 minutes. Pour into greased muffin pan. Bake at 450° for about 10 minutes or until golden brown

APPLE RAISIN BREAKFAST MUFFINS

$\frac{1}{2}$ cup fructose	1 egg, lightly beaten
$\frac{1}{3}$ cup softened butter	$\frac{1}{2}$ teaspoon sea salt
$1\frac{1}{2}$ cups unbleached flour	$\frac{1}{4}$ cup golden raisins
$\frac{1}{4}$ teaspoon ground nutmeg	$\frac{1}{4}$ teaspoon ground cinnamon
$1\frac{1}{2}$ teaspoons aluminum free baking powder	$\frac{1}{2}$ cup milk
$\frac{1}{2}$ cup apple, peeled & chopped	

Preheat oven to 350°. Butter 12 muffin cups or use cupcake papers. Using an electric mixer on low speed, cream the fructose, butter and egg until blended. Stir the flour, baking powder, salt, nutmeg and cinnamon together. Add the flour mixture alternately with the milk, beating well after each addition. Be sure to begin and end with the flour mixture. Stir in the apple and raisins. Fill muffin cups ⅔ full. Bake for 25 minutes or until golden brown. Remove muffins from oven and immediately dip in melted butter, then in cinnamon/sugar mixture. It takes about ¼ cup melted butter and ½ cup sugar mixed with 1 teaspoon cinnamon.

SWEET POTATO NUT BREAD

1 cup fructose	$\frac{1}{3}$ cup softened butter
1 cup mashed sweet potatoes	2 eggs, lightly beaten
2 teaspoons aluminum free baking powder	$\frac{1}{2}$ teaspoon sea salt
2 cups unbleached flour, sifted	$\frac{1}{2}$ teaspoon ground ginger
$\frac{1}{4}$ teaspoon aluminum free baking soda	$\frac{1}{4}$ cup milk
$\frac{1}{2}$ teaspoon ground cinnamon	$\frac{1}{4}$ teaspoon ground cloves
$\frac{1}{2}$ cup toasted walnuts	

Preheat oven to 350°. Butter a 9-by-5-by-3-inch pan. Using an electric mixer on medium speed, cream the butter and fructose until fluffy. Add the eggs one at a time, beating well. Beat in the sweet potato and milk just until blended. Sift the flour, baking powder, baking soda, salt, ginger, cloves and cinnamon and stir into the sweet potato mixture. Beat on low speed for 2 minutes. Stir in the nuts and put in prepared pan and bake for 50 to 60 minutes. Remove from pan and allow to cool completely before wrapping. This bread is really better the next day.

Autumn Bread

½ cup softened butter

2 large eggs, lightly beaten

2 cups unbleached flour, sifted

1 teaspoon aluminum free baking soda

¾ cup shredded cheddar cheese

1½ cups apple, peeled & chopped

⅔ cup fructose

½ teaspoon sea salt

½ teaspoon apple pie spice

½ cup chopped walnuts

¼ cup chopped dates

⅓ cup apple juice

Preheat oven to 350°. Butter a 9-by-5-by-3-inch loaf pan. Using an electric mixer on medium speed, cream the butter and fructose until fluffy. Add the eggs to the creamed mixture and beat well. Stir together the flour, baking soda, salt and apple pie spice. Add to the creamed mixture alternately with the apple juice. Stir in the cheese, walnuts, dates and apples, mixing well. Spoon the dough into the buttered loaf pan and bake for 50 to 60 minutes. Bread is done when a toothpick inserted in the center comes out clean. Allow to cool in the pan for 10 minutes and then remove and cool completely on a wire rack before slicing.

Nutty Citrus Bread

2 cups unbleached flour

½ teaspoon aluminum free baking soda

½ cup chopped walnuts

1 tablespoon chopped orange peel

¼ cup tangerine juice

1 tablespoon lemon juice with ¼ teaspoon lemon peel

1 tablespoon lime juice with ¼ teaspoon lime peel

¾ cup fructose

½ teaspoon sea salt

1 large egg, beaten

½ cup orange juice

2 tablespoons melted butter

Preheat oven to 350°. Butter a 8-by-4-by-2-inch loaf pan. Stir together the flour, fructose, baking soda and salt. Stir in the walnuts. Combine the beaten egg, orange peel, orange juice, tangerine juice, lemon juice, lemon peel, lime juice, lime peel and melted butter. Add to the dry ingredients and stir just until moistened. Spoon the batter into the loaf pan and bake for 50 to 60 minutes. Bread is done when a toothpick inserted in the center comes out clean. Cool completely, wrap tightly and store overnight before slicing.

COUNTRY STYLE CORNBREAD

2 cups yellow cornmeal

2 tablespoons unbleached flour

1 teaspoon aluminum free baking soda

1 large egg, lightly beaten

1 tablespoon aluminum free baking powder

¼ cup fructose

1 cup milk

¼ cup melted butter

1 cup sour cream

Preheat oven to 370°. Put the cornmeal, fructose, flour, baking powder, baking soda and salt in a bowl and mix well. In a separate bowl, mix together the milk, sour cream and melted butter until well blended. Add the milk mixture to the flour mixture, stirring just until moistened. Pour batter into the prepared pan and bake for 20 minutes or until toothpick inserted in center comes out clean or the bread is a golden brown color.

RAISIN BROWN RICE MUFFINS

1 cup cold cooked short grain brown rice

1¼ cups unbleached flour, sifted

2 teaspoons aluminum free baking powder

4 tablespoons butter, melted

1 cup raisins

½ teaspoon sea salt

2 tablespoons fructose

1 cup milk

2 eggs, beaten

Sift together flour, baking powder, salt and fructose. Combine milk, eggs, butter and rice. Quickly combine the two mixtures. ***Do not over beat***, as this will make heavy muffins. Pour into 12 buttered muffin tins. Bake in a 425° oven for 20 to 25 minutes or until lightly browned.

BANANA NUT MUFFINS

2 cups unbleached flour

1 tablespoon aluminum free baking powder

1 cup milk

⅓ cup grape seed oil

½ cup chopped walnuts

⅛ cup fructose

½ teaspoon sea salt

1 egg, beaten

¾ cup mashed banana

Preheat oven to 400°. Grease a 12-cup muffin pan. Sift flour, fructose, baking powder and salt into medium bowl; make a well in the center. Mix the milk, egg, oil, banana and walnuts in a small bowl. Pour mixture into well. Mix batter just until moistened; do not overmix. Spoon batter into prepared muffin cups. Bake until a toothpick inserted in center comes out clean or until muffins are golden brown, about 15 minutes.

BANANA NUT BREAD

¾ cup softened butter

8 ounces softened cream cheese

3 cups unbleached flour

½ teaspoon aluminum free baking powder

½ teaspoon aluminum free baking soda

2 large eggs

1 cup fructose

½ teaspoon sea salt

1½ cups mashed banana

½ teaspoon vanilla extract

1 cup chopped pecans

Beat butter and cream cheese at medium speed with an electric mixer until creamy. Gradually add fructose, beating until light and fluffy. Add eggs, one at a time, beating just until blended after each addition. Combine flour, baking powder, baking soda and salt; gradually add to butter mixture, beating at low speed just until blended. Stir in bananas, pecans and vanilla. Spoon batter into 2 greased and floured 8-by-4-inch loaf pans. Bake at 350° for 1 hour or until a toothpick inserted in the center comes out clean and sides pull away from pan. Cool bread in pans on wire racks for 10 minutes. Remove from pans and cool for 30 minutes on wire racks before slicing.

ZUCCHINI BREAD

1½ cups unbleached flour	1 teaspoon ground cinnamon
½ teaspoon aluminum free baking soda	¼ teaspoon sea salt
¼ teaspoon aluminum free baking powder	¼ teaspoon ground nutmeg
½ cup fructose	¼ cup olive oil
1 cup finely shredded unpeeled zucchini	1 egg
¼ teaspoon finely shredded lemon peel	½ cup chopped walnuts
1 cup milk	

In a mixing bowl combine flour, cinnamon, baking soda, salt, baking powder and nutmeg. In another mixing bowl combine fructose, shredded zucchini, oil, 1 cup milk, egg and lemon peel; mix well. Add flour mixture; stir just until combined. Stir in chopped walnuts. Pour batter into a greased loaf pan. Bake at 350° for 55 to 60 minutes or until a toothpick inserted in the center comes out clean. Cool for 10 minutes on a wire rack. Remove bread from pan; cool thoroughly on a wire rack. Wrap and store overnight before slicing.

PUMPKIN BREAD

2 cups whole wheat flour	1 cup brown sugar
1 tablespoon aluminum free baking powder	1 teaspoon ground cinnamon
¼ teaspoon sea salt	⅛ teaspoon ground ginger
¼ teaspoon aluminum free baking soda	¼ teaspoon ground nutmeg
1 cup canned pumpkin	½ cup milk
2 eggs	⅓ cup olive oil
½ cup chopped walnuts	½ cup raisins

In a large mixer bowl combine 1 cup of the flour, brown sugar, baking powder, cinnamon, salt, soda, nutmeg and ginger. Add pumpkin, milk, eggs and oil. Beat with an electric mixer on low speed until blended, then on high speed for 2 minutes. Add remaining flour; beat well. Stir in nuts and raisins. Pour batter into a greased loaf pan. Bake at 350° for 60 to 65 minutes or until a toothpick inserted in the center comes out clean. Cool for 10 minutes on a wire rack. Remove from the pan; cool thoroughly on a wire rack. Wrap and store overnight before slicing.

BERRY BANANA WALNUT BREAD

1½ cups whole wheat flour

½ teaspoon aluminum free baking soda

¾ cup mashed strawberries

½ cup fructose

½ cup mashed ripe banana

1½ teaspoon finely shredded orange peel

¾ teaspoon cinnamon

¼ teaspoon nutmeg

2 beaten eggs

¼ cup olive oil

1 cup chopped walnuts

¼ teaspoon sea salt

In a bowl combine flour, cinnamon, soda, nutmeg and salt. In another bowl stir together eggs, fructose, banana, berries, oil and orange peel. Add to flour mixture, stirring just until combined. Stir in nuts. Pour into a greased loaf pan. Bake in a 350° oven for 60 to 70 minutes or until a toothpick inserted in the center comes out clean. Cool for 10 minutes. Remove from pan; cool on a wire rack. Wrap and store overnight before slicing.

SODA BREAD

2 cups unbleached flour

1 teaspoon aluminum free baking powder

½ teaspoon aluminum free baking soda

¼ teaspoon sea salt

3 tablespoons butter

2 beaten eggs, seperated

¾ cup buttermilk

In a bowl combine flour, baking powder, soda and salt. Cut in butter until mixture resembles coarse crumbs. Combine 1 egg and buttermilk; add to flour mixture. Stir just until moistened. On a lightly floured surface, knead gently for 12 strokes. On a greased baking sheet, shape dough into a 6-inch round loaf. Cut a 4-inch cross, ¼-inch deep, on the top. Brush with the remaining egg. Bake at 375° for about 35 minutes or until golden. Cool on a wire rack.

STRAWBERRY BREAD

5 tablespoons + 1 teaspoon butter, softened	$\frac{1}{2}$ teaspoon ground cinnamon
1 pint strawberries, mashed	$\frac{1}{4}$ teaspoon sea salt
$1\frac{3}{4}$ cups whole wheat flour	$\frac{1}{2}$ cup fructose
1 teaspoon aluminum free baking soda	2 large eggs
$\frac{1}{4}$ teaspoon aluminum free baking powder	$\frac{1}{3}$ cup water

Preheat oven to 350°. Butter a loaf pan. In a small saucepan, bring strawberries to a boil over medium heat. Cook, stirring, 1 minute. Set aside. In a medium bowl, whisk together flour, baking soda, cinnamon, baking powder and salt; set aside. With an electric mixer, cream butter, fructose and eggs in a mixing bowl until light and fluffy. Add flour mixture alternately with water, beginning and ending with flour. Fold in reserved strawberries. Scrape batter into prepared pan, smoothing top. Bake until a toothpick inserted in the center comes out clean, about 1 hour. Cool in pan 10 minutes. Run a knife around edges; invert onto a rack. Re-invert; cool completely.

APPLE OATMEAL BREAD

$1\frac{1}{2}$ cups whole wheat flour	1 teaspoon sea salt
1 tablespoon unbleached flour	1 teaspoon ground cinnamon
1 apple, peeled and cored	1 cup cooked oatmeal
$\frac{1}{4}$ cup chunky applesauce	$\frac{1}{2}$ cup milk
1 large egg, lightly beaten	2 tablespoons rolled oats
$\frac{1}{4}$ cup light brown sugar	

Preheat oven to 350°. Place flour, baking powder, salt and cinnamon in a medium bowl. Whisk to combine. Grate apple into large bowl using large holes of box grater. Add cooked oatmeal, milk, applesauce, egg and brown sugar. Add flour mixture; mix until just combined. Divide batter between two loaf pans. Sprinkle oats over loaves. Bake about 1 hour or until golden on top.

NOTES

The Salad Cart

7

Fruit
Veggies
Rice
Chicken
Tuna

FRUIT GALORE SALAD

Dressing Ingredients:

16 ounces plain organic yogurt

½ cup fresh strawberries, mashed

¼ cup fresh lemon or lime juice

3 tablespoons pure honey

1 teaspoon rum extract

1 teaspoon poppy seed

Mix all ingredients until well blended. Cover tightly and refrigerate until ready to use.

Fruit Salad Ingredients:

3 cups fresh pineapple, cut in chunks

3 bananas, peeled, sliced and tossed with

1 cup of orange juice

1½ cups green seedless grapes, cut in half

1 cup fresh passion fruit, cut in small chunks

1 cup fresh mango, cut in small chunks

3 sweet plums, pitted and cut into 6 to 8 wedges

2 navel oranges, peeled, seeded and cut in slices

1 cup sweet cherries, pitted and cut in half

2 cups fresh strawberries, each cut into 4 wedges

Gently combine all of the fruit salad ingredients until well mixed. Add the dressing and stir until blended. Cover tightly and chill for at least 4 hours before serving. If desired, garnish with fresh sprigs of mint before serving. **Serves 8-10**

SOUTHWESTERN SALAD

1 cup cooked Black Japonica rice

2 cups rinsed black beans

1 large tomato, seeded and diced

1 bunch green onions, diced

1 each green & red bell pepper, diced

¼ cup sliced black olives (optional)

1 cup fresh corn

1¼ cups mild salsa

2 teaspoons cumin powder

2 tablespoons fresh lime juice

2 cloves garlic, minced

¼ teaspoon cilantro, chopped

Combine cooked, cooled rice with all ingredients. Toss lightly. Chill and serve. **Serves 8-10**

FRESH SWEET PEA & RICE SALAD

2 cups sweet peas, steamed & chilled	2 cups steamed rice
½ cup chopped & peeled plum tomatoes	½ cup chopped onion
¼ cup chopped sweet yellow pepper	¼ cup chopped celery
½ cup chopped fresh parsley	1 tablespoon light olive oil
1¼ cup low fat sour cream	1 tablespoon red wine vinegar

Toss peas, rice, onion, tomatoes, celery, sweet pepper and parsley in a large bowl, mixing well. Whisk together sour cream, vinegar and olive oil until well blended. Pour over pea mixture and mix gently. Cover and chill for 1 hour before serving.
Serves 6

KENTUCKY POTATO SALAD

2 pounds. small red potatoes, steamed & cut in half	½ cup chopped basil
	1 pound fresh green beans, steamed
1 cup chopped celery	1 cup chopped sweet red pepper
1 cup chopped onion	1 cup fresh grape tomatoes, cut in half
4 boiled eggs, sliced	

Combine all of the ingredients and toss gently. Cover and refrigerate while making the dressing.

Dressing Recipe:

1 cup extra virgin olive oil	¼ cup fresh lemon juice
2 cloves garlic, minced	1 teaspoon sea salt
½ teaspoon hot sauce	4 tablespoons Dijon mustard
½ cup balsamic vinegar	1 tablespoon fructose

Combine all ingredients in a bowl and whisk vigorously until well blended. Pour dressing over the salad and gently toss. If not serving immediately, cover tightly and refrigerate. **Serves 6**

DELIGHTFUL DELUXE CARROT SLAW

8 large carrots, coarsely grated

1 cup golden raisins, soaked in hot apple juice

8 ounces organic vanilla yogurt

1 tablespoon apple juice

½ teaspoon ground cinnamon

1 cup crushed pineapple

1 cup chopped pecans

2 tablespoons pure honey

2 teaspoons apple cider vinegar

Mix the carrots, pineapple, raisins, and pecans in a bowl. Whisk the remaining ingredients together, blending thoroughly. Pour the yogurt mixture over the carrot mixture and stir until well blended. Cover tightly and refrigerate at least 4 hours before serving. **Serves 6-8**

BERRY SPINACH SALAD

2 pints sliced strawberries

½ cup toasted slivered almonds

12 ounces fresh baby spinach

Place almonds on oiled cookie sheet; bake until golden. Combine spinach and strawberries in a large bowl; toss with ½ cup Strawberry Poppy Seed Dressing just before serving. Top with almonds.

Strawberry Poppy Seed Dressing:

½ cup fructose

1 tablespoon minced onion

½ cup fresh strawberries

½ teaspoon Worcestershire sauce

¼ cup sesame seeds, toasted

½ cup cider vinegar

¼ teaspoon sea salt

1 cup olive oil

2 tablespoons poppy seeds

In blender, pulse together the fructose, vinegar, onion, strawberries, Worcestershire sauce and salt 2 or 3 times or until smooth. With blender running, add oil in a slow, steady stream; process until smooth. Stir in seeds; chill 24 hours. **Serves 2-4**

FRUITY SLAW

2 cups shredded cabbage

1 cup cubed honeydew melon

1 cup pineapple chunks, drained

1 cup halved strawberries

1/4 teaspoon poppy seed

1/3 cup lemon yogurt

In a mixing bowl combine cabbage, honeydew, pineapple, strawberries and poppy seed. Cover and chill up to 3 hours. Just before serving, add lemon yogurt. Toss gently until the cabbage and fruit are coated. Transfer slaw to a salad bowl, if desired. **Serves 4**

SALMON STUFFED EGGS

1 dozen boiled eggs, peel &
   cut in half lengthwise

1/2 cup low fat sour cream

1/2 cup salmon, drained & flaked

1/4 cup chopped green onions

1/4 cup chopped red bell pepper

1/4 cup chopped dill pickle

2 teaspoons dijon mustard

1 tablespoon minced parsley

Sweet paprika

1/4 cup chopped celery

Remove yolks from egg whites, set whites aside. In a medium bowl, mash the egg yolks with a fork. Stir the salmon, onion, bell pepper, celery, dill pickle, sour cream, mustard and parsley into the mashed egg yolks and mix well. Stuff the egg whites with the salmon mixture, being sure to mound the mixture high. Cover well and refrigerate until ready to serve. Sprinkle paprika lightly over the eggs just before serving. **Makes 12 eggs.**

BEAN SALAD

1 can green beans

1 can red kidney beans, undrained

1/4 cup fructose

1 small onion, chopped

1 can yellow beans

1/2 cup vinegar

3/4 cup olive oil

Mix all ingredients until well blended; chill. **Serves 4**

GARDEN MACARONI SALAD

3 cups cooked macaroni (small shells)	1 cup diced celery
2 cups fresh young sweet peas, steamed	¼ cup diced carrots
½ cup diced sweet yellow pepper	1 cup diced sweet onion
1 cup seedless cucumber, peeled & chopped	2 boiled eggs, chopped
½ cup sweet diced pickles	½ cup chopped parsley
1 cup sliced black olives (optional)	

Place all of the ingredients in a large bowl and toss well. Cover tightly and refrigerate while making the dressing.

Dressing Recipe:

1½ cups low fat sour cream	2 tablespoons dijon mustard
2 tablespoons sweet pickle juice	1 teaspoon garlic powder

Whisk all of the ingredients together until well blended. Stir the dressing into the salad and mix well. Cover salad tightly and refrigerate until ready to serve. Place the salad on lettuce leaves and sprinkle with sweet paprika just before serving.
Serves 6-8

CHICKEN COUSCOUS SALAD

2 cups chicken broth	1½ cups plain couscous
3 cups cubed, cooked skinless chicken breast	4 cups mixed fruit
½ cup plain, nonfat yogurt	1 tablespoon olive oil
¼ teaspoon nutmeg	⅛ teaspoon cinnamon
¼ cup orange juice	1 teaspoon lemon juice

In a medium saucepan, bring the broth to a boil over high heat. Stir in the couscous, cover, and remove from heat. Let stand for 5 minutes, then remove the saucepan lid, fluff with a fork, and transfer couscous to a large bowl. Chill, uncovered, for 10 to 15 minutes. Remove the couscous from the refrigerator, and add the chicken and fruit; toss to mix. In a small bowl, mix the yogurt, oil, nutmeg, cinnamon, orange juice and lemon juice. Add the yogurt mixture to the chicken mixture and stir gently. Serve each portion on a bed of leaf lettuce.
Serves 6-8

ASPARAGUS RICE SALAD

1½ pounds. fresh asparagus,   ½ cup diced celery
     cut in 1½ inch pieces   1 cup raw baby carrots, sliced
3 cups cooked wild rice   1 cup grape tomatoes, cut in half
1 cup diced sweet onion   ½ cup chopped yellow pepper

Place all of the ingredients in a large bowl and toss until mixed well. Cover bowl tightly and refrigerate while making the dressing.

Dressing Recipe:

½ cup extra virgin olive oil   ¼ cup red wine vinegar
1 tablespoon fresh lemon juice   1½ tablespoon dijon mustard
1 tablespoon fructose   Pinch of sea salt
¼ teaspoon ground black pepper   ½ teaspoon minced garlic
2 teaspoons dried basil   1 teaspoon dried rosemary
½ teaspoon dried thyme

Put vinegar, lemon juice, mustard, salt, pepper, fructose and garlic in a bowl, whisking vigorously until all ingredients are well blended. Very slowly add the olive oil, beating constantly with the whisk. Stir in the basil, rosemary and thyme until well blended. Remove salad from the refrigerator and add dressing, tossing until well blended. Cover salad tightly and refrigerate at least 8 hours before serving, removing from refrigerator and tossing 3 or 4 times. Be sure to re-cover completely and tightly each time before placing back in refrigerator. Gently toss just before serving. **Serves 6-8**

If desired, garnish with one of the following just before serving:

½ cup pine nuts
½ cup toasted walnuts
½ cup croutons
½ cup diced cucumbers
1 cup sliced fresh mushrooms

Navy Bean & Turkey Ham Salad

1 pound dry navy beans, cooked but not seasoned
¾ pound cooked cubed nitrate-free turkey ham
½ cup chopped yellow pepper
½ cup chopped red pepper
1½ cups chopped plum tomatoes

1 diced purple onion
1 cup diced celery
½ cup sliced black olives
1 cup chopped cucumber

Place all of the ingredients in a large bowl and toss until evenly mixed. Cover tightly and refrigerate while you make the dressing.

Dressing Recipe:

½ cup white vinegar
2 tablespoons. spicy brown mustard
1 teaspoon hot sauce
1 cup light olive oil

2 cloves garlic, minced
1 teaspoon ground pepper
½ teaspoon dried oregano
1 teaspoon fructose

Place all ingredients except olive oil in a bowl and whisk vigorously while slowly adding the oil in a steady stream. Remove the salad from the refrigerator and add the dressing, tossing until well mixed. Cover bowl and refrigerate at least 8 hours before serving. Gently toss again before serving. **Serves 6**

Note: This salad is even better if allowed to set in the refrigerator overnight. If desired, sprinkle ½ cup of fresh chopped parsley or basil over the top just before serving.

Summer Salad

1 cup cooked long grain wild rice
1 cup cooked, cubed chicken breast
1 medium tomato, seeded & diced
½ teaspoon dried tarragon
1 bunch green onions, chopped
⅓ cup cooked green peas

4 tablespoons rice vinegar
1 tablespoons olive oil
1 clove garlic, minced
½ teaspoon sea salt
¼ teaspoon black pepper

Combine cooked, cooled rice with all ingredients. Toss lightly. Chill and serve.
Serves 4-6

BEST EVER CHICKEN SALAD

1 pound roasted boneless chicken breast strips	½ cup sliced onions
1 pound fresh baby leaf spinach	1 cup sliced mushrooms
1 cucumber, peeled and diced	1 peeled tomato, chopped

Place spinach on a serving platter, place chicken strips on top, then follow with mushrooms, onions, cucumber, and tomato. Serve with the following salad dressing on the side. **Serves 4-6**

Dressing Recipe:

8 ounces fat free sour cream	¼ cup light olive oil
2 tablespoons. balsamic vinegar	1 tablespoon fresh lemon juice
1 teaspoon fructose	¼ teaspoon sea salt
¼ teaspoon black pepper	2 tablespoons chopped parsley

Place all ingredients in a jar. Cover tightly and shake well. Chill thoroughly. Shake well before using.

Note: Pine nuts may be sprinkled on top of salad if desired.

TRULY A MEAL TUNA SALAD

1 (12 ounce) can albacore tuna, drained & flaked	1½ cups fresh green beans, steamed
	4 tablespoons fresh lemon juice
4 cups cannellini beans, cooked & drained	1 cup chopped purple onion
4 tablespoons light olive oil	½ teaspoon sea salt
1 teaspoon grated lemon peel	½ teaspoon minced garlic
¼ teaspoon ground black pepper	6 cups baby spinach
1 cup cherry tomatoes, cut in half	1 tablespoons chopped rosemary

In a large bowl, whisk the olive oil, lemon juice, lemon peel, salt, black pepper, garlic and rosemary together until well blended. Add the cannellini beans, tuna, onions, tomatoes and green beans and gently toss until well mixed. Cover tightly and chill until ready to serve. When ready to serve, toss salad again and serve on beds of fresh raw baby spinach. **Serves 8-10**

WILD RICE SALAD WITH CHEESY BRUSCHETTA

½ pound mixed mushrooms, sliced (button, shitake, cremini)	¾ cup light vinaigrette salad dressing
	2 teaspoons olive oil
1 cup long grain wild rice	2 tablespoon Dijon mustard
3 teaspoons dried thyme, divided	½ cup Gorgonzola
1½ teaspoons pepper, divided	8 cups salad greens
16 slices French baguette bread	½ cup toasted walnuts

Cook rice according to package directions, then stir in mushrooms, 1 ½ teaspoons of the thyme and 1 teaspoon of the pepper. Meanwhile, heat oven to 350 degrees. Combine remaining thyme, Gorgonzola, olive oil and remaining pepper and spread on bread slices. Bake on baking sheet until edges are browned, about 15 minutes.

Whisk salad dressing and mustard together. Toss salad greens with enough dressing to coat them and divide among 4 serving dishes. Spoon rice mixture into the center and sprinkle with walnuts. Arrange bruschetta around the edges. **Serves 12-14**

JUBILEE SALAD

1 cup cooked Jubilee rice	½ cup minced parsley
¼ cup low-fat Italian vinaigrette	1 cup diced celery
1 large tomato, seeded & diced	1 tablespoon chopped basil
1 bunch green onions, minced	Sea salt & pepper to taste
4 ounces cubed natural cheddar	

Add vinaigrette, salt and pepper to cooled rice. Toss lightly. Add remaining ingredients and toss. If desired, add more vinaigrette to taste. Chill. Serve on a bed of lettuce and garnish with parsley. **Serves 4**

WILD RICE PECAN SALAD

1 cup uncooked long grain wild rice
1 cup uncooked short grain brown rice
2 cups chopped celery
1 cup chopped scallions
1½ cups dried sweet cranberries

4 cups water
1 teaspoon olive oil
½ teaspoon sea salt
1 cup chopped cilantro
2 cups chopped pecans

Dressing:

½ cup balsamic vinegar
2 navel oranges (for ¾ cup juice & 3 tablespoons zest)

2 tablespoons honey
1 tablespoon Dijon mustard
½ cup olive oil

In a large saucepan, combine water, wild rice, oil and salt. Simmer about 30 minutes. Add brown rice and simmer 30 minutes longer or until rice is tender. Drain and add chopped celery, scallions, cranberries, pecans and cilantro. In blender, put mustard, orange juice and zest, honey and olive oil. Process in blender until mixed. Pour over rice and vegetables. Stir and chill. **Serves 6-8**

GARDEN RICE SALAD

1 cup Black Japonica rice
1½ cups sliced mushrooms
1 cup fresh snow peas, halved or diagonal
4 teaspoons garlic flavored olive oil
4 to 6 cups assorted field greens
½ cup shaved Parmesan cheese

2 tablespoons olive oil
1 cup sliced red pepper
½ cup sliced scallions
1 cup balsamic vinegar
Sea salt & pepper to taste

Cook rice according to package directions and cool. Place cooled rice in a large bowl. Heat the olive oil in a large skillet over high heat. Add the sliced mushrooms. Season with salt and pepper to taste. Sauté 5 minutes. Add the snow peas, red pepper, and scallions. Stir-fry 3 minutes, or just until vegetables are tender-crisp. Fold the stir-fry, balsamic vinegar and 1 tablespoon of the garlic flavored oil into the rice. Serve the rice salad over the field greens. Just before serving, drizzle the salad with the remaining garlic flavored oil and shaved Parmesan. Serve warm or cooled. **Serves 4-6**

MEDITERRANEAN SALAD

1 cup cooked Wehani rice

1/4 cup sliced olives (optional)

1 to 2 tablespoons balsamic vinegar

1/2 cup julienned sundried tomatoes

1/4 cup natural Parmesan cheese

1/2 teaspoon dried rosemary, crushed

2 tablespoons olive oil

2 cloves garlic, minced

1/2 teaspoon sea salt

1 to 2 tablespoons lemon juice

1 tablespoon minced basil

1 teaspoon black pepper

Optional Ingredients:

1 each red and green bell pepper, seeded & finely chopped

1/2 cup diced carrots

1 medium tomato, seeded & finely chopped

1/2 cup capers

Place hot rice in a large bowl. Combine oil, lemon juice, vinegar, garlic, salt, rosemary and pepper in small jar or blender. Shake or blend well and pour over rice. Toss lightly and let cool. Add remaining ingredients. Serve chilled or at room temperature. **Serves 4-6**

BLACK BEAN SALAD

1 red bell pepper

1 yellow bell pepper

1 cup corn, drained

4 tablespoons red wine vinegar

1 can black beans, drained

1 teaspoon lime juice

Tortilla chips

1 green bell pepper

1 clove garlic, minced

1/2 cup red onion, diced

1 teaspoon cilantro

1/4 cup olive oil

freshly ground pepper

Seed and dice all bell peppers. In a salad bowl, combine bell peppers, onion, corn, garlic and cilantro. Toss to mix. Add olive oil, vinegar, lime juice and salt and pepper to taste. Toss again. Add black beans, toss well and serve with tortilla chips or place on a bed of lettuce. **Serves 6**

HAWAIIAN SALAD

3 cups cooked short grain brown rice

2 cups pineapple chunks, reserve liquid

2 cups cooked chicken, cut in bite-sized pieces

2 cups sliced celery

Sea salt & pepper to taste

¾ cup organic mayonnaise

Combine rice, pineapple, celery and chicken. Blend ½ cup pineapple juice with the mayonnaise. Add to rice and chicken mixture. Toss lightly. **Serves 6-8**

FESTIVAL SALAD

2 cups cooked, chilled long grain brown rice

2 organic eggs, boiled and chopped

½ cup cooked, cubed chicken breast

½ cup organic mayonnaise

½ cup slivered smoked turkey

Sea salt and pepper to taste

½ cup chopped celery

1 tablespoon chopped chives

1 tablespoon olive oil

1 tablespoon wine vinegar

¼ cup chopped parsley

Combine all ingredients except oil, vinegar and mayonnaise, by tossing lightly. Sprinkle oil and vinegar over mixture. Add mayonnaise and season to taste. Refrigerate for several hours for enhanced flavor. **Serves 6-8**

COUNTRY WILD RICE SALAD

1 cup cooked country wild rice

1 each red & green bell pepper, diced

1¼ cup chopped green onions

1 cup cooked, finely chopped chicken

½ cup organic mayonnaise

¼ cup sliced black olives

1¼ cup chopped celery

2 tablespoons fresh lemon juice

1 teaspoon curry powder

Combine cooked, cooled rice with all ingredients. Toss lightly. Chill. Serve on a bed of lettuce and garnish with bell pepper slivers and olives. **Serves 6-8**

FIESTA LAYERED SALAD

1 (9 ounce) package Arrowhead Mills
  cornbread mix
$\frac{1}{4}$ cup lime juice
1 teaspoon ground cumin
$\frac{1}{2}$ cup chopped cilantro
$\frac{1}{2}$ teaspoon sea salt
3 green onions, chopped
6 plum tomatoes, chopped
Garnish: green onion curls

1 (11 ounce) can whole kernel
  corn, drained
4 ounces chopped green chiles
$\frac{1}{2}$ cup organic mayonnaise
4 cups romaine lettuce, shredded
1 (15 ounce) can black beans, drained
1 cup shredded cheddar
1 red pepper, chopped

Prepare cornbread mix according to package directions, add chiles. Cool and crumble. Process mayonnaise, cilantro, lime juice, cumin and salt in a food processor or blender until smooth, stopping to scrape down sides. Layer a 4-quart bowl with half of the lettuce, half of the cornbread, one-third of the mayonnaise mixture and half each of beans, corn, cheese, red pepper, onions and tomatoes. Repeat layers. Top with remaining mayonnaise mixture. Cover and chill 1 to 2 hours. **Serves 4**

SPRING SALAD

1 roasted chicken, chilled
2 cups sliced strawberries
4 ounces crumbled bleu cheese
$\frac{1}{2}$ cup honey roasted cashews
$\frac{1}{4}$ teaspoon black pepper

8 cups mixed greens
1 lemon, halved
3 tablespoons olive oil
$\frac{1}{4}$ teaspoon sea salt

Remove and discard skin from chicken. Pull meat from bones, discarding bones. Shred meat. Place greens on a platter. Top with chicken, strawberries, cheese and nuts. Drizzle with juice from lemon and oil. Sprinkle with salt and pepper. **Serves 6-8**

NINE DAY COLE SLAW

3 pounds cabbage

2 onions

1/4 cup fructose

2 tablespoons mustard seed

1 green pepper

1 cup vinegar

1 cup olive oil

2 tablespoons sea salt

Chop cabbage, pepper and onions. Combine remaining ingredients in a medium saucepan and bring to a boil; pour over vegetables and store in refrigerator in covered jars. Delicious for 9 days. **Serves 8-10**

SAUERKRAUT SALAD

2 jars sauerkraut

1 cup diced green peppers

1 small can water chestnuts

1/3 cup olive oil

3/4 cup fructose

1 cup chopped onion

1 cup diced celery

1/3 cup water

2/3 cup vinegar

Mix together the sauerkraut, peppers, onion, celery and water chestnuts. Heat the remaining ingredients until fructose dissolves. Pour over vegetables and chill. **Serves 4-6**

WILD RICE SALAD

1 (6 ounce) package quick cook long grain/wild rice

4 tablespoons olive oil

1/2 cup raisins

1/4 teaspoon sea salt

1/4 teaspoon pepper

2 green onions, chopped

2 cups chopped cooked chicken

1/2 cup dried cranberries

1 granny smith apple, peeled & chopped

1/3 cup white balsamic vinegar

1 package toasted sliced almonds

Cook rice according to package directions; cool. Stir together chicken with all ingredients except almonds. Add rice. Cover and chill for 8 hours. Sprinkle with almonds just before serving. **Serves 6-8**

SPINACH-ORANGE SALAD

4 cups torn fresh spinach

2 oranges, peeled and sectioned

¾ cup sliced fresh mushrooms

¼ teaspoon poppy seed

¼ cup toasted slivered almonds

2 tablespoons olive oil

1 tablespoon lemon juice

1 tablespoon honey

⅛ teaspoon garlic powder

Place spinach in a large salad bowl. Add oranges and mushrooms. Toss lightly to mix. For dressing, in a screw-top jar combine oil, lemon juice, honey, poppy seed and garlic powder. Cover and shake well. Pour the dressing over the salad. Toss lightly to coat. Sprinkle with toasted almonds. **Serves 4**

CREAMY CUCUMBERS

½ cup sour cream

½ teaspoon fructose

1 large cucumber, halved lengthwise and sliced

1 teaspoon sea salt

1 tablespoon lemon juice

¼ teaspoon dried dill weed

1 small onion, sliced thin

Dash of pepper

Stir together the sour cream, lemon juice, fructose, dill weed, salt and pepper. Add cucumber and onion slices; toss to coat. Cover and chill for 2 to 48 hours, stirring often. Stir before serving. **Serves 2**

CARROT SALAD

3 medium carrots, shredded

⅓ cup raisins

⅓ cup organic mayonnaise

¼ cup toasted slivered almonds

1 small apple, chopped

1 teaspoon lemon juice

Milk

In a mixing bowl combine carrots, apple and raisins. Sprinkle with lemon juice. Add mayonnaise. Stir gently to coat well. Cover and chill for 2 to 24 hours. If dressing becomes too thick, stir in a little milk. Before serving, sprinkle with toasted almonds. **Serves 4-6**

PEA SALAD

1 (10 ounce) package frozen peas
1 cup cubed cheddar cheese
2 tablespoons chopped onion
$\frac{1}{3}$ cup organic mayonnaise
2 tablespoons diced pimento (optional)
6 medium tomatoes

2 boiled eggs, chopped
$\frac{1}{4}$ cup chopped celery
$\frac{1}{8}$ teaspoon pepper
$\frac{1}{4}$ teaspoon sea salt
Leaf lettuce

Cook peas according to package directions. Thoroughly drain the cooked peas and cool. In a large bowl combine peas, cheese, eggs, celery, onion and pimento. Combine mayonnaise, salt and pepper. Add to pea mixture; toss to mix. Cover and chill for 4 to 24 hours. Stir mixture well. If desired, cut each tomato into 8 wedges, cutting to, but not through, the bottom. Place tomatoes atop lettuce. Fill tomatoes with pea mixture. **Serves 4-6**

COMPANY CHICKEN SALAD

2 whole roasted chickens, skinned
    & de-boned or 6 cooked skinless,
    boneless chicken breasts
1 large yellow onion, chopped
6 celery stalks, finely chopped
$1\frac{1}{2}$ cups broken pecan pieces
3 cups red seedless grapes, sliced in half
$1\frac{1}{2}$ cups raisins, soaked in hot water

$\frac{1}{2}$ cup mayonnaise
1 cup low fat sour cream
$\frac{1}{4}$ teaspoon sea salt
$\frac{1}{4}$ teaspoon pepper
1 apple, finely chopped

Drain raisins. Tear or chop chicken into small bite-size pieces. In large bowl, mix together all ingredients. Refrigerate for two hours. Serve on a bed of mixed greens or spread on whole wheat bread or croissants. **Serves 12-14**

MACARONI SALAD

1 cup elbow macaroni
¾ cup cubed cheddar cheese
½ small green pepper, chopped
¼ cup organic mayonnaise
2 tablespoons sweet pickle relish
¼ teaspoon sea salt

1 stalk celery, diced
½ cup green peas
⅓ cup chopped onion
¼ cup sour cream
2 tablespoons milk

Cook macaroni according to package directions. Drain and rise with cold water. Drain again. In a mixing bowl combine macaroni, cheese, celery, green pepper, peas and onion. Stir gently to combine. For dressing, mix mayonnaise, sour cream, milk, pickle relish and salt. Toss dressing with macaroni mixture. Cover and chill for 4 to 24 hours. Stir in additional milk, if necessary. **Serves 2-4**

RAMEN BOK CHOY SALAD

2 packages ramen noodles
3 tablespoons slivered almonds, chopped
¼ cup cider vinegar
1 bok choy (Chinese white cabbage), shredded

¼ cup fructose
¼ cup olive oil
2 tablespoons soy sauce
6 green onions, chopped

Place noodles and almonds on buttered cookie sheet. Bake at 350° for 8 to 10 minutes or until golden brown; set aside. Bring fructose, oil, vinegar and soy sauce to a boil in a saucepan over medium heat. Remove from heat and cool. Place bok choy and green onions in a large bowl. Drizzle with fructose mixture. Add ramen noodle mixture, tossing well. Serve immediately. **Serves 2-4**

CRANBERRY CABBAGE SLAW

$\frac{1}{4}$ cup organic mayonnaise

1 tablespoon sweet pickle relish

$\frac{1}{4}$ teaspoon pepper

$\frac{1}{8}$ teaspoon celery seed

$\frac{1}{4}$ cup chopped celery

$\frac{1}{4}$ cup chopped red sweet pepper

1 tablespoon mustard

2 tablespoons honey

$\frac{1}{8}$ teaspoon sea salt

$\frac{1}{3}$ cup chopped walnuts

$\frac{1}{4}$ cup chopped onion

$\frac{1}{4}$ cup dried cranberries

In a small bowl stir together mayonnaise, pickle relish, mustard, honey, pepper, salt and celery seed. In a large mixing bowl combine cabbage, walnuts, celery, onion, red pepper and cranberries. Add mayonnaise mixture to cabbage mixture and toss to coat. Cover and chill at least 1 hour or up to 6 hours. **Serves 4**

CINNAMON FRUIT SALAD

1 cup unpeeled apricot halves

2 teaspoons lemon juice

2 inches stick cinnamon, broken

2 medium oranges, peeled and sliced

1 cup strawberries, halved

1 teaspoon fructose

1 cup pineapple chunks

Dash of ground nutmeg

Leaf lettuce

Fresh mint sprigs

For dressing, in a blender container or food processor bowl place undrained apricots. Cover and blend or process until smooth. In a saucepan combine blended apricots, fructose, lemon juice, cinnamon and nutmeg. Bring to boiling; reduce heat. Cover and simmer for 10 minutes. Remove cinnamon. Meanwhile, in a mixing bowl stir together orange slices and pineapple chunks. Add dressing, stirring carefully to coat. Cover and chill for several hours. Just before serving, stir in strawberry halves. Spoon fruit mixture onto 6 lettuce-lined plated. If desired, garnish with fresh mint sprigs. **Serves 4-6**

HONEY CHICKEN SALAD

4 cups chopped chicken

1 cup sweetened dried cranberries

½ cup chopped pecans, toasted

½ cup organic mayonnaise

½ cup orange blossom honey

3 celery ribs, diced

¼ cup raisins

¼ teaspoon sea salt

1 cup sour cream

¼ teaspoon pepper

Stir together chicken, celery, cranberries, raisins and pecans. Whisk together mayonnaise, sour cream, honey, salt and pepper. Add to chicken mixture, stirring gently until combined. Garnish with additional toasted pecans, if desired.
Serves 6

TOMATO CUCUMBER SALAD

2 pints cherry tomatoes, halved

1 small seedless cucumber, sliced

3 tablespoons fresh dill

3 tablespoons chopped scallions

Dressing:

¼ cup organic mayonnaise

¼ cup seasoned rice-wine vinegar

¼ cup sour cream

1 tablespoon fresh lime juice

For dressing, whisk together all ingredients in a large bowl until blended. Add tomatoes, cucumber, scallions and dill. Stir gently to mix and coat. **Serves 2-4**

The Dinner Table

Main Entrees:
Fish,
Chicken,
Turkey

8

HEARTY MEATBALLS

Sauce Ingredients:

8 cups plum tomatoes, peeled & chopped

1 tablespoon fructose

1 large clove garlic, minced

2 teaspoons low sodium soy sauce

½ cup chopped fresh carrots

1 bay leaf

1 teaspoon dried oregano

½ teaspoon thyme

1 cup minced onion

Combine all of the ingredients and bring to a slow boil, lower to a simmer and cover. Simmer sauce for 30 minutes, stirring 2 or 3 times.

Preheat oven to 350°.

Meatball Ingredients:

1 pound ground nitrate-free
    Italian turkey sausage

1 pound lean ground beef

½ cup chopped celery

½ cup chopped onion

2 eggs, lightly beaten

1 teaspoon sea salt

1 cup cooked long grain rice

¾ cup chopped green pepper

⅓ cup chopped parsley

1½ tablespoon spicy brown mustard

¼ teaspoon ground red pepper

Combine all ingredients and mix well. Form the meat mixture into 1 to 2 inch balls. Place the meatballs in a large glass baking dish and pour sauce over them. Cover baking dish with foil and bake on middle oven rack for 1 to 1½ hours, depending on the size of the meatballs. **Serves 6**

OUT OF THIS WORLD BEEF SHORT RIBS

6 pounds beef short ribs	4 cups water
1 cup pineapple juice	6 bay leaves
2 cloves garlic, peeled & left whole	$\frac{1}{2}$ teaspoon sea salt

Place all ingredients in a large pot and bring to a boil. Cover and simmer for 30 minutes.

Preheat oven to 325°.

Remove ribs from pot and place in a single layer in a large roasting pan. Place ribs in oven for 30 minutes. Make sauce while the ribs are in the oven.

Sauce Recipe:

$\frac{1}{4}$ cup olive oil	$\frac{1}{2}$ cup chopped onion
1 clove garlic, peeled & minced	2 cups tomato puree
4 tablespoons fructose	3 tablespoons honey
$\frac{1}{4}$ cup vinegar	$1\frac{1}{4}$ teaspoon dry mustard
2 teaspoons Worcestershire sauce	1 teaspoon sea salt
$\frac{1}{2}$ teaspoon dried basil	$\frac{1}{4}$ teaspoon dried rosemary
1 teaspoon paprika	

Combine olive oil, onion and garlic in medium saucepan and sauté for 6 to 8 minutes or until the onion is soft and clear. Add the remaining ingredients and bring to a simmer. Simmer sauce for 15 minutes, stirring often.

Remove the ribs from the oven and drain off fat. Pour half of the sauce evenly over the ribs and put back in the oven for 20 minutes. Remove from oven, turn the ribs over and pour the remaining sauce over them. Bake for an additional 20 minutes. Remove from oven and evenly sprinkle the following mixture over them.

$\frac{1}{4}$ cup flour, $\frac{1}{4}$ cup fructose and $\frac{1}{4}$ teaspoon allspice, blended well together.

Place back in oven and bake for 15 minutes. Allow ribs to set for 20 minutes before serving. **Serves 8-10**

SPINACH STUFFED MEATLOAF

Stuffing Ingredients:

1 pound baby spinach, sautéed lightly & chopped   ¼ cup sour cream

1 cup goat cheese, finely crumbled   Pinch of sea salt

¼ teaspoon black pepper

Place all ingredients in a bowl, mixing until well blended. Set aside while preparing the meat mixture.

Preheat oven to 375°.

Meatloaf Ingredients:

1 pound lean ground beef   2 eggs, lightly beaten

1 pound ground nitrate-free turkey sausage   ¼ cup chopped parsley

¼ cup diced green pepper   ¼ cup diced red onion

½ cup dry oat bread crumbs   1 teaspoon minced garlic

1 teaspoon fennel seed   ½ teaspoon sea salt

¼ teaspoon black pepper

Put all of the ingredients in a large bowl. Using your hands, mix until well blended. Using a large 9-by-5-by-3-inch non-stick loaf pan, layer the meat mixture and stuffing mixture. Make a total of 4 layers. Keep the stuffing mixture 1 inch away from the sides of the pan. Make sure the first and last layers are the meat mixture. Lightly press down on the top layer of the meat mixture on the outer edges only. Cover tightly with foil and place in oven for 1 hour. Remove foil and bake for an additional 45 minutes. Remove from oven and allow to stand for 20 minutes before transferring to a serving dish. **Serves 4**

MEATLOAF SURPRISE

1½ pounds lean ground beef

1 pound nitrate-free ground turkey sausage

1½ cups diced onions

1 teaspoon dried oregano

1 tablespoon dried basil

2 tablespoons prepared mustard

2 egg whites

1 cup pretzels, coarsely crushed

2 tablespoons tomato paste, mixed with
   1 tablespoon balsamic vinegar

½ pound ground chicken

3 tablespoons light olive oil

4 cloves garlic, minced

1 teaspoon dried thyme

1½ teaspoon hot sauce

⅛ teaspoon black pepper

1 whole egg

Preheat oven to 350°.

Heat olive oil in skillet over medium heat. Add the onions, garlic, oregano, thyme and basil. Cook about 5 minutes. Put the onion mixture in a large bowl and add beef, chicken, turkey sausage, egg whites, whole egg, pretzels, mustard, hot sauce, black pepper and tomato paste/vinegar mixture. Using your hands, blend mixture completely. Put the mixture in a large glass baking dish and shape into a loaf. Bake on middle oven rack for 1 hour and 20 minutes. Remove from oven and baste with glaze below.

Meatloaf Glaze:

3 tablespoons tomato sauce

1 tablespoon molasses

1 tablespoon prepared mustard

Mix until completely blended. Brush all over the top and sides of the meatloaf. Return meatloaf to oven for 30 minutes. Remove from oven and allow to set for 30 minutes before transferring to a serving dish. **Serves 4**

OUR FAVORITE BARBECUE

3 pounds lean beef stew meat, cubed

1 diced green pepper

1 (6 ounce) can tomato paste

½ cup fructose

1 teaspoon hot sauce

2 teaspoons low sodium
   Worcestershire sauce

1 cup diced onion

½ cup diced celery

¼ cup white vinegar

1 clove garlic, minced

2 teaspoons Dijon mustard

1 teaspoon sea salt

Preheat oven to 300°.

Place all ingredients in a dutch oven and stir until well combined. Place on a burner and just bring to a boil, stirring constantly. Cover tightly and place on the middle rack in oven. Cook for 5 hours, stirring once every hour. Remove from oven and break up any big chunks of meat. This is very good served on a toasted roll or over rice. **Serves 4-6**

BEEF STIR FRY

½ cup low sodium beef broth

3 tablespoons low sodium soy sauce

1 large clove garlic, minced

1 pound top round steak, cut in strips

1 medium bell pepper, cut in strips

1 cup fresh mushrooms, thinly sliced

1 teaspoon ground ginger

5 teaspoons olive oil

¾ teaspoon grated orange peel

1¼ cup sliced carrots

1 cup sliced green onion

½ cup chopped celery

Combine broth, soy sauce, ginger, garlic and orange peel in a small bowl. Whisk until well blended, set aside. In a large non-stick skillet, heat the oil over high heat. Add the strips of steak and stir-fry until no longer pink, about 4 minutes. Using a large slotted spoon, remove the steak and put on a plate. Add the bell pepper, carrots, celery, onions and mushrooms to the skillet and stir-fry for 3 minutes. Stir in the broth mixture and continue to stir-fry until the vegetables are tender but still crisp. Add the steak back to the skillet and stir-fry for 3 more minutes. This is very good served over rice or Chinese noodles. **Serves 6**

CORNBREAD POT PIE

½ pound nitrate-free ground turkey sausage	1 pound ground beef
½ cup diced green bell pepper	1 cup diced sweet onion
½ cup diced baby carrots	1 cup chopped cabbage
2 cups tomatoes, peeled & chopped (use juice)	1 teaspoon minced garlic
¼ teaspoon ground black pepper	½ teaspoon sea salt
½ teaspoon caraway seeds	½ teaspoon paprika
¼ teaspoon hot sauce	

Cook the meat until brown, stirring and breaking into bite size chunks. Remove the meat but leave the drippings and add the onion, bell pepper and carrots and cook for 10 minutes. Put the meat, sautéed vegetables and the rest of the ingredients in a large glass casserole dish, mixing well.

Preheat oven to 400°.

Mix the following ingredients until well blended:

1 cup whole wheat flour	1 teaspoon sea salt
1 cup stone ground corn meal	1 cup milk
1½ sticks butter, melted & cooled	1 lightly beaten egg
2 teaspoons aluminum free baking powder	1 tablespoon honey

Drop this batter by spoonfuls on top of the meat and vegetable mixture. Place the casserole dish on the middle oven rack and bake for 20 to 25 minutes or until the cornbread is golden brown. **Serves 4**

Note: Any ground meat or a combination of any ground meats may be used in place of the beef and turkey sausage.

GRANDPA'S FAVORITE CASSEROLE

2 pounds beef steak, cut in bite size pieces	1 medium onion, sliced
6 baking potatoes, sliced ¼ inch thick	½ pound shredded cheddar
1½ cup sliced mushrooms	

Using a large glass baking dish, layer all of the ingredients in 2 to 3 layers each. Be sure to layer so that the last of the cheese is the top layer.

Preheat oven to 375°.

Combine 1 cup fresh milk, ⅓ cup butter, 1 teaspoon salt, ½ teaspoon ground black pepper, 1 teaspoon minced garlic, 1 teaspoon dried crushed thyme and ½ teaspoon paprika in a small sauce pan. Bring mixture to a low simmer, stirring constantly and simmer until butter is melted and the mixture is hot. Pour the hot butter mixture evenly over the meat/vegetable mixture, cover tightly with foil, being careful not to let the foil touch the cheese on top. Place the baking dish in oven for 45 minutes. Remove the foil and put back in the over for 15 more minutes. Allow to stand for 20 to 30 minutes before serving.

Note: This is also very good made with chicken breast or nitrate free turkey sausage in place of the steak. **Serves 4-6**

HOBO BEEF STEW

2 pounds lean ground beef	6 tablespoons butter
½ cup diced red pepper	1½ cups chopped onion
½ cup diced green pepper	1 cup diced celery
4 cups chopped tomatoes	1 tablespoon minced garlic
½ cup chopped parsley	1 tablespoon paprika
½ teaspoon black pepper	1 teaspoon sea salt
¼ teaspoon red pepper	6 cups boiling water
3 cups potatoes, peeled & cut in cubes	1 cup beans, your choice

In a large pot, melt the butter. Add the meat and cook until brown and crumbly. Add the rest of the ingredients, stirring well and bring to a boil. Cover the pot and reduce heat to low. Simmer for 45 minutes, stirring often. **Serves 6-8**

BEST EVER RICE

1 pound lean ground beef	1 medium chopped onion
2 tomatoes, peeled & diced	2 cloves garlic, minced
¼ cup diced green pepper	½ cup chopped celery
½ teaspoon black pepper	½ teaspoon sea salt
½ teaspoon thyme	1 teaspoon fructose

Brown meat, stirring to break up. Remove from skillet and set to the side. Put onions, garlic, green pepper, and celery in skillet and cook over medium heat for 10 minutes, stirring often. Add tomatoes (including juice), salt, fructose, black pepper and thyme to onion mixture and cook 10 minutes longer. Add cooked meat and cook for 10 more minutes. Serve over hot rice.

Recipe for rice: Place 3½ cups water, 1 tablespoon olive oil, 1 teaspoon salt and 1½ cups long grain rice in a heavy pot and bring to a boil, stirring well. Lower heat, cover tightly and simmer for 20 minutes. Allow rice to stand covered 5 minutes before serving.

Place rice on serving platter and top with meat mixture. Garnish with fresh chopped parsley. **Serves 4-6**

BARBECUED STEAK

3 pounds beef steak, cut in strips	3 tablespoons light olive oil
1½ cups diced plum tomatoes	1 cup tomato sauce
¼ cup low sodium Worcestershire sauce	2 cloves garlic, minced
¼ cup apple cider vinegar	1 tablespoon paprika
3 tablespoons light brown sugar	½ teaspoon chili powder
2 teaspoons spicy brown mustard	1 teaspoon sea salt
½ cup finely chopped purple onion	½ teaspoon black pepper

Heat the oil in a large, deep skillet. Add the steak and brown on both sides. While the steak is browning, make the sauce. In a bowl, whisk the rest of the ingredients together until well blended. Pour the sauce over the steak and bring to a boil, stirring often. Lower heat until sauce is simmering. Cover skillet and cook for about 1½ hours or until steak is tender. Sprinkle with ¼ cup fresh chopped parsley just before serving, if desired. **Serves 4**

BAKED GROUPER WITH SAUCE

2 pounds grouper fillets, cut in serving size pieces	2 tablespoons Dijon mustard
¼ cup diced onion	½ cup chopped plum tomatoes
½ teaspoon minced garlic	2 teaspoons diced sweet pepper
2 tablespoons honey	2 tablespoons organic mayonnaise

Preheat oven to 450°.

Place the fish in an ungreased baking dish and bake in oven for 5 to 6 minutes. The fish should flake easily when tested with a fork. Remove from oven and drain off any liquid. Combine the rest of the ingredients, stirring until well mixed. Pour the sauce evenly over the fish. Return the fish to the oven and bake for 4 more minutes. Place fish on a serving dish and pour sauce over it. If desired, garnish with fresh chopped parsley. **Serves 4**

OVEN BEEF ROAST

3 pound eye of round roast

1/4 cup unbleached flour

1/4 teaspoon ground black pepper

4 cloves garlic, minced

1/4 cup chopped parsley

1 pound whole baby carrots

1 pound small button mushrooms, whole

4 cups beef broth

2 tablespoons light olive oil

1 teaspoon sea salt

1/2 teaspoon red pepper

2 teaspoons chopped thyme

1 1/2 cup pearl onions

2 cups chopped celery

2 tablespoons tomato paste

Stir together the flour, salt, red pepper and black pepper until well blended. Rinse and pat dry the roast and roll in the flour mixture until completely coated. Heat olive oil in a large pot over medium heat and add the roast, keeping the rest of the flour. Brown the roast, turning to brown all sides. Remove roast, add the garlic, thyme and parsley, sautéing and stirring constantly for 2 to 3 minutes. Add the rest of the flour mixture, stirring constantly until the mixture is light brown and all of the flour is absorbed. Slowly add the broth, stirring constantly and bring to a slow steady boil. Cover pot and reduce heat. Allow to simmer while over preheats.

Preheat oven to 375°.

Put roast in oven and cook for 1 hour. Remove from oven and stir the tomato paste into the broth and cook for 30 more minutes. Remove roast and add the carrots, celery, onions and mushrooms. Cover the pot and return to the oven for 30 more minutes. Remove the roast and vegetables and arrange on a serving dish. Bring the remaining juices to a low boil, stirring constantly. Simmer for 8 to 10 minutes or until reduced and slightly thickened. **Serves 6**

BEEF ROAST WITH WHOLE POTATOES & SPECIAL SAUCE

4 pound eye of round roast	¼ cup balsamic vinegar
¼ cup Extra virgin olive oil	2 tablespoons Dijon mustard
1 teaspoon hot sauce	2 teaspoons fresh lemon juice
2 teaspoons low sodium soy sauce	3 cloves garlic, minced
1 teaspoon coarsely ground black pepper	

Place all of the ingredients above in a bowl. Whisk the mixture until well blended. Using the point of a paring knife, pierce the roast all over about an inch deep. Put the roast in a large ziploc freezer bag, pour vinegar mixture over the roast and seal bag tightly. Place bag in the refrigerator for 6 to 8 hours, shaking bag occasionally.

Preheat oven to 400°.

Remove roast from bag, place on a rack in a roasting pan. Discard vinegar mixture. Scrub 1 baking potato per person and arrange around roast. Place pan in oven and roast for 30 minutes. Then, turn oven down to 325° and roast for 1 hour and 30 minutes. Roast will be medium. Make the sauce while the roast cooks. See sauce recipe below.

Special Sauce:

2 tablespoons extra virgin light olive oil	¼ cup diced onions
¼ cup diced carrots	¼ cup diced celery
½ teaspoon dried thyme	3 tablespoons minced parsley
4 tablespoons prepared mustard with horseradish	1 cup milk
1 teaspoon cornstarch	

Over medium heat, warm olive oil in saucepan. Add onions, carrots and celery, stirring often and cook for 6 minutes or until soft. Stir the cornstarch into the milk until well blended and lump free. Add the mustard and thyme to the milk mixture. Slowly stir the milk mixture into the vegetables, stirring constantly until mixture is very warm and thickens slightly. Remove mixture from heat and stir in parsley. Pour sauce into a gravy boat or small bowl. Remove roast from oven and allow to set for 20 minutes. Place on serving dish and arrange potatoes around roast or place on a separate dish. **Serves 6-8**

MOM'S DAY OFF OVEN STEW

2 pounds beef stew meat, cut in 1 inch pieces	1 cup chopped celery
5 medium potatoes, cut in eighths	$\frac{1}{2}$ cup diced red pepper
2 large carrots, cut in 1 inch pieces	$\frac{1}{2}$ cup chopped parsley
1 medium onion, cut in eighths	1 tablespoon soy sauce
1 (28 ounce) can chopped stewed tomatoes	$\frac{1}{4}$ teaspoon black pepper
$\frac{1}{4}$ teaspoon hot sauce	2 teaspoons dried thyme
1 teaspoon dried basil	1 cup lima beans
1 cup sliced mushrooms	$1\frac{1}{2}$ cups boiling water

Preheat oven to 275°.

Combine all of the ingredients, stir gently and pour into a large glass casserole dish. Cover and place on middle oven rack. Cook stew for 5 hours, stirring gently every hour. Remove from oven and allow to stand for 30 minutes. Stir well before serving. **Serves 6**

DELUXE FRANKS

8 all natural franks, beef or turkey (nitrate free)	1 medium sliced onion
$\frac{1}{2}$ cup diced green pepper	1 cup diced celery
1 (28 ounce) can diced tomatoes	1 clove garlic, minced
2 tablespoons light olive oil	2 tablespoons brown mustard

Heat olive oil in a deep sauté pan. Add onion, celery, garlic, and green pepper. Sauté over medium low heat for 8 minutes, stirring often. Stir in tomatoes including the juice and add the mustard, stirring well. Bring the vegetable mixture to a low boil, add the franks and bring back to a low simmer. Cover and cook for 20 minutes.

Serve on all grain or whole grain buns that have been toasted. **Serves 4-6**

TURKEY SAUSAGE STUFFED POTATOES

2 cups ground cooked turkey sausage (nitrate free)	¼ cup shredded cheddar
1 cup low fat sour cream	4 large baking potatoes
2 tablespoons chopped chives	½ cup shredded swiss cheese
1 teaspoon minced garlic	2 tablespoons chopped red pepper
1 tablespoon chopped celery	½ cup chopped tomatoes
1 teaspoon sea salt	½ teaspoon black pepper

Preheat oven to 425°.

Place potatoes in baking pan and place in over for 45 to 60 minutes or until done. Remove potatoes from oven and allow to cool enough to handle. Cut a slice from the top of each potato and gently scoop out inside and cube, being sure to keep potato skins intact.

Toss cubed potatoes and all other ingredients together and carefully replace back in potato skins. Return to oven for 15 minutes. Remove potatoes from oven and sprinkle shredded cheddar cheese on top and return to oven for 2 to 3 more minutes, or until cheese is melted.

Add a fresh spinach and mushroom salad and you have a very good and complete meal. **Serves 4**

HOLIDAY CHICKEN & RICE

1 cup long grain brown rice	1 bouillon cube
½ pound fresh sliced mushrooms	2 cloves garlic, minced
8 ounces diced chicken breast	1 tablespoon olive oil
½ teaspoon rosemary	½ teaspoon black pepper
½ cup water	½ cup chicken stock

Sauté garlic in olive oil briefly. Add rice and sauté until rice is coated with the oil. Turn heat to medium-high. Add mushrooms and cook until tender-crisp. Add chicken and cook for 5 minutes. Add remaining ingredients, turn heat to low and simmer for 45 minutes. **Serves 4-6**

Poached Salmon with Lemon & Fresh Herb Butter

2 pounds fresh salmon fillets, about 1 inch thick

1 cup chicken broth

1 teaspoon fresh grated lemon rind

1/8 teaspoon ground black pepper

1/4 cup chopped chives

2 tablespoons fresh lemon juice

2 tablespoons unsalted butter

Put all of the ingredients above except the salmon in a large skillet and bring to a soft boil, stirring well. Add the salmon and lower heat until the liquid is simmering softly. Cover the skillet and simmer the salmon for 20 minutes or until it flakes when tested gently with a fork. While the salmon is cooking, make the sauce below.

Lemon and Fresh Herb Butter:

3 tablespoons unsalted butter, softened

1/4 teaspoon fresh grated lemon rind

2 tablespoons fresh chopped parsley

1 teaspoon fresh lemon juice

1 tablespoon fresh chives

1/2 teaspoon chopped thyme

Put all of the ingredients in a small bowl and stir until well blended.

Remove the salmon from the poaching liquid and place on a serving dish. While the salmon is still warm, spread each fillet with the lemon/herb butter. **Serves 8**

Fresh Tuna Burgers

2 pounds white albacore tuna, chopped

4 tablespoons low sodium soy sauce

1/2 teaspoon ground black pepper

1/2 cup dried bread crumbs

1/4 cup fresh chopped parsley

1/4 cup diced onion

2 teaspoons grated ginger

1 teaspoon fresh lemon juice

4 tablespoons sesame seeds

Preheat oven broiler. In a large bowl, combine the tuna, onion, soy sauce, ginger, pepper and lemon juice. Stir in the breadcrumbs, sesame seeds and parsley. Shape the mixture into 4-inch round patties and place on a broiler pan. Broil for 5 minutes, turn and broil 3 minutes. **Serves 8**

PAN SEARED GROUPER WITH LEMON GARLIC CREAM SAUCE

2 pounds grouper fillets,
  cut in serving size pieces
2 teaspoons fresh lemon juice
$\frac{1}{2}$ teaspoon sea salt

$\frac{1}{4}$ teaspoon paprika
$\frac{1}{8}$ teaspoon ground black pepper
$\frac{1}{2}$ cup unbleached flour
$\frac{1}{4}$ cup olive oil

Sprinkle the lemon juice on both sides of the fish. Put the salt, pepper, paprika and flour in a large ziploc bag and shake to blend ingredients. Pour the olive oil in a non-stick skillet and warm over medium heat. Put the fish in the Ziploc bag with the flour. Shake gently to coat the fish completely with the flour mixture. Place the fish in the hot skillet and allow to cook until light golden brown, about 3 minutes. Carefully turn fish over and repeat cooking process. Place fish on a warm serving dish and keep warm while making the sauce.

Do not wash the skillet! Use the same skillet to make the sauce.

Lemon Garlic Cream Sauce:

$\frac{1}{4}$ cup butter
2 teaspoons fresh lemon juice
$\frac{1}{2}$ cup low fat sour cream

2 cloves garlic, minced
1 teaspoon fresh parsley

Melt the butter in the skillet. Add the garlic and sauté over low heat, stirring constantly. Stir the lemon juice, parsley and sour cream into the garlic butter mixture. Stirring mixture constantly, heat for 2 to 3 minutes. When the sauce is very warm and smooth, drizzle it over the fish. **Serves 8**

DELUXE SALMON CASSEROLE

3 (6½ ounce) salmon, drained & flaked

16 ounces cooked egg noodles

1 cup low fat sour cream

¾ cup organic mayonnaise

1½ cups shredded Colby cheese

½ teaspoon ground black pepper

4 chopped plum tomatoes

1 cup sliced celery

½ cup sliced green onion

2 teaspoons Dijon mustard

½ teaspoon crushed thyme

½ teaspoon sea salt

1 small sliced zucchini

½ teaspoon crushed dill

Preheat oven to 350°. Butter a 3-quart casserole dish.

In a large bowl, mix the cooked noodles, drained salmon, celery and green onions. Blend the sour cream, mustard, mayonnaise, thyme, dill, salt and pepper into the noodle mixture and stir until well blended. Spoon the mixture into the buttered casserole dish. Evenly spread half of the sliced zucchini on top of the noodle mixture. Repeat layers and sprinkle the shredded cheese evenly over the top. Place on the middle oven rack and bake uncovered for 30 minutes or until bubbly and hot. Remove casserole from oven and sprinkle the chopped tomato over the top. Serves **6-8**

BAKED HADDOCK WITH VEGETABLES

2 pounds fresh haddock, cut in serving size pieces	
1 teaspoon fresh lemon juice	¼ teaspoon ground black pepper
1 teaspoon sea salt	1 cup fresh mushrooms
½ cup sliced green onion	½ cup chopped plum tomatoes
¼ cup melted butter	½ cup chopped green pepper
1 tablespoon orange juice	⅓ cup minced parsley

Preheat oven to 350° and butter a large glass baking dish.

Sprinkle the lemon juice, salt and black pepper on both sides of the fish. Place the fish in a single layer in the buttered dish. Mix the mushrooms, onions, tomatoes and green peppers and spoon evenly over the fish. Blend the melted butter and orange juice together and pour over fish and vegetables. Cover with foil and bake for 25 minutes or until fish flakes easily with a fork. Sprinkle with minced parsley before serving. **Serves 8-10**

TURKEY SAUSAGE FILLED ACORN SQUASH

2 medium acorn squash	½ cup chopped onion
1 pound ground turkey sausage (nitrate free)	½ cup chopped celery
¼ cup raisins, soaked in boiling water	½ cup chopped apple

Preheat oven to 350°.

Cut washed squash in half lengthwise and remove seeds. Place cut side down in buttered glass baking dish. Place on middle oven rack and bake for 50 to 60 minutes or until fork tender. Place sausage, onion, celery and apple in skillet and cook until sausage is browned and vegetables are tender crisp. Pour off fat. Remove squash from oven and allow to cool enough to handle. Remove squash from shells and reserve shells. In a mixing bowl, mix squash, ½ teaspoon salt, 1 tablespoon dijon mustard, 1 tablespoon light brown sugar and 1 tablespoon milk. Beat squash mixture on low until fluffy. Return squash/sausage mixture to reserved squash shells and return to 350° oven for 15 minutes. **Serves 4**

EASY GOURMET CHICKEN BREASTS

3 tablespoons chopped parsley	1½ tablespoons chopped thyme
1 tablespoon chopped rosemary	1½ tablespoons minced garlic
4 tablespoons chopped chives	¼ cup olive oil
2 tablespoons balsamic vinegar	½ cup butter
4 chicken breasts, flattened slightly	1½ cup sliced mushrooms
1½ cup chopped tomatoes	½ cup sliced olives (optional)

Combine all herbs, olive oil and vinegar with a wire whisk until well blended. Place chicken in a single layer in a glass dish. Pour the herb/oil mixture over the chicken and wrap tightly. Place in refrigerator for 4 hours, turning after 2 hours. Melt butter, add chicken and sauté for 20 minutes, turning once. Remove chicken and set aside. Sauté mushrooms in same skillet for 5 minutes, remove and set aside. Put chicken back in skillet and add tomatoes and olives. Simmer for 10 minutes or until chicken is done. Remove chicken and place on serving dish. Add the mushrooms back to the skillet and simmer for 5 minutes. Pour hot mixture over chicken just before serving and sprinkle with additional parsley. **Serves 4-6**

ISLAND CHICKEN & PINEAPPLE

2 pounds boneless, skinless chicken breast, in bite size chunks	¼ cup fructose
	¼ teaspoon ground ginger
1 small red onion, coarsely chopped	2 tablespoons olive oil
1 medium chopped green pepper	1 cup pineapple juice
1½ cups chopped pineapple	¼ cup unsalted butter

Melt the butter in a large skillet but do not allow to brown. Add the olive oil and chicken and cook until done. Remove chicken from skillet, leaving all the liquid. Add the onion and green pepper to the liquid in the skillet and sauté for 10 minutes, stirring often. Add the chopped pineapple, stir well and remove from heat. Mix the pineapple juice, fructose and ginger together in a small sauce pan and heat until sugar is melted, stirring constantly. Add this mixture to the skillet mixture and stir well. Put the cooked chicken back in the skillet with the pineapple/vegetable/sauce mixture and cook for 10 minutes or until heated and starting to thicken, stirring often. **Serves 8**

SURPRISE OVEN CHICKEN

5 chicken breasts, skinned, boned & cut in half	2 cups milk
2 tablespoons fresh lemon juice	1 tablespoon minced garlic
1 cup whole wheat flour	1 teaspoon sea salt
1 teaspoon hot sauce	1 teaspoon crushed oregano
1 cup salty pretzels, crushed	¼ cup olive oil

In a large glass bowl, combine the milk, lemon juice, garlic, salt and hot sauce. Add the chicken and stir well. Cover tightly and refrigerate overnight, turning chicken 2 or 3 times.

Preheat oven to 400°. Mix the flour, pretzels and oregano until well blended. Remove the chicken from the milk mixture and roll in the flour mixture. Allow to set on wax paper for 15 minutes. Spread the olive oil on a large baking sheet and place in over for 15 minutes. Remove the hot pan from the oven and place the chicken on it for 3 minutes and then turn chicken. Return to the oven and cook chicken for 30 to 35 minutes or until the juices run clear. **Serves 6**

DIJON CHICKEN & RICE

2 cups cooked black japonica rice	¼ cup honey
¾ cup organic mayonnaise	2 tablespoons Dijon mustard
1 teaspoon horseradish	sliced orange as garnish
6 chicken breast halves	

Mix mayonnaise, honey, mustard and horseradish in a bowl. Brush mixture on chicken breasts. Broil or grill the chicken breasts until done. Spread the rice on a platter as a bed for the chicken breasts. Arrange the chicken breasts on the rice and garnish with the sliced orange. **Serves 8-10**

CHICKEN & DUMPLINGS

4 skinless chicken breasts (not boneless)   1 small diced onion
1 cup diced celery   ½ cup diced carrots
4 peppercorns, left whole   2 teaspoons sea salt
½ cup chopped parsley   ¼ teaspoon dried thyme
¼ teaspoon minced fresh garlic   1 bay leaf
8 cups water

Place all of the ingredients in a 4-quart pot and bring to a boil. Reduce to a simmer, cover and cook for 45 minutes. While the chicken is simmering, prepare the dumplings as follows.

3 cups whole wheat flour   ¼ teaspoon sea salt
6 tablespoons cold unsalted butter   2 large beaten eggs
½ cup cold milk (or water or buttermilk)

Sift the flour and salt together in a large bowl. Cut in cold butter until crumbly. Mix the eggs and milk and pour into the flour and butter mixture. Stir until a ball forms. Lightly flour a clean surface. Place the dough on floured area and knead 4 or 5 times, working gently with the dough. Roll the dough out to about a ¼-inch thick. Cut the dough in 2-by-1-inch pieces.

Remove the chicken from the broth and allow to cool enough to handle. Remove the bones, cut chicken in bite size pieces and set aside. Bring broth to a low boil, carefully drop dumplings into the broth and simmer for 8 minutes, stirring carefully 2 or 3 times. Put the chicken back in the pot and gently stir. Simmer for about 8 more minutes. Do not cover pot after adding dumplings! **Serves 6**

Remember to remove bay leaf before serving.

Note: May be garnished with ½ cup chopped fresh parsley and 2 hard boiled eggs, sliced or chopped.

PREACHER'S COMING ROAST CHICKEN

8 pound roasting chicken, rinse & pat dry

1½ cups chopped pineapple

1 cup baby carrots, cut in half

1 medium purple onion, cut in 8 wedges

1 green pepper, coarsely chopped

4 tablespoons unsalted butter, softened

½ teaspoon sea salt

¼ teaspoon black pepper

¼ teaspoon dried thyme

¼ teaspoon dried rosemary

¼ teaspoon dried oregano

¼ teaspoon dried sage

Preheat oven to 400°. Combine the pineapple, carrots, onions and green pepper, stirring until well mixed. Spoon all of the pineapple mixture into the cavity of the chicken. Stir the butter and all herbs together until well blended. Place the stuffed chicken on a rack in a roasting pan and rub with the butter/herb mixture

Roast chicken for 45 minutes. Reduce heat to 375°; roast for 1 hour and 45 minutes longer or until the juices run clear when chicken is pierced. Remove chicken from oven and scoop mixture out of the cavity and place on a serving dish. Allow chicken to set for 30 minutes before serving. **Serves 6**

JAPONICA CHICKEN STIR FRY

1 cup cooked black japonica rice

1 pound mixed vegetables

Assorted colorful bell peppers, cut in strips

½ pound diced chicken breast

⅛ cup teriyaki sauce

1 tablespoon olive oil

Using a wok or heavy skillet, stir-fry the marinated drained chicken cubes over high heat for 5-10 minutes. Add the rice, stirring constantly. Add the vegetables, cover and let steam for 10 minutes. If softer vegetables are desired, add ¼ cup water.

Add chopped colored bell peppers for added color, slivered almonds, or sliced mushrooms. **Serves 12-14**

CHICKEN WITH FRESH VEGETABLES & BASIL

1½ pound chicken breasts, cut in bite size pieces
1 cup red pepper, cut in thin strips
1 cup yellow pepper, cut in thin strips
2 cups green beans, cut in thing strips
2 cups grape tomatoes, cut in half
2 cups young asparagus, ends removed
1½ cups basil leaves, torn in half
1 cup low sodium chicken broth

3 tablespoons olive oil
2 tablespoons butter
1½ cups sliced onion
1 teaspoon sea salt
⅛ teaspoon black pepper
1 teaspoon fresh lemon juice
2 teaspoons grated lemon peel
½ cup crumbled feta

Heat olive oil in a large deep non-stick skillet. Add the chicken, sautéing and stirring for 10 minutes. Remove the chicken and set aside. Add the butter to the skillet and when it melts, stir in the peppers, onions, beans, asparagus, salt and pepper. Cook for 6 minutes or until vegetables are tender but still crisp. Add the tomatoes, broth, lemon juice and lemon peel and stir until well mixed. Simmer for 3 minutes, add chicken and basil and heat for 2 more minutes. Remove from heat and stir in the feta cheese just before serving. **Serves 6-8**

ITALIAN STUFFED CHICKEN BREASTS

4 boneless skinless chicken breast halves
1 cup cooked wehani rice
¼ cup finely shredded mozzarella cheese
1 tablespoon chopped fresh basil

⅛ teaspoon black pepper
¼ teaspoon sea salt
¼ cup minced tomato
Olive oil cooking spray

Season chicken breasts with ¼ teaspoon pepper and salt. Combine rice, tomato, cheese, basil and remaining ¼ teaspoon pepper. Spoon rice mixture on top of pounded chicken breasts; fold over and secure sides with wooden toothpicks soaked in water. Wipe off outsides of chicken breasts with paper towel. Coat a large skillet with cooking spray and place over medium-high heat until hot. Cook stuffed chicken breasts for 1 minute on each side or until just golden brown. Transfer chicken to shallow baking pan. Bake at 350° for 8 to 10 minutes.

Serves 4-6

STUFFED CORNISH HENS

4 cornish hens, rinse & pat dry	$\frac{1}{2}$ cup chopped onion
1 cup chopped celery	$\frac{1}{4}$ cup fresh parsley
$\frac{1}{2}$ cup butter	$\frac{1}{2}$ teaspoon sea salt
3 cups bread, in small cubes	$\frac{1}{4}$ teaspoon black pepper
$\frac{1}{2}$ teaspoon dried thyme	$\frac{1}{4}$ teaspoon dried rosemary
1 cup sliced button mushrooms	$\frac{1}{2}$ teaspoon dried sage

Preheat oven to 350°. Sauté the onions and celery in the butter until they are soft. Add half of the bread cubes and stir well. Combine the rest of the bread cubes and all other ingredients in a bowl. Pour the butter mixture in and toss until well mixed. Stuff the hens loosely and tie legs together. Place hens breast side up on a rack in a baking pan.

Baste Recipe:

$\frac{1}{2}$ cup melted butter	1 teaspoon marjoram
1 teaspoon sweet basil	1 teaspoon sea salt
$\frac{1}{8}$ teaspoon black pepper	2 tablespoons honey
$\frac{1}{4}$ cup red wine vinegar	

Heat all ingredients to a low simmer, stirring well. Baste the hens and place in oven for 75 to 80 minutes, brushing with the warm baste several times. Remove from oven and allow to set 15 minutes. Untie legs and place on a serving platter. **Serves 4-6**

SMOKY RICE ROUND

$1\frac{1}{2}$ cups brown basmati	$\frac{1}{2}$ cup diced pimentos
2 cups grated smoked gouda cheese	2 teaspoons minced dried onion
$\frac{1}{2}$ cup chopped walnuts, toasted	$\frac{3}{4}$ cup milk

Generously oil an 8 cup ring mold and set aside. Cook rice according to package directions. Stir in remaining ingredients and quickly press into prepared mold. Let stand for 5 minutes and turn out onto a platter. **Serves 10-12**

FAMILY REUNION CHICKEN

2 chickens, cut up, rinse & pat dry	1 teaspoon celery salt
1 cup unbleached flour	1 teaspoon garlic powder
1/2 teaspoon chili powder	1/8 teaspoon black pepper
1/3 cup olive oil	

Combine flour, celery salt, garlic powder, chili powder and pepper in a large ziploc bag. Seal the bag very tightly and shake until all ingredients are well mixed. Add the chicken to the bag 3 to 4 pieces at a time, close bag tightly and shake until the chicken is completely coated. Place the coated chicken in a single layer on a baking pan and set aside while making the sauce.

Preheat oven to 350°.

2/3 cup tomato puree	1/3 cup water
2 teaspoons fresh lemon juice	3 tablespoons honey
1/4 cup apple cider vinegar	2 cloves garlic, minced
3 tablespoons light brown sugar	1 cup chopped onion
2 teaspoons Dijon mustard	1 teaspoon hot sauce
1/2 cup melted butter	

Stir all of the ingredients together in a saucepan and bring to a simmer over medium heat. Simmer for 10 minutes, stirring often. Pour 1/4 of the sauce over the chicken and bake in oven for 1 hour. Turn chicken over every 20 minutes and baste with more of the sauce. Remove the chicken and place on a serving dish.
Serves 12-14

MAMA MIA CHICKEN & ITALIAN TURKEY SAUSAGE

6 pound boneless chicken breasts, cut in half	¼ cup tomato paste
2 pounds turkey sausage (nitrate free), diced	1 cup tomato puree
6 cups plum tomatoes, peeled & crushed	¼ cup red wine
1 cup chicken broth	1 large diced onion
1 yellow pepper, cut in thin strips	1 cup diced celery
1 red pepper, cut in thin strips	7 cloves garlic, minced
1 teaspoon dried oregano	½ teaspoon dried thyme
½ teaspoon dried rosemary	1 teaspoon hot sauce

Preheat oven to 350°. Using a large roasting pan, combine all ingredients except the chicken and sausage. Stir until well blended. Arrange the chicken and sausage on top of the sauce, put in preheated oven and cook for 2½ hours, being sure to baste with the sauce several times. Arrange on a large platter and sprinkle with freshly grated romano cheese and ½ cup chopped fresh basil.

Note: This will easily feed 10 to 12 people or you can freeze any leftovers for up to one month.

SMOKED CHICKEN RISOTTO

1 whole roasted chicken, skinned and sliced	2 cloves garlic, crushed
4 cups leeks, julienne sliced	5 cups chicken broth
2 cups mushrooms, sliced	6 roma tomatoes, diced
1 cup parmesan cheese	2 tablespoons olive oil
2 cups white Arborio rice	2 sprigs fresh rosemary
Pepper to taste	

Cook rice in saucepan with 4 cups chicken broth and two sprigs of rosemary until almost done. In large pan, sauté over medium heat, add olive oil, leeks, garlic and mushrooms. Sauté for 3 minutes, add chicken and tomatoes, and sauté for 2 minutes more. Add rice to pan (discard rosemary), toss and cook for 3 to 4 minutes, add pepper and parmesan cheese, stirring to melt and combine.

Serves 6-8

TURKEY SAUSAGE VEGETABLE PIE

1 baked 9-inch pastry crust

½ pound ground turkey sausage (nitrate free)

1 cup peeled, chopped potato

¼ cup chopped red pepper

⅛ teaspoon black pepper

6 eggs

3 ounces fresh shredded cheddar cheese

1 cup chopped onion

¼ cup chopped celery

¼ cup fresh parsley

½ teaspoon sea salt

4 tablespoons melted butter

8 ounces low fat sour cream

Cook sausage until it is brown and crumbly and drain well. Stir melted butter, potatoes, onion, peppers and celery together in a skillet and cook over medium heat. Cook for 10 minutes or until potatoes are soft and lightly brown. Stir mixture often. Remove from heat and allow to cool slightly. Combine eggs, sour cream, salt, pepper and parsley in a large bowl. Beat well with a wire whisk. Add the sausage and the potato mixture to the egg mixture and stir well with. Pour the mixture into the pastry crust. Very gently stir the cheese in. Bake uncovered on middle rack for 30 to 40 minutes or until a butter knife gently inserted in the center comes out clean. Allow to stand 15 minutes before serving. **Serves 4-6**

Note: May be garnished with any of the following

½ cup peeled diced tomato

½ cup lightly sautéed, sliced mushrooms

½ cup of your favorite salsa.

CHEESY BROCCOLI & RICE CASSEROLE

1½ cups cooked long grain brown rice

1 can cream of chicken soup

1½ pounds fresh broccoli

½ cup milk

1 cup diced cheddar

Cook broccoli until tender. Drain well, add all other ingredients and stir well. Put in casserole dish, cover and bake in a 350° oven for 25 to 30 minutes. **Serves 4**

SMOKED TURKEY & RICE LOAF WITH TOMATO SALSA

Salsa Recipe:

2 cups chopped plum tomatoes	½ cup diced celery
½ cup chopped purple onion	¼ cup chopped cilantro
¼ cup diced green pepper	1 tablespoon lime juice
1 tablespoon lemon juice	1 teaspoon minced garlic
½ teaspoon sea salt	⅛ teaspoon black pepper
½ teaspoon hot pepper sauce	

Stir all ingredients together until well blended. Put salsa in a container and cover tightly. Refrigerate for at least 4 hours.

Loaf Recipe:

2 pounds ground smoked turkey	½ cup milk
2 eggs, lightly beaten	¼ chopped parsley
1¼ cups cooked long grain rice	1 teaspoon celery seed
½ cup diced purple onion	½ teaspoon sea salt
⅛ teaspoon ground black pepper	2 tablespoons Dijon mustard

Put all ingredients in a large bowl. Using hands, mix until well blended. Put the mixture in a loaf pan and wrap tightly. Place in refrigerator and chill for 1 hour.

Preheat oven to 350°.

Un-mold loaf onto a baking sheet and place on the middle rack in oven for 1 hour. Let loaf rest for 20 minutes before transferring to a serving dish.

This is also good served with the following sauce:

1 cup low fat sour cream	½ cup diced tomato
2 teaspoons Dijon mustard	2 tablespoons minced chives
2 tablespoons minced celery	½ teaspoon minced garlic

Mix all of the ingredients until well blended and warm slightly. **Serves 6-8**

JAPONICA RICE RAVIOLI

1 cup black japonica rice
2 teaspoons vegetable bouillon crystals
1½ cups water
2 tablespoons minced green onion
½ teaspoon dried Italian herbs
48 chilled wonton wrappers
1 cup chicken broth

1 tablespoon organic butter
¼ cup chopped walnuts
1 tablespoon minced parsley
1 clove garlic
4 quarts salted water
1 egg with 1 tablespoon water

Sauce:

2 tablespoons butter
1 ounce crumbled bleu cheese

4 ounces cream cheese
1 cup whipping cream

Garnish:

2 tablespoons butter
1 tablespoon minced sweet red pepper

Parsley sprigs

In 2-quart saucepan with lid, melt butter over medium-low heat. Stir walnuts into butter, cooking until nuts are lightly toasted. Remove nuts with a slotted spoon and set aside. Add rice, water, bouillon crystals, parsley, onion, herbs and garlic to saucepan. Bring mixture to a full boil over high heat. Stir, cover, and reduce heat to medium-low. Simmer 45 to 50 minutes until grains "bloom" and water is absorbed. Stir in reserved toasted walnuts. (Mixture may be made ahead and refrigerated at this point, but does not need to be. The warm rice may be used.) Remove from heat and allow to sit for 15 minutes as you prepare wonton wrappers.

Bring salted water to a full boil in a large kettle or stockpot. Lay wonton wrappers on the counter and brush each with egg wash. Place a heaping tablespoonful of rice mixture in the centers of half the wonton wrappers. Cover with another wrapper, pressing edges together well to seal, forcing out as much air as possible. Slide ravioli into boiling water, a few at a time to maintain boil. Cook 3 minutes, remove and drain. Keep warm.

To make sauce, melt butter in a medium saucepan. Stir in whipping cream, cream cheese and bleu cheese, simmering over low heat until cheese is melted.
Serves 8-10

To serve, place ravioli on serving plates, spooning cream sauce over and around them. Sprinkle with sliced green onion, parsley and a little minced sweet red pepper or pimento if desired.

TURKEY SAUSAGE RICE PIZZA

Crust:

4 cups cooked basmati rice	2 eggs, beaten
3 cups grated cheddar cheese	1½ teaspoon powdered garlic
2 tablespoons oregano	

Topping:

1½ cups tomato sauce	1 cup diced green pepper
1 pound browned turkey sausage (nitrate free)	1 cup diced red pepper
2 cups grated mozzarella cheese	Olive oil cooking spray

Preheat oven to 375°. Brown sausage in saucepan on stove, drain and let cool. To the cooked rice, add grated cheddar, ½ tablespoon garlic, 1 tablespoon oregano, and slightly beaten eggs and mix together well. Spread rice mixture over 12-inch round pizza pan that has been sprayed with olive oil cooking spray. Spread tomato sauce evenly over rice crust. Sprinkle 1 tablespoon garlic and 1 tablespoon oregano over tomato sauce. Sprinkle green peppers, red peppers and sausage over pizza. Put in oven and cook for 10 to 15 minutes. Cover top of pizza with mozzarella cheese and cook for another 10 to 15 minutes. Let cool 5 to 10 minutes before cutting into slices. **Serves 6**

TUNA & RICE CASSEROLE

3 cups hot cooked brown basmati	2 cups sliced celery
7 ounces white albacore tuna	1 tablespoon organic butter
3 eggs, boiled and chopped	3 tablespoons fresh lemon juice
1 cup organic mayonnaise	3 to 4 ounces breadcrumbs

Sauté celery in butter until tender crisp. Add basmati, tuna, eggs and lemon juice. Fold in mayonnaise. Season to taste. Turn into shallow buttered 1½-quart casserole dish. Top with breadcrumbs. Bake at 350° for 20 minutes. **Serves 6-8**

ZUCCHINI RICE CASSEROLE

3 cups cooked long grain brown rice

2 cups grated cheddar cheese

2 onions, thinly sliced

2 zucchinis, sliced

8 ounces low fat sour cream

5 tomatoes, thinly sliced

In a 13-by-9-inch baking pan, layer the following ingredients in order: rice (on the bottom of the pan), onion, zucchini, cheese, tomatoes and sour cream. Bake at 350° for 40 minutes or until cheese melts. **Serves 4**

SQUASH & CHICKEN CASSEROLE

3 cups cubed cooked chicken

4 cups cooked squash

½ cup chicken broth

½ cup milk

1 can cream of chicken soup

25 crackers, crumbled

6 eggs, beaten

2 teaspoons sea salt

1 stick butter, melted

1½ teaspoon onion salt

⅛ teaspoon black pepper

Add 1 teaspoon salt to squash, then add butter and all remaining ingredients; mix well. Add 1 teaspoon salt to chicken and pour into squash; blend well. Bake in large buttered casserole dish at 350° for 45 minutes or until bubbly in center. **Serves 8-10**

BEEF STROGANOFF

1 pound ground beef

1 can cream of mushroom soup

1 (4 ounce) can sliced mushrooms, drained

2 teaspoons Worcestershire sauce

1 cup low fat sour cream

1 large onion, chopped

1 clove garlic, minced

Brown beef, onion and garlic in 10-inch skillet; drain. Combine soup and sour cream in bowl; blend thoroughly. Add soup mixture and mushrooms to meat; heat through and serve immediately over noodles or rice. **Serves 4-6**

BAKED RED SNAPPER

3 pounds red snapper

2 to 3 slices tomato

Breadcrumbs

1 small onion

Butter

Sea salt & pepper

Dressing:

1 cup breadcrumbs

1 teaspoon chopped parsley

½ teaspoon sea salt

4 tablespoons butter

1 teaspoon lemon juice

¼ teaspoon pepper

Mix dressing; stuff fish and place in greased baking dish. Season with salt and pepper, dot with butter and grate onion over the top. Top with tomato slices and breadcrumbs. Bake at 350° for 45 minutes. **Serves 8-12**

ANGEL HAIR CHICKEN

2 tablespoons olive oil, divided

2 chicken breasts, cut into 1-inch cubes

1 zucchini, sliced diagonally, in ¼-inch pieces

1 package frozen broccoli, thawed

¼ cup grated parmesan cheese

2 cloves garlic, minced

⅔ cup chicken broth

1 teaspoon dried basil

12 ounces angel hair pasta

Heat 1 tablespoon oil in a medium skillet over medium heat; add chicken. Cook, stirring, until chicken is cooked through, about 5 minutes. Remove from skillet and drain on paper towels. Heat remaining oil in same skillet. Begin heating water for pasta. Add zucchini to skillet; cook, stirring for 4 minutes. Add broccoli and garlic to skillet; cook, stirring for 2 minutes longer. Cook pasta according to package directions. While pasta is cooking, add chicken broth, basil and cheese to skillet. Stir to combine. Return chicken to skillet. Reduce heat and simmer for 4 minutes. Drain pasta. Place in a large serving bowl. Top with chicken and vegetable mixture. **Serves 6-8**

BROILED SIRLOIN STEAK

1 to 2½ pounds sirloin steak, 1½ in thick   ½ cup butter
¼ cup chopped fresh parsley   ¼ cup minced onion
2 tablespoons Worcestershire sauce   ⅛ teaspoon black pepper
½ teaspoon dry mustard

Lightly score edges of steak at 1-inch intervals. Preheat broiler. Combine butter, parsley, onion, Worcestershire sauce, pepper and mustard in a small saucepan. Heat, stirring continually, over low heat, until butter melts. Reserve ¼ of the mixture. Place steak on broiler pan. Brush with butter mixture. Cook, basting frequently with butter mixture, about 6 minutes per side for medium. Place steak on serving platter. Cut thin slices across the grain. Drizzle reserved butter mixture over steak. **Serves 8-10**

SALMON & ZUCCHINI TERIYAKI

7 tablespoons low-sodium teriyaki sauce   2 salmon fillets
Sesame seeds   4 scallions, chopped
2 small zucchini, thinly sliced   Olive oil

Combine 5 tablespoon teriyaki sauce and fish in a zip-top plastic bag. Seal and marinate for 20 minutes. Toast sesame seeds in a large non-stick skillet over medium heat, and set aside. Drain fish, discarding marinade. Add fish to skillet and cook for 5 minutes on each side on medium-low heat. Add the zucchini, scallions and 2 teaspoons oil to skillet. Sauté for 4 minutes or until lightly browned. Stir in 2 tablespoons teriyaki sauce. Sprinkle with sesame seeds and serve with the salmon. **Serves 4**

CLASSIC ROAST CHICKEN

1 (3½ pound) roasting chicken   1 stalk celery
½ teaspoon dried thyme   ½ teaspoon sea salt
1 tablespoon butter, softened and divided   1 onion, quartered

Preheat oven to 475°. Slice celery. Sprinkle inside of cavity of chicken with thyme and salt; add 1 teaspoon butter, sliced celery and onion. Rub outside of chicken with remaining butter. Place chicken breast side down on rack in roasting pan. Add enough water to cover bottom of pan. Roast for 10 minutes. Reduce temperature to 375°. Roast for 20 minutes longer. Turn chicken breast side up. Roast until chicken is browned, about 30 to 45 minutes. **Serves 6**

HONEY DIJON CHICKEN

⅓ cup Dijon mustard   ⅓ cup honey
2 tablespoons chopped fresh dill   1 teaspoon grated orange peel
1 (2½ pound) chicken, quartered

Preheat oven to 400°. Combine mustard and honey in a small bowl. Stir in dill and orange peel. Oil a baking sheet. Place chicken, skin side down, on prepared pan. Brush sauce on top of chicken; coat well. Turn chicken over. Gently pull back skin and brush meat with sauce. Gently pull skin back over sauce. Brush skin with remaining sauce. Bake until juices run clear when thickest portion of meat is pierced with a knife, about 30 minutes. **Serves 6**

BAKED SALMON WITH FRUIT SALSA

6 skinless salmon fillets   1 tablespoon Cajun seasoning
1½ tablespoons olive oil   Fruit salsa

Place salmon fillets in roasting pan; sprinkle evenly on 1 side with Cajun seasoning. Drizzle with oil. Cover and chill for 2 hours. Bake salmon at 350° for 20 to 25 minutes or until fish flakes with a fork. Serve with fruit salsa. For fruit salsa, use recipe for pineapple salsa and add ½ cup diced mangos. **Serves 6**

GRILLED CHICKEN WITH PINEAPPLE

4 skinned and boned chicken breasts

1 teaspoon chili powder

2 teaspoons paprika

Lime slices for garnish

1 tablespoons olive oil

2 teaspoons garlic salt

Pineapple salsa

Place chicken between 2 sheets of heavy duty plastic wrap; flatten to ½-inch thickness using a meat mallet or rolling pin. Rub evenly with olive oil and sprinkle evenly with chili powder, garlic salt and paprika. Grill chicken, covered with grill lid, over medium-high heat for 4 minutes on each side or until done. Serve with pineapple salsa and garnish with lime slices.

Pineapple Salsa:

¼ cup diced red bell pepper

2 tablespoons chopped cilantro

2 tablespoons lime juice

1 tablespoon chopped mild pepper

1 tablespoon agave nectar

2 tablespoons brown rice syrup

2 tablespoons orange juice

1 tablespoon butter

1 can diced pineapple

Stir together red bell pepper, brown rice syrup, agave nectar, cilantro, orange juice, lime juice and mild pepper. Melt butter in large skillet over medium-high heat; add drained pineapple and cook for 2 minutes or until pineapple is golden brown. Combine pineapple with red bell pepper mixture and blend well. **Serves 4**

PEANUT BUTTER CHICKEN

1 skinned and boned chicken

¾ teaspoon paprika

1 tablespoon olive oil

1 (14 ounce) can chicken broth

½ teaspoon ground black pepper

3 tablespoons natural chunky peanut butter

¾ teaspoon sea salt

¾ teaspoon dried thyme

⅓ cup maple syrup

⅓ cup balsamic vinegar

¼ teaspoon ground red pepper

Sprinkle chicken evenly with salt, paprika and thyme. Cook chicken in hot oil in a large non-stick skillet over medium-high heat 2 minutes on each side or until golden brown. Stir in chicken broth, syrup, vinegar, black pepper and red pepper. Bring to a boil. Cover, reduce heat to low and simmer for 15 minutes. Remove chicken to a serving platter and keep warm. Reserve liquid in skillet. Whish peanut butter into reserved liquid and boil over medium-high heat, uncovered, for 5 minutes or until sauce is thickened; spoon sauce evenly over chicken. **Serves 6**

BROILED LEMON SALMON

4 salmon fillets

½ teaspoon coarsely ground pepper

3 tablespoons fresh lemon juice, divided

1 teaspoon dried rosemary

2 cups hot cooked brown rice

½ teaspoon sea salt

1 teaspoon grated lemon rind

2 tablespoons olive oil, divided

4 cups raw baby spinach

Sprinkle salmon fillets evenly with salt and pepper. Place fillets, lemon rind, 1 tablespoon lemon juice, 1 tablespoon oil and rosemary in large zip-top plastic bag. Seal and turn to coat. Chill for 30 minutes. Remove fillets from marinade, discarding marinade. Place fillets, skin side down on a rack coated with olive oil in broiler pan. Broil fish 5 ½ inches from heat for 10 to 12 minutes or until fillets flake easily with a fork. Arrange rice and spinach on a serving platter; top with salmon fillets. Whisk together remaining 2 tablespoons lemon juice and 1 tablespoon oil; drizzle evenly over fillets. Garnish with rosemary and lemon slices, if desired. **Serves 4**

BAKED APPLE LAMB CHOPS

6 lamb chops, ¾-inch thick

3 apples, cored and halved

3 to 4 potatoes, peeled and halved

Hot milk to cover bottom of skillet

2 tablespoons butter

Sea salt

Paprika

¼ cup brown sugar

Brown chops in butter; season with salt and paprika. Place apples on them skin sides down; sprinkle with brown sugar. Cover bottom of skillet with hot milk; add potatoes. Cover and bake at 350° for 30 to 40 minutes. Turn potatoes and baste to brown uniformly. **Serves 6**

LASAGNA

1 medium onion, chopped

1 tablespoon olive oil

1 bay leaf, finely crushed

2 (8 ounce) cans tomato sauce

12 to 14 lasagna noodles

1 teaspoon basil leaves

Mozzarella cheese

8 ounces cottage cheese

1 clove garlic, minced

2 pounds ground beef

Sea salt and pepper

1 (6 ounce) can tomato paste

1 tablespoon parsley flakes

2 eggs

American cheese

Lightly brown meat, onion and garlic in oil; drain off excess fat. Add salt, pepper, parsley flakes, basil leaves, bay leaf, tomato sauce and tomato paste; simmer uncovered for about 30 minutes. Add water to keep soupy. Mix cottage cheese and eggs. Grate about 8 ounce of mozzarella and American cheese and mix. Arrange 2 layers each as follows: meat sauce, lasagna, cottage cheese, cheese. Makes 1 large greased 13-by-9-inch or 2 small casseroles. Bake at 375° for 30 minutes. Note: freezes well; prepare as directed except do not bake; cover with foil and freeze; thaw and bake. **Serves 8-10**

CLASSIC MEAT LOAF

2 pounds ground beef

1 small onion

2 cups oatmeal

¾ cup milk

⅓ cup catsup

1 teaspoon Worcestershire sauce

1 teaspoon sea salt

2 teaspoons onion juice

2 eggs

Pepper

½ cup water

Meat Sauce:

2 tablespoons butter

2 tablespoons unbleached flour

Dash of pepper

¾ cup catsup

½ teaspoon sea salt

1 to 2 teaspoons onion powder

1 cup milk

Combine salt, pepper, eggs, onion and meat; add oatmeal moistened with milk, catsup and sauce. Shape into loaf; roast at 400° for 1½ hours, basting frequently with ½ cup hot water. To make meat sauce, blend flour, salt, pepper, onion and milk in saucepan. Stir until thick; add catsup. Serve with meat. **Serves 4-6**

SWEET AND SOUR CHICKEN

1½ pound boneless chicken, cut in 1-inch cubes

Sea salt and pepper

½ cup pineapple juice

1 tablespoon cornstarch

1 20 ounce can pineapple chunks, drained

Olive oil

½ cup barbecue sauce

¼ cup vinegar

Cooked rice

1 green pepper, in strips

Brown meat in small amount of oil; season with salt and pepper. Stir in mixture of barbecue sauce, reserved pineapple juice, vinegar and cornstarch; cover and simmer for 35 minutes. Add pineapple and green pepper; simmer 10 minutes longer. Serve with hot rice. **Serves 4**

SHEPHERD'S PIE

1¼ pound red potatoes, cut into chunks

1 cup low fat cottage cheese

½ cup shredded sharp cheddar, divided

2 tablespoons whole wheat flour

4 cups frozen mixed vegetables

3 cloves garlic, peeled

1 pound lean ground beef

¾ cup beef broth

1 tablespoon catsup

Cover potatoes and garlic with water in large saucepan. Bring to a boil on high heat. Reduce heat to low; simmer 20 minutes or until potatoes are very tender. Drain; return to saucepan. Meanwhile, place cottage cheese in food processor container; cover. Process until smooth and thick, scraping down the sides of the container once. Add to potatoes in saucepan. Mash to desired consistency. Stir in ¼ cup of the shredded cheese. Preheat oven to 375°. Brown meat in large skillet. Stir in flour; cook for 1 minute. Add vegetables, broth and catsup; continue cooking for 5 minutes. Spoon meat mixture into 8-inch square baking dish. Cover with mashed potatoes; top with remaining shredded cheese. Bake for 20 minutes or until heated through and cheese is melted. **Serves 6-8**

LEMON HERB CHICKEN

4 chicken breasts

1 tablespoon grated lemon zest

3 garlic cloves, minced

¾ teaspoon pepper

1 tablespoon dried tarragon

4 bay leaves, crushed

1½ teaspoons sea salt

3 teaspoons olive oil

In a small bowl, mix together the lemon zest, cloves, tarragon, bay leaves, oil, salt and pepper. Stir until well blended. Heat grill to medium. Rub 6 teaspoons of the herb mixture under the skins of the chicken breasts. Sprinkle with salt and pepper. Lightly oil grates. Place chicken on grill. Cook, turning several times, until chicken is cooked through but still juicy, about 30 to 40 minutes. **Serves 4**

GARLIC LIME SALMON

1 pound wild salmon	2 tablespoons chopped garlic
2 tablespoon + 1 teaspoon lime juice	¼ teaspoon sea salt
½ cup sour cream	⅛ teaspoon chili powder
1 teaspoon grated lime peel	2 tablespoons olive oil
Chopped fresh cilantro	

In a large bowl, combine salmon, 2 tablespoons lime juice, garlic and salt. Marinate in refrigerator for 15 minutes. Meanwhile, in a small bowl, blend sour cream, remaining lime juice, chili powder and lime peel. Set aside. Remove salmon from marinade, reserving marinade. In a 12-inch skillet, heat oil over medium-high heat; cook salmon, flipping occasionally, 4 minutes. Add reserved marinade and bring to a boil over high heat. Continue cooking, stirring occasionally, until salmon is cooked through, 1 to 2 minutes. Drizzle with sour cream mixture and sprinkle with cilantro. **Serves 2-4**

ORANGE HONEY CHICKEN

6 skinned chicken breasts	1 can tomato sauce
⅔ cup honey	¼ cup soy sauce
½ cup finely chopped onion	2 teaspoons onion powder
¼ cup red wine vinegar	1½ teaspoons garlic powder
2 teaspoons finely shredded orange peel	1½ teaspoons ground ginger
1 teaspoon barbecue seasoning	

In a large saucepan combine tomato sauce, honey, onion, soy sauce, vinegar, onion powder, orange peel, garlic powder, ginger and barbecue seasoning. Bring to a boil; reduce heat. Simmer, uncovered, for 10 minutes, stirring occasionally. Remove saucepan from heat; cool sauce completely. Place chicken in large baking dish. Pour about 3 cups of the sauce over chicken. Cover and refrigerate for 4 to 12 hours. To grill, remove chicken from marinade, reserving marinade to brush on during grilling. Place on grill for 25 to 30 minutes, turning and basting occasionally with some of the reserved marinade. Discard any remaining marinade. In a small saucepan heat the remaining sauce to serve with the chicken. **Serves 6**

APRICOT CHICKEN ROLL-UPS

1⅓ cups dried apricots, snipped	½ cup dried cranberries
⅔ cup fine dry breadcrumbs	3 tablespoons honey
1½ teaspoon ground ginger	2 tablespoons fresh parsley
1 tablespoon unbleached flour	1 teaspoon paprika
1 tablespoon finely shredded parmesan cheese	¼ teaspoon fructose
½ teaspoon sea salt	½ teaspoon oregano, crushed
¼ teaspoon garlic powder	¼ teaspoon onion powder
2 tablespoons butter	2 eggs
6 medium skinless, boneless chicken breast	1 teaspoon paprika

Preheat oven to 350°. Coat a 3-quart rectangle baking dish with butter; set aside. Stir together apricots, cranberries, honey and ginger; set aside. Stir together breadcrumbs, parsley, flour, cheese, paprika, fructose, salt, oregano, garlic powder, onion powder and ¼ teaspoon pepper. Cut in butter until mixture resembles fine crumbs. Transfer to a shallow dish. Place eggs in another shallow dish; beat lightly with a fork. With a meat mallet lightly pound each chicken breast between two pieces of plastic wrap into a rectangle slightly less than ¼-inch thick. Remove wrap. Spoon a scant ¼ cup of apricot mixture onto center of each chicken breast. Fold in bottom and sides. Roll up. Secure with toothpicks. Dip in egg, then in crumb mixture. Place in prepared dish. Bake for 35 to 40 minutes or until no pink remains. **Serves 6**

CHICKEN TETRAZZINI

3 tablespoons butter

1 medium onion, chopped

1 green bell pepper, chopped

7 ounces spaghetti, cooked

1 cup shredded cheddar cheese

1 can cream of mushroom soup

½ cup grated parmesan cheese

½ teaspoon pepper

1 garlic clove, minced

2 cups milk

3 tablespoons whole wheat flour

3 cups cooked chicken

1 teaspoon sea salt

½ cup sliced mushrooms

2 tablespoons chopped parsley

Melt butter in a large skillet over medium heat; add onion, bell pepper and garlic, and sauté until tender. Stir in flour; cook, stirring constantly, 1 minute. Gradually stir in milk; cook over medium heat, stirring constantly, until thickened and bubbly. Stir in pasta, chicken, ¾ cup of the cheddar cheese, soup, mushrooms, parmesan cheese, parsley, salt and pepper. Spoon into a lightly buttered 2-quart baking dish. Bake at 350° for 20 minutes; sprinkle with remaining ¼ cup cheddar cheese, and bake 5 more minutes. **Serves 4**

BEEF & SPINACH SHELLS

2 (10 ounce) packages frozen spinach, thawed

1 medium onion, chopped

½ teaspoon sea salt, divided

1 (16 ounce) jar marinara sauce

1 (16 ounce) container cottage cheese

¼ cup grated parmesan cheese

1 pound ground beef

¼ teaspoon ground nutmeg

½ teaspoon pepper, divided

1 large egg

18 jumbo shells, cooked

Drain spinach well. Cook ground beef in a large skillet, stirring until it crumbles and is no longer pink; drain. Return beef to skillet and stir in nutmeg, ¼ teaspoon salt, ¼ teaspoon pepper and marinara sauce. Set aside. Stir together spinach, cottage cheese, egg, parmesan cheese, remaining salt and remaining pepper. Spoon evenly into shells. Spread half of sauce mixture on bottom of a lightly buttered 13-by-9-inch baking dish. Arrange shells over sauce; pour remaining sauce over shells. Bake, covered, at 350° for 30 minutes. **Serves 8**

WALNUT CRUSTED SALMON

2 tablespoons whole wheat flour

4 (1-inch thick) pieces of wild salmon

1 cup walnuts, toasted & chopped

2 teaspoons water

$\frac{1}{8}$ teaspoon sea salt

1 large egg white

1 teaspoon cayenne pepper

Apricot Sauce:

1 cup apricot preserves

2 tablespoons chopped cilantro

1 teaspoon cider vinegar

3 tablespoons red onion slivers

1 jalapeno pepper, seeded & minced

Heat oven to 450°. Butter a baking sheet or large casserole dish. Mix flour, salt and pepper on a sheet of wax paper. Beat egg white and water in shallow bowl. Spread walnuts on another sheet of wax paper. Coat fish in flour mixture, dip in egg white mixture then press into walnuts to coat. Arrange on pan. Bake 5 to 10 minutes until fish is barely opaque at center when tested with tip of knife. In medium saucepan combine sauce ingredients. Stir and bring to a simmer. Remove from heat. Serve over fish. **Serves 4**

ARTICHOKE CHICKEN

4 skinned & boned chicken breasts

1 (14 ounce) can quartered artichoke hearts

1 can cream of chicken soup

$\frac{1}{4}$ cup fresh chopped cilantro

$\frac{1}{4}$ cup diced red bell pepper

$\frac{1}{2}$ teaspoon sea salt

$\frac{1}{2}$ teaspoon pepper

1 tablespoon olive oil

1 teaspoon ground cumin

$\frac{3}{4}$ cup salsa

Sprinkle chicken evenly with salt and pepper. Brown chicken in hot oil in a large skillet over medium-high heat. Remove from skillet, and place chicken in an 11-by-17-inch baking dish. Top with artichoke hearts. Stir together soup, salsa, cumin and bell pepper. Pour sauce over chicken mixture. Bake at 350° for 30 minutes. Sprinkle with cilantro. **Serves 4**

PHYLLO CHICKEN

8 skinned & boned chicken breasts

4 cups chopped fresh spinach

1 medium onion, chopped

8 ounces cream cheese, softened

1 cup shredded mozzarella cheese

1/2 cup shredded cheddar cheese

1/2 teaspoon ground nutmeg

16 frozen phyllo pastry sheets, thawed

1 teaspoon sea salt

1/2 teaspoon pepper

2 tablespoons olive oil

1 egg yolk, lightly beaten

1/2 cup crumbled feta

1 tablespoons unbleached flour

1/2 teaspoon ground cumin

Melted butter

Place chicken between 2 sheets of plastic wrap, and flatten to 1/8 inch thickness, using a meat mallet or rolling pin. Sprinkle evenly with salt and pepper and set aside. Sauté spinach and onion in hot oil in a large skillet over medium-high heat 3 to 4 minutes or until onion is tender. Remove from heat, and stir in cream cheese until blended. Stir in mozzarella cheese, feta, cheddar cheese, the beaten egg yolk, flour, nutmeg and cumin. Spoon 1/4 cup spinach mixture on center of each chicken breast half and roll up like a jelly roll. Unfold phyllo sheets on a lightly floured surface. Stack 2 phyllo sheets, brushing with melted butter between sheets. Place 1 chicken roll on short side of phyllo stack; gently roll up, folding in long side. Repeat procedure with remaining pastry, melted butter and chicken. Place rolls in a shallow pan, and brush with melted butter. Bake at 350° for 35 to 40 minutes or until done. **Serves 10-12**

PARMESAN CRUSTED CHICKEN

6 skinless chicken breasts

1/4 cup Italian seasoned bread crumbs

1/4 cup parmesan cheese

1/2 cup low fat sour cream

Combine sour cream and cheese. Spread on chicken, then roll in bread crumbs. Bake at 425° for 20 minutes or until chicken is done and no longer pink. **Serves 6**

BAKED FRIED CHICKEN

1 whole skinned, cut up chicken	3 eggs, beaten
2 cups crushed sweet flake cereal	½ cup whole wheat flour
½ teaspoon sea salt	¼ teaspoon pepper
¼ teaspoon fructose	¼ cup olive oil

In a large bowl mix flakes, salt pepper and fructose. Place beaten eggs in separate bowl. Place oil in large cast iron skillet and heat. Dip each piece of chicken in egg, whole wheat flour then press to side down into flake mixture. Place each piece of chicken top side down in hot oil. Cook each piece of chicken about 1 minute and then place in oiled baking dish top facing up. Sprinkle lightly with salt and pepper. Cover and bake at 350° for 30 minutes. Uncover and bake until flakes start to lightly brown. **Serves 6**

TOMATO BASIL CHICKEN

⅔ cup soft breadcrumbs	⅓ cup crumbled feta
1 tablespoon chopped fresh basil	¼ teaspoon sea salt
¼ teaspoon pepper	3 tablespoons olive oil
2 tablespoons lemon juice	Tomato basil cream
4 skinned & boned chicken breast halves	

Stir together breadcrumbs, feta, basil, salt and pepper. Whisk together olive oil and lemon juice until blended. Dip chicken into oil mixture, and dredge in breadcrumb mixture, pressing to coat. Place in a lightly buttered 11-by-7-inch baking dish. Bake at 375° for 30 minutes or until chicken is done. Serve with tomato basil cream. **Serves 4**

Tomato Basil Cream:

1 cup spaghetti sauce	2 tablespoons sour cream
1 tablespoon chopped fresh basil	

Cook all ingredients in a small saucepan over low heat, stirring often, about 5 minutes.

CHICKEN FRIED RICE

4 skinned & boned chicken breasts, chopped

3 tablespoons olive oil, divided

1 medium onion, chopped

1 package frozen green peas, thawed

$\frac{1}{8}$ teaspoon turmeric

$\frac{1}{2}$ teaspoon fructose

$\frac{1}{2}$ cup chopped roasted cashews

2 eggs, lightly beaten

1 clove garlic, minced

$\frac{1}{2}$ teaspoon grated ginger

5 cups cooked rice

$\frac{1}{4}$ cup light soy sauce

$\frac{1}{8}$ teaspoon pepper

$\frac{1}{4}$ cup sliced green onion

In a large skillet, stir fry eggs in 1 tablespoon of the oil. Remove eggs. Add 1 tablespoon oil and stir fry chicken. Add last of the oil, onions, garlic, ginger, peas, rice and turmeric. Stir fry for 3 minutes. Mix together soy sauce, fructose and pepper. Add to skillet and stir fry for 5 minutes. Stir in eggs and cashews; top with green onions. **Serves 6**

BEEF BURRITO CASSEROLE

1 pound lean ground beef or ground turkey

4 tablespoons olive oil

2 cans refried beans

$1\frac{1}{2}$ cups low fat sour cream

$\frac{1}{2}$ cup Cajun pepper, chopped

$1\frac{1}{2}$ cups shredded cheddar cheese

1 teaspoon sea salt, divided

8 corn tortillas

1 cup chopped cilantro

1 clove garlic, minced

2 cups cooked rice

1 cup salsa

In large skillet, brown meat with $\frac{1}{2}$ teaspoon salt. Drain and set aside. In same skillet, add oil, pepper, onion and garlic. Sauté until onions are tender. Stir in meat, rice and cilantro. In a 13-by-9-inch casserole dish, line with 4 tortillas. Spread meat mixture on top of tortillas. Top with 4 more tortillas. Spread 1 cup sour cream over tortillas. Mix $\frac{1}{2}$ cup sour cream, $\frac{1}{2}$ teaspoon salt and refried beans together in bowl until smooth and creamy. Spread bean mixture over sour cream. Spread salsa over sour cream and top with cheese. Bake at 350° for 30 minutes. **Serves 6**

SALMON WITH HERBED RICE

8 (6 ounce) salmon fillets	¼ to ½ teaspoon sea salt
¼ teaspoon pepper	2 tablespoons butter
1 small onion, chopped	2 garlic cloves, minced
3 tablespoons fresh lime juice	2 tablespoons chopped parsley
¼ cup slivered almonds, toasted	Lime slices for garnish

Sprinkle fish evenly with salt and pepper. Set aside. Melt butter in a large, heavy skillet over medium-high heat. Add onion, and sauté 8 minutes or until onion is tender. Add garlic, and sauté 2 to 3 minutes. Stir in lime juice. Remove from heat. Arrange fish, skin side down, on a lightly greased broiler pan. Broil, 5 inches from heat, for 7 to 10 minutes or until fish flakes with a fork. Using a wide metal spatula, lift fish from skin, leaving skin on rack. Transfer to a serving dish filled with herbed rice. Place fish on top of rice. Sprinkle evenly with toasted almonds and parsley.

Herbed Rice:

3 cups uncooked basmati rice	2 cups water
4 cups chicken broth	½ cup olive oil, divided
2 garlic cloves, minced	1 teaspoon sea salt
1 large onion, chopped	1 cup chopped cilantro
½ teaspoon ground cinnamon	

In a large skillet, sauté onions and garlic in ¼ cup oil. Add dry rice. Stir over medium heat for 3 minutes. Remove from heat. In a 2-quart pot with lid, add water, broth, salt and contents from skillet. Cover and bring to a boil. Reduce heat to low and simmer for 35 minutes. Add cilantro and cinnamon. Mix well and return to a simmer. Remove from heat, leaving lid on. Set aside and allow steam to finish cooking the rice, about 20 to 30 minutes. Stir and fluff with fork. **Serves 8-10**

CHICKEN IN BLACK BEAN SAUCE

4 boneless, skinless chicken breasts

2 (10 ounce) cans diced tomatoes

2 (10 ounce) cans black beans, drained

1 bag whole kernel corn, thawed & drained

1 clove garlic, minced

1 cup cooked basmati rice

½ cup fresh chopped cilantro

1 tablespoon ground cumin

1 teaspoon chili powder

1 teaspoon garlic salt

1 tablespoon olive oil

1 small onion, diced

½ cup grated cheddar

Cut chicken into ½-inch pieces. In large ziploc bag, combine cumin, chili powder and garlic salt. Shake and remove 2 tablespoons of mixture and reserve. Add chicken to bag, seal and toss to coat. In large bowl, stir together reserved spice mixture, diced tomatoes, black beans and corn. In large skillet, sauté minced garlic, onion and chicken in olive oil over medium heat for 6-8 minutes or until chicken is browned. Add tomato mixture and bring to a boil. Add rice. Remove from heat and sprinkle with cheese and cilantro. **Serves 6**

RAISIN COUSCOUS CHICKEN

1 (14½ ounce) container broth

3 tablespoons olive oil, divided

½ cup raisins

⅓ cup chopped fresh parsley

2 celery ribs, diced

4 skinned, boned chicken breast halves, cut in strips

¼ cup water

½ cup couscous

1 tablespoon lemon juice

¼ cup slivered almonds

3 garlic cloves, pressed

Bring broth, ¼ cup water, and 1 tablespoon oil to a boil in a saucepan over medium heat. Stir in couscous. Cover, reduce heat and simmer 15 minutes or until liquid is absorbed and couscous is tender. Fluff with a fork. Stir in raisins, parsley, almonds, lemon juice and celery. Heat remaining 2 tablespoon oil in a large skillet over medium heat. Add garlic, and sauté 2 to 3 minutes or until tender. Add chicken and sauté 8 minutes or until browned. Spoon couscous onto a serving platter; top with chicken.

CHICKEN FAJITAS

4 boneless, skinless chicken breasts	1 green bell pepper
8 whole grain flour tortillas	1 yellow bell pepper
1 large onion	1 red bell pepper
1/4 cup raspberry marmalade	2 tablespoons olive oil
1/4 cup olive oil	1 garlic clove, minced
dash of salt & pepper	

Slice chicken and all vegetables in thin strips. Mix the 1/4 cup oil, marmalade, garlic, salt and pepper. Place mixture in freezer bag with the chicken and refrigerate overnight. Place vegetables in a separate bag and refrigerate overnight. In large skillet, cook chicken in 2 tablespoons oil until no longer pink. Add the vegetables. Sauté until onions are tender. Steam or cook tortillas on a griddle. Spoon vegetables and chicken into tortillas (about 2 tablespoons) and fold in half. Top with sour cream and hot sauce. **Serves 6-8**

CHICKEN & SPINACH PIZZA

1 large whole wheat pizza crust	1 teaspoon olive oil
1/2 cup onion, finely sliced	2 cups cooked chicken
1 cup frozen spinach, thawed & squeezed	3/4 cup pizza sauce
1 (4 ounce) package tomato-basil feta cheese	

Brush crust with olive oil. Spread sauce evenly over crust. Top with spinach, onions and chicken. Sprinkle evenly with cheese. Bake at 350° for 20 minutes or until crust is light golden brown and cheese has melted. **Serves 4-6**

In my Kitchen

I preheat a memory.

I fold in family and old friends with new.

I bake a smile and lots of laughter.

What a nice warm place to be.

Sharon at 1-1/2 years old in her first kitchen.
Do you like that fancy "refrigerator?"

Birthdays are a big deal at the Broer home.
Austin and his homemade "Lion King" cake.

Harrison and his 3rd birthday
homemade safari cake.

*Savannah, Alexis and
Harrison make Father's Day
muffins for their daddy.*

*Austin cooks up a quick burrito.
Even a teenager can cook.*

*Savannah and Ted:
A "Kodak moment"
in the kitchen.*

Take time to bake a birthday cake. It's much more special than a grocery store cake. Alexis, the "horse lover" enjoys her "Spirit" cake.

Chef Harrison makes popcorn for family movie night.

Ted and Austin enjoy Sharon's home cooked southern meal of black-eyed peas, cornbread and sweet potatoes after a cold day on the slopes.

Toys and action figures make
great toppers for children's
birthday cakes.
Austin's 4th birthday
pirate cake.

Alexis helps clean up the dishes.

Ted's 37th birthday cake.
Sharon used a cut-out of an
Acura NSX for the topper.

Harrison and Alexis make their
first morning toast.

Austin's 8th birthday
"Toy Story" cake.
Popsicle sticks were used
for the headboard
and footboard.

Harrison taste tests the batter
for Ted's birthday cake.

Birthday cakes are excellent "memory makers;" so take lots of photos. Alexis is so excited to have a "Princess cake". Sharon bought the castle and princess' from Disney Village and dressed up the bottom of the cake with a pink bow.

Ted in the kitchen with his girls, Savannah, Alexis and Sharon.

Healthy 4th of July cake using blue berries for the stars and red licorice for the stripes.

Savannah's first birthday almond cake.

Harrison and Alexis learn the valuable lesson of "taking turns" even while helping in the kitchen.

*Savannah celebrates her 2nd birthday and Alexis
celebrates her 4th birthday with a combined
"pony party" including a live pony and
a "Hummingbird" cake (see page 201 for recipe).
Their birthdays are two weeks apart.*

*Harrison, Savannah and Alexis patiently wait for
a piece of Ted's "German Chocolate" birthday cake (see page
206 for recipe). Sharon used "happy birthday" candles
to decorate the cake.*

The Vegetable Platter

Side Dishes:
Veggies,
Rice and
Casseroles

9

SWEET POTATO & APPLE BAKE

4 large sweet potatoes	½ cup firm butter
4 granny smith apples, cored	½ cup brown rice syrup
1 cup raisins, steeped in boiling water and drained	

Preheat oven to 375°.

Boil sweet potatoes just until fork tender. Remove from heat and allow to cool enough to handle. Butter a large glass baking dish. Gently remove skin from sweet potatoes and slice in ¼ inch thick slices and place in buttered dish. Dot ¼ cup butter evenly on top of the potatoes and drizzle with ¼ cup of the brown rice syrup. Slice the apples into ¼ inch thick slices and arrange on top of the potatoes. Dot with the remaining butter and brown rice syrup. Sprinkle the drained raisins evenly on top and cover tightly with foil. Place baking dish in oven and bake for 30 minutes. **Serves 6**

EASTER COINS

1 pound fresh carrots	3 tablespoons butter
2 tablespoons honey	¼ teaspoon minced ginger

Wash and scrape carrots and cut into ¼ inch slices. Steam until fork tender. In a small saucepan, melt the butter over low heat. Stir the honey and ginger into the melted butter and cook for 2 to 3 minutes, stirring constantly. When the honey and ginger have completely blended with the melted butter and the mixture is very warm, pour it over the carrots. Gently toss the mixture with the carrots and pour into a serving dish. **Serves 4-6**

CREAMY FRIED FRESH CORN

8 slices turkey, chopped

1 cup chopped onion

½ cup chopped red bell pepper

¼ cup chopped green bell pepper

8 ounces cream cheese, diced

4 cups corn kernels

1 teaspoon fructose

½ teaspoon sea salt

¼ teaspoon red pepper

½ cup buttermilk

Cook turkey in a large skillet until heated through. Remove turkey and drain on paper towels. Add the corn, onions and both kinds of bell pepper to the drippings in the skillet. Sauté over medium heat for about 8 minutes, stirring often. Stirring constantly, add the cream cheese and buttermilk. Cook until cheese is completely melted. Stir in the fructose, salt and red pepper until well mixed. Pour mixture into a serving dish and sprinkle with the cooked crumbled turkey. **Serves 4-6**

LIMA BEAN & TOMATO SKILLET

1 pound baby lima beans, shelled

1 thinly sliced purple onion

1 cup chicken broth

8 plum tomatoes, peeled & cut in wedges

¼ cup chopped parsley

⅛ cup butter

¼ cup olive oil

2 teaspoons fructose

1 teaspoon dried thyme

Heat olive oil and butter in a skillet. Add lima beans, onions, chicken broth, fructose and thyme and stir until all the ingredients are well mixed. Cover and cook over medium heat for about 20 minutes. Put the tomato wedges over the lima bean mixture. Cover and cook 5 more minutes. Stir gently and spoon into a serving dish. Sprinkle ¼ cup fresh chopped parsley over the top. **Serves 4-6**

MASHED POTATOES SUPREME

3 pounds potatoes, unpeeled	½ teaspoon sea salt
½ teaspoon minced garlic	¼ teaspoon black pepper
3 tablespoons unsalted butter, softened	2 tablespoons chopped chives
½ cup milk, warmed	

Preheat oven to 350°.

Put potatoes in a large pan, cover with water and bring to a boil. Boil until fork tender. Remove potatoes from water and allow to cool enough to handle. Peel potatoes and cut in chunks. Place potatoes in a baking dish and bake for 10 minutes. Remove potatoes from oven and put in a large bowl. Mash potatoes with a potato masher. Add butter, salt, pepper, chives and garlic, mixing well. Slowly stir in the warm milk until potatoes reach the desired consistency. If desired, garnish with ¼ cup fresh chopped parsley. **Serves 8-10**

SKY FRIES

4 large baking potatoes, unpeeled	½ cup olive oil
½ teaspoon ground black pepper	1 teaspoon Sea salt
1 teaspoon garlic powder	1 tablespoon dried parsley
1 teaspoon dried rosemary	

Boil potatoes uncovered for 20 minutes. Remove from water and allow to cool enough to handle.

Preheat oven to 400°. Cut potatoes length wise into eighths (peeling optional). Mix the rest of the ingredients well. Add the potatoes, stirring gently (do not break up potatoes). Make sure all of the potatoes are well coated with the olive oil mixture. Place potatoes in a single layer on a large baking sheet and bake for 10 to 12 minutes. Carefully turn over and bake 10 to 15 minutes longer or until tender, brown and slightly crisp. Remove from oven and transfer to a serving dish. **Serves 6-8**

GRANNY'S SUNDAY POTATOES

3 pounds potatoes, unpeeled	1 cup chopped celery
1 medium onion, chopped	1 cup diced carrots
½ cup sweet red pepper	½ teaspoon Sea salt
½ teaspoon ground black pepper	1 cup milk
2 ounces grated parmesan cheese	½ cup butter
2 ounces fresh cheddar cheese	½ cup chopped parsley

Boil potatoes uncovered until fork tender. Remove from water and allow to cool enough to handle. Melt the butter in a medium size saucepan, but do not allow to brown. Add the onion, celery, carrots and sweet red pepper to the melted butter and sauté for 10 minutes, stirring often. Slowly stir in the milk and heat for 5 minutes. Add the cheeses, stirring constantly until melted.

Preheat oven to 350°.

Slice potatoes (peeling optional) and place ⅓ of them in a glass baking dish. Pour ⅓ of the cheese mixture on top and continue layering potatoes and cheese mixture until all is used. Bake uncovered for 20 to 30 minutes or until warm and light brown.

Garnish with the chopped parsley before serving. **Serves 6-8**

Note: If cheese mixture is too thick, simply add more warm milk before layering with the potatoes.

GREEN BEANS, COMPANY STYLE

1½ pounds fresh green beans, trim ends only
1 small onion, peeled and cut into wedges
1 cup baby carrots, cut in thin sticks
1 cup sliced mushrooms
¾ cup chicken stock
3 tablespoons olive oil

½ teaspoon sea salt
½ teaspoon black pepper
1 teaspoon dried basil
½ teaspoon dried oregano
2 cloves garlic, minced
¼ cup chopped parsley

In separate pans, steam the green beans and carrots just until they are tender. Remove from pans and set aside. Warm the olive oil in a large non-stick skillet. Add the onions, garlic, salt, pepper, basil, oregano and mushrooms and cook for about 5 minutes, stirring often. Add the chicken broth and bring to a soft boil. Add the green beans and carrots. Simmer for 5 minutes. Transfer to a serving dish and sprinkle with the chopped parsley. **Serves 8-10**

SAUTÉED FRESH SPINACH MELEE

3 pounds fresh baby spinach, rinsed
1 pound sliced mushrooms
1½ cups cherry tomatoes, cut in half
2 tablespoons extra virgin olive oil
2 tablespoons balsamic vinegar or lemon juice

1 cup sliced onion
1 teaspoon minced garlic
½ teaspoon sea salt
½ teaspoon black pepper
2 teaspoons fructose

Heat the olive oil in a skillet over medium heat. Add the onion and garlic and sauté for 3 or 4 minutes, stirring often. Add mushrooms and cook 5 more minutes, stirring often. Remove from skillet and set aside. Add spinach to same skillet (do not wash skillet) and sauté about 8 minutes, stirring often until spinach has started to wilt. Add the mushroom mixture back to the skillet and stir. Mix the vinegar, salt, pepper, fructose and tomatoes together and add to the spinach mixture. Cook for 5 minutes, stirring often. **Serves 4**

Oven Roasted Vegetable Bonanza

2 large baking potatoes, cut in eight wedges

1 medium onion, cut in chunks

1½ pounds young asparagus,
remove woody ends

8 ounces whole baby carrots

2 red peppers, chopped

1 pound button mushrooms

Place all ingredients in a large bowl and toss gently. Combine the following ingredients until well blended: ½ cup extra virgin light olive oil, 1 teaspoon Salt, ½ teaspoon Ground black pepper, 1 tablespoon Fresh lemon juice and ½ teaspoon Hot sauce. Pour over the vegetables and toss gently until lightly coated.

Preheat oven to 400°. Line an extra large baking dish with foil and place the potatoes on the pan and roast for 10 minutes. Carefully turn the potatoes over and roast for 10 more minutes. Add the rest of the vegetables. Roast for 10 to 15 minutes or until tender but still crisp. Remove from oven and arrange on a serving dish. Drizzle with the following sauce.

1 teaspoon grated lemon peel

1 teaspoon fresh lemon juice

⅓ cup chopped parsley

½ cup butter

1 clove garlic, minced

Combine all ingredients except the parsley in a saucepan and heat over low heat, stirring constantly. Remove from heat and stir in the parsley. **Serves 4-6**

Lemon Pesto Rice

1 cup long grain white rice

2 tablespoons butter

1 tablespoon prepared organic pesto

½ cup grated parmesan cheese

7 tablespoons chopped green onions

2 cups chicken broth

2 tablespoons fresh lemon juice

2 teaspoon fresh lemon zest

Sea salt & pepper to taste

¼ cup diced pistachios

In a saucepan, combine rice, broth and butter. Add the lemon juice, pesto, lemon zest, salt and pepper. Bring to a boil. Reduce heat, cover and simmer for about 25 minutes. Add the parmesan cheese, green onions and pistachios. Stir well and serve. **Serves 4-6**

FRESH VEGETABLE & MUSHROOM RISOTTO

6 cups chicken broth	1½ tablespoons light olive oil
3 fresh carrots, diced	1 small red onion, diced
3 cloves garlic, minced	1 zucchini, diced
½ cup diced sweet yellow pepper	1½ cups Arborio rice
½ pound asparagus, cut in 1 inch pieces	½ cup chopped basil
1½ cups sliced mushrooms	2 teaspoons fresh lemon juice
1 teaspoon sea salt	½ teaspoon fresh black pepper

Simmer broth in a pot until ready to use. Put the olive oil in a large, deep skillet and warm. Add the carrots, onion and garlic and sauté for 7 minutes, stirring often. Add the yellow pepper, zucchini, asparagus and mushrooms and cook for about 12 minutes or until tender but still crisp. Add the rice to the skillet and cook for 7 minutes, stirring often. Add 1 cup of the warm broth to the mixture and stir constantly. Allow broth to be absorbed before adding the next cup of broth. Continue adding broth, stirring constantly, until all of the broth has been used. Place in a serving dish and garnish as desired. **Serves 4-6**

BLACK JAPONICA

1 cup black japonica rice	1 bouillon cube
½ pound fresh sliced mushrooms	2 cloves garlic, minced
2 tablespoons olive oil	½ teaspoon rosemary
½ teaspoon black pepper	1 cup water
1 cup diced red, yellow & green peppers	

For the mushrooms, use mixed varieties. Shitakes are terrific in this dish with sliced white mushrooms. Sauté garlic in olive oil briefly. Add mushrooms and cook until tender-crisp. Add rice and sauté until it is coated with oil. Turn heat to medium-high. Add water, bring to a boil, turn heat to low and simmer for 45 minutes. Toss with peppers before serving. **Serves 4-6**

FIVE VEGETABLE SCALLOP

5 cups potatoes, peeled & sliced   1½ cups chopped onion
1 cup chopped sweet green pepper   1 cup sliced celery
1 cup baby carrots, cut in fourths lengthwise

Place all of the above ingredients in a pot, add just enough water to cover the vegetables and bring to a boil. Continue to boil for about 6 minutes. Drain vegetables and set aside while making the sauce.

Preheat oven to 375°.

Butter a large glass baking dish

Sauce:

4 tablespoons butter   1 teaspoon sea salt
2 tablespoons unbleached flour   ½ teaspoon black pepper
2 teaspoons Dijon mustard   1½ cups milk
1¼ cups of your favorite grated cheese   ½ cup grated cheddar

Melt the butter over low heat and add the flour, stirring until you have a smooth paste. Slowly add the milk, stirring constantly. Add the salt, pepper and 1¼ cups of cheese. When the cheese has melted and been blended into the sauce, remove from heat. Layer the vegetable mixture and the cheese sauce into the prepared baking dish. Starting with a layer of vegetables, make a total of four layers, making sure a layer of cheese sauce is on top. Completely cover the dish with foil and put on middle oven rack. Bake for 1 hour. Remove foil and sprinkle the ½ cup cheddar cheese on top. Do not re-cover! Put back in the oven for 10 minutes or until cheese has melted and started to brown slightly. **Serves 6-8**

HEARTY MASHED POTATOES

3 pounds Yukon Gold potatoes, unpeeled
1 cup diced celery
1 small purple onion, diced
$\frac{1}{2}$ teaspoon ground black pepper
1 cup milk, warmed

$\frac{1}{2}$ pound diced baby carrots
$\frac{1}{4}$ cup chopped parsley
2 cloves garlic, minced
1 teaspoon sea salt
$\frac{1}{2}$ cup unsalted butter

Put potatoes in a large pot and boil until fork tender, about 30 minutes. Remove potatoes and allow to cool enough to handle. Melt the butter in a large skillet over low heat. Add the carrots, celery, onion, garlic, salt and pepper. Sauté for 10 minutes, stirring often.

Preheat oven to 350°. Peel potatoes and place in a baking pan and bake for 10 minutes. Remove potatoes from oven and cut up and place in bowl. Add the mixture in the skillet to the potatoes and beat with an electric mixer on medium while slowly adding the warm milk. Beat the potato mixture until fluffy. Stir in the fresh parsley and serve. **Serves 6**

DELUXE GREEN BEANS

6 slices turkey , cooked & crumbled
1$\frac{1}{2}$ pounds fresh green beans, ends trimmed
$\frac{1}{4}$ cup minced purple onion
2 cups sliced mushrooms
$\frac{1}{2}$ teaspoon dried oregano
$\frac{1}{4}$ teaspoon ground black pepper
2 teaspoons fructose
1 tablespoon extra light olive oil

1 teaspoon minced garlic
$\frac{1}{4}$ cup chopped parsley
1 teaspoon minced fresh dill
$\frac{1}{2}$ teaspoon sea salt
2 tablespoons lemon juice
3 tablespoons unsalted butter

Steam the beans for 10 minutes or until tender but still crisp. Melt the butter in a large skillet. Add the onion, mushrooms, parsley and garlic. Sauté for 7 minutes, stirring often. Add the rest of the ingredients one at a time until the mixture is well blended. Add the green beans to the skillet and sauté over medium low heat for 5 minutes. Transfer to a serving dish and sprinkle with the crumbled turkey. **Serves 6-8**

VEGETABLE RICE BAKE

2 cups long grain rice
3 cups chicken broth
1½ cups sliced mushrooms
1¼ cups milk with 1 tablespoon lemon juice
3 tablespoons unsalted butter

1 cup chopped onion
¼ cup diced celery
1 teaspoon sea salt
⅛ teaspoon black pepper

Preheat oven to 350°.

Sauté the mushrooms, onion and celery in the butter for about 5 minutes. Mix the rice, milk, lemon juice, broth, salt, pepper and mushroom mixture in a large bowl, stirring well. Butter a 2½ to 3-quart casserole dish and pour rice mixture into it. Cover well with foil and bake for about 70 minutes. Remove the foil and sprinkle with ¼ cup fresh grated romano cheese. Return to oven and bake for an additional 15 minutes. **Serves 6-8**

SWEET POTATO PECAN CASSEROLE

6 sweet potatoes, cooked, peeled & mashed
½ cup fructose
1 cup pecans, chopped
1 cup orange slices, chopped

1 teaspoon sea salt
6 tablespoons melted butter
1 cup pineapple, chopped
1 cup shredded coconut

Preheat oven to 350°

Butter a 3-quart casserole dish

Put the sweet potatoes, fructose, salt and melted butter in a bowl and stir until smooth. Add the pineapple, orange pieces, coconut and pecans, stirring until well mixed. Put into the buttered casserole dish. Sprinkle ⅓ cup fructose, ¼ cup chopped pecans and ¼ cup shredded coconut. Drizzle with ¼ cup melted butter. Place on middle oven rack and bake for 30 minutes. **Serves 8-10**

DELUXE BAKED BEANS WITH SMOKED TURKEY

3 cups dry navy beans, sort & rinse

1 pound smoked turkey

1 cup chopped sweet red pepper

1/3 cup fructose

4 teaspoons spicy brown mustard

1/2 teaspoon black pepper

1 large onion, diced

1 cup diced celery

1 cup tomato sauce

1/2 cup honey

1 teaspoon sea salt

Put the beans in a heavy pot with 10 cups of water and boil for 5 minutes. Remove pot from heat and cover, let stand for 2 hours. Do not drain off liquid! Add the salt and black pepper to the beans and bring back to a boil. Lower to a simmer and cook for 1 hour. Drain all but 2 cups of the liquid off. Save the liquid! Put the beans and 2 cups of the liquid in a 3-quart casserole dish. Mix cooked turkey, onion, sweet pepper, celery, honey, fructose, mustard and tomato sauce in with the beans, stirring until well mixed. Cover and bake at 350° for about 3 hours. Stir the beans occasionally. If needed, stir in a little more of the reserved liquid. Do not allow beans to cook dry. **Serves 8-10**

MY FAVORITE PEAS

2 pounds sweet peas, steamed

1/2 teaspoon black pepper

1 cup diced turkey

1/2 teaspoon dried rosemary

1 cup sliced mushrooms

1 cup diced onion

1 teaspoon sea salt

1/4 cup unsalted butter

1 clove garlic, minced

1/2 cup chicken broth

In skillet, sauté the onion, garlic, turkey and mushrooms in the butter for 5 minutes. Add the rest of the ingredients and stir until well mixed. Bring the mixture to a simmer and allow to cook for about 10 minutes. Stir often and do not allow mixture to boil. **Serves 6-8**

VEGETABLE SMORGASBORD

½ cup butter

1½ cups chopped onion

1 cup chopped sweet green pepper

3 cups chopped plum tomatoes

1½ cups fresh small lima beans

1 cup chicken broth

1 teaspoon ground black pepper

2 cloves garlic, minced

1 cup chopped celery

1 cup sliced okra

3 cups fresh corn

1 cup sliced baby carrots

1½ teaspoons sea salt

Sauté the garlic, onion, sweet pepper and celery in the butter over medium heat. Cook until vegetables are tender, stirring constantly. Add the tomatoes and bring to a boil. Lower heat and simmer for about 10 minutes. Stir in all of the remaining ingredients and bring back to a boil. Lower heat and simmer for 15 minutes or just until vegetables are tender. **Serves 8-10**

CITRUS AND HONEY GLAZED CARROTS

4 cups baby carrots, steamed

1 strip lemon peel

2 teaspoons fresh lemon juice

⅛ teaspoon ground nutmeg

2 teaspoons grated orange peel, finely chopped

1½ cups orange juice

¼ cup honey

⅛ teaspoon ground ginger

½ teaspoon sea salt

⅛ teaspoon black pepper

In a medium saucepan, combine the orange juice, lemon peel, honey, lemon juice, ginger, nutmeg, orange peel, salt and pepper. Bring to a boil over medium heat, stirring constantly. Add the steamed carrots and bring back to a boil. Reduce heat to low and allow the carrots to cook until most of the liquid has evaporated. Be sure to stir the mixture often to coat all of the carrots with the glaze. Pour into a serving dish. **Serves 6-8**

GREEN BEANS & ONIONS WITH MUSTARD SAUCE

1½ pounds green beans, steamed
   with ends trimmed
2 teaspoons fresh lemon juice
¼ cup butter
¼ cup milk

3 tablespoons spicy whole
   grain mustard
½ cup diced purple onion
½ cup chicken stock
½ cup diced tomato

Put the steamed green beans in a serving dish and evenly drizzle with the lemon juice. In a saucepan over medium heat, melt the butter and sauté the onion for 4 minutes. Stir the broth, milk and mustard into the onion mixture. Simmer the sauce until it thickens slightly, stirring constantly. Spoon the warm sauce over the green beans and sprinkle with the diced tomatoes. **Serves 6-8**

CURRIED RICE

1 cup long grain rice
½ cup chopped mixed dried fruit
½ cup toasted almond slivers
2½ cups chicken broth
2 teaspoons butter

¼ cup golden raisins
4 teaspoons minced onion
2 teaspoons curry powder
½ teaspoon sea salt

Combine the curry powder, salt, chicken broth and butter in a saucepan and bring to a boil. Stir in the rice, dried fruit, almonds, raisins and onion. Allow mixture to boil for 1 minute, stirring constantly. Reduce heat to low and cover saucepan tightly. Simmer rice undisturbed for 30 minutes. Remove from heat and allow to set for 5 minutes. Fluff with a fork before serving. **Serves 4**

This is very good served with roasted chicken or grilled fish.

EGGY VEGETABLE CASSEROLE WITH CHEESY MUSHROOM SAUCE

8 large eggs, beaten well
½ cup diced sweet red pepper
¼ cup diced baby carrots
½ cup sweet peas, steamed
¼ cup milk

¼ cup diced onion
½ cup sliced celery
¼ cup chopped parsley
1 clove garlic, minced

Preheat oven to 350°. Butter a glass baking dish (12-by-8-by-2-inch).

In a large bowl, whisk all of the above ingredients until well blended. Pour mixture into the prepared baking dish and bake for 35 to 40 minutes or until a knife inserted in the center comes out clean.

Cheesy Mushroom Sauce:

2 cups chicken broth
½ cup shredded cheddar cheese
1 cup sliced mushrooms

2 tablespoons butter
2 tablespoons cornstarch

Stir the cornstarch into ½ cup of broth until smooth. Warm the remaining broth and butter to the boiling point. Slowly whisk the cornstarch mixture into the hot broth. Cook mixture, whisking constantly until smooth and starting to thicken. Stir in the mushrooms and cheese until well mixed. Cut the casserole into serving size portions and top with the sauce. If preferred, sauce can be served on the side.

Serves 6-8

STIR FRY VEGETABLES

3 tablespoons olive oil

2 tablespoons chopped fresh thyme

1/8 teaspoon ground black pepper

1/2 pound sliced mushrooms

1/2 pound broccoli florets

1 cup chicken broth

2 cloves garlic, minced

1/2 teaspoon sea salt

2 medium onions, sliced

1/2 pound cauliflower florets

1/2 pound baby carrots

In a large non-stick skillet, heat the olive oil, garlic, thyme, salt and pepper for 3 minutes, stirring constantly. Add the onions, mushrooms, cauliflower, broccoli and carrots and sauté for 5 minutes, stirring often. Stir the broth into the vegetable mixture and cook for 5 more minutes, stirring often. **Serves 6**

APPLE AND PEPPER SKILLET

1 red bell pepper, julienned

1 yellow bell pepper, julienned

1 green bell pepper, julienned

1 tablespoon low sodium soy sauce

1/4 teaspoon crushed dried rosemary

1/4 cup toasted pine nuts

2 apples, sliced

3 tablespoons olive oil

1 medium onion, sliced

2 cloves garlic, minced

1/2 teaspoon dried basil

In a large skillet, sauté the peppers, onion and apples in the olive oil until tender but still crisp. Add the soy sauce, garlic, rosemary and basil and cook for 5 minutes, stirring constantly. Pour into a serving dish and sprinkle with pine nuts. **Serves 4-6**

BRUSSEL SPROUTS & ONIONS

2 pounds fresh brussel sprouts, trim and
    cut an 'x' in each core
1/4 pound turkey sausage
1 cup chopped onion
1/4 teaspoon ground black pepper

1 cup chicken broth
2 teaspoons olive oil
1 teaspoon celery seeds
1 teaspoon caraway seeds
1/8 teaspoon sea salt

Place brussel sprouts in a saucepan and cover with water. Bring to a boil. Cook for 8 minutes or just until tender. In a large skillet, cook turkey sausage. Using a slotted spoon, remove turkey sausage and place on paper towels. Add the olive oil and onion to the drippings in the skillet and cook for 5 minutes. Stir the broth, celery seeds, caraway seeds, salt and pepper into the skillet. Cook mixture uncovered until most of the liquid is gone. Drain the brussel sprouts and add to the onion mixture and cook for 3 minutes. Stir the cooked turkey sausage into the brussel sprouts mixture and pour into a serving dish. **Serves 6-8**

BAKED RICE

1 cup brown basmati rice
1 1/2 cups beef or chicken broth

1 cup water
1 tablespoon butter

Melt butter in 2-quart casserole dish. Add rice, broth and water. Stir and cover. Place in 350° oven for 1 hour. Remove cover for the last 10 minutes if you prefer it a bit crunchy.

Easy additions:

Some or all of these can be stirred in raw before cooking:

1/2 cup chopped onions
1/4 cup scallions

1/4 cup sweet red pepper

These should be cooked before adding and added after the rice has cooked:

Diced cooked chicken

sautéed mushrooms

Serves 4-6

RICE PILAF WITH BLEU CHEESE, PEARS AND PECANS

¾ cup chopped shallots

1 cup white basmati rice

¾ cup chopped dried pears

1½ cups shredded cooked chicken

4 ounces Bleu cheese crumbles

2 tablespoons olive oil

2 cloves garlic, minced

2 cups chicken broth

2 teaspoons chopped rosemary

⅔ cup toasted pecans

Heat oil in heavy saucepan over medium heat. Add shallots and sauté until golden, about 5 minutes. Add garlic and sauté 30 seconds more. Stir in rice and dried pears. Add chicken broth, bring to a boil. Reduce heat to low; cover and cook until rice is tender and liquid is absorbed, about 18 minutes. Remove lid and stir in chicken, rosemary and half of the bleu cheese; cook 2 minutes to warm through. Season to taste with pepper. Transfer pilaf to bowl. Sprinkle with remaining bleu cheese and pecans to serve. **Serves 4-6**

CURRIED RISOTTO WITH SOUR CHERRIES

1 cup Arborio rice

1 small onion, diced

5 cups chicken or vegetable broth

¼ cup dried sour cherries

1 tablespoon hot mango chutney (hot optional)

1 teaspoon olive oil

1 teaspoon curry powder

2 teaspoons thyme

¼ cup milk

½ cup parmesan cheese

Simmer broth in saucepan. In deep thick-walled pot heated to medium hot, add olive oil. Add onion and sauté until onion is translucent. Add rice and stir until grains are coated. Add curry and thyme and stir. Add broth 1 cup at a time, stirring continuously, until each cup is absorbed. Cook time is about 20 minutes. Add sour cherries, milk, chutney and cheese, stirring gently. Cook another 5 minutes and serve. **Serves 4-6**

BASIC RISOTTO

1 cup white Arborio rice
1 large onion, chopped
$\frac{1}{4}$ cup grated parmesan cheese

1 tablespoon olive oil
4-5 cups hot stock/water

Heat olive oil in a heavy non-stick 2-quart pot. Sauté onion in oil until translucent. Add rice and stir until grains are coated with oil. Add 1 cup hot stock or water, stirring until liquid is absorbed. Continue cooking for about 20 minutes, adding the remaining liquid 1 cup at a time. This rice creates its own creamy sauce; add additional liquid if creamier texture is desired. Remove from heat, stir in cheeses and serve immediately. For variety, add fresh herbs and chopped vegetables during the last 5 minutes of cooking. **Serves 4**

HOLIDAY RISOTTO

6 cups chicken broth
2 shallots, minced
1$\frac{1}{2}$ cups Arborio rice
1 tablespoon chopped thyme

3 tablespoons olive oil
3 cloves garlic, minced
$\frac{1}{4}$ cup milk

In large saucepan, simmer chicken broth and keep warm. In separate heavy saucepans, heat olive oil over medium heat and sauté shallots and garlic for 2 minutes. Add rice and cook for 1 minute, ensuring that all the grains are coated. Add 1 cup of chicken broth, cooking and stirring until liquid is absorbed. Add chicken broth $\frac{1}{2}$ cup at a time, stirring until completely absorbed. Rice will be cooked in 19 minutes. Add the remaining chicken broth, milk and thyme. Stir briskly to combine and serve immediately. **Serves 4-6**

VEGETABLE PILAF

¼ cup chopped onion	3 tablespoons olive oil, divided
2 cups chicken or vegetable broth	1 cup wild rice
2 teaspoons dried basil	8 ounces mushrooms
1 large zucchini, cut into 1-inch pieces	Sea salt & pepper to taste
1 large red pepper, cut into 1-inch pieces	1 medium tomato, chopped

Heat oven to 425°. Heat 1 tablespoon oil in heavy, large saucepan over medium heat. Add onion and sauté until lightly browned. Add rice, chicken broth and 1 teaspoon basil. Bring to a boil. Cover and simmer at low heat until rice is tender, about 45 minutes. Meanwhile, in 15-by-1-by-1-inch pan, combine mushrooms, zucchini and red pepper. Add remaining 2 tablespoons oil, remaining 1 teaspoon herbs, salt and pepper. Toss to coat. Bake 15 minutes; stir in tomatoes. Bake 5 minutes more or until vegetables are tender. Stir vegetables into rice. Garnish with fresh herb sprigs if desired. **Serves 4-6**

CHEESY ASPARAGUS RISOTTO

1½ cups white Arborio rice	2 tablespoons olive oil
1 large onion, chopped	2 cloves garlic, chopped
4½ cups stock	½ cup romano cheese
½ pound asparagus, chopped into ½ inch pieces	

In a deep pot, sauté onion and garlic in olive oil until translucent. Add rice and stir with a wooden spoon. Add ½ cup of stock and stir until it is absorbed. Add the asparagus pieces. Continue adding stock in ½ cup portions as the rice dries out. Continue cooking for about 20 minutes until rice is cooked. Typical risotto is characterized by firm grains in a creamy smooth base. Remove from heat, stir in cheese and serve immediately. **Serves 4-6**

REGAL BASMATI

2 cups brown basmati rice

1 teaspoon whole cumin seeds

1 large onion, chopped

½ cup frozen green peas

4 cups water or broth

3 tablespoons olive oil

⅛ teaspoon black pepper

¼ teaspoon sea salt

In a heavy skillet or Dutch oven with a lid, heat oil and cumin seeds. Stir for a few seconds, add onions and cook until translucent. Add rice and continue cooking for 3 to 4 minutes. Add liquid and bring to a boil. Cover and reduce heat to low and cook 45-50 minutes. Stir in peas the last few minutes of cooking. **Serves 4**

MEXICAN RICE

1½ cups short grain rice

3 cups chopped tomatoes, reserve liquid

1 large onion, diced

1 bell pepper, diced

⅛ teaspoon cayenne pepper

3 cups broth

2 stalks celery, diced

2 cloves garlic, minced

½ cup fresh cilantro

1 tablespoon olive oil

Heat oil in deep skillet or 3-quart saucepan. Sauté onion until translucent. Add rice and cook for 1 minute. Add bell pepper, celery and liquid. Bring to a boil, reduce heat and simmer for 50 minutes. Mixture should be creamy not dry. **Serves 4-6**

RICE PILAF

2 cups long grain brown rice

4 cups broth or water

2 cups fresh chopped parsley

2 teaspoons olive oil

Sea salt & pepper to taste

½ cup slivered almonds

Heat a heavy skillet on medium heat. Add oil and stir with wooden spoon. Add rice and continue stirring for 5 minutes or until grains are toasted. Add broth or water, cover tightly and cook for 45 minutes. Stir in parsley and almonds and continue cooking for 5 minutes. **Serves 4-6**

WILD MUSHROOM RISOTTO

1 cup Arborio rice

¼ cup onion, finely chopped

½ ounce chopped thyme

¼ ounce basil

1 quart chicken broth

2 ounces grated parmesan cheese

Pinch of sea salt

1 medium Portobello mushroom, sliced

1 head garlic, minced

½ ounce chopped rosemary

¼ cup chopped parsley

¼ qt. milk

½ pound butter

1 ounce olive oil

Pinch of white pepper

Warm olive oil in a pot, sauté onion and garlic until translucent and add rice. Sauté rice until it becomes pearl white in color, start stirring in chicken broth with wooden spoon until rice becomes tender to the tooth. Slowly add in the milk and diced butter. Add herbs and cheese, stirring constantly until well incorporated; season with salt and pepper. Place sliced Portobello mushroom on top and garnish with basil leaves. **Serves 4**

ITALIAN BASMATI

2 cups cooked brown basmati rice

½ cup grated parmesan cheese

1 tablespoon olive oil

¾ cup rehydrated sundried tomatoes, chopped

1 tablespoon dry basil

½ teaspoon pepper

½ teaspoon sea salt

Put cooked basmati into large mixing bowl. Toss hot rice with remaining ingredients using wooden spoons to avoid breaking grains. Serve immediately. **Serves 4-6**

WILD RICE DRESSING

3-4 slices turkey, minced

1 cup wild rice

2¼ cups chicken broth

1½ cups total diced carrots, & green beans

2 onions, minced

1 tablespoon butter

Fresh thyme & sage

2 cups whole grain bread cubes

Sauté turkey and onions with butter over medium heat to brown lightly. Add rice and sauté for 2 to 3 minutes. Add chicken broth, pepper to taste, and a few sprigs of thyme tied together with a few sage leaves. Cover and simmer at low heat for 25 minutes, stir in diced fresh veggies and continue to simmer, covered, for 25 minutes or longer. Rice will be tender, but still a bit soupy. Add bread cubes and stir into hot rice. If rice cooked dry, add a splash of stock with bread. **Serves 4-6**

BAKED CREAM SPINACH

1 (10 ounce) package frozen spinach, thawed

1 medium onion, chopped

2 tablespoons unbleached flour

½ teaspoon sea salt

¼ teaspoon pepper

1 cup parmesan cheese

2 tablespoons butter

2 garlic cloves, minced

3 large eggs

¼ teaspoon nutmeg

1 cup milk

Drain spinach well, pressing between paper towels to remove all excess liquid. Melt butter in a large skillet over medium heat; add onion and garlic, and sauté 5 minutes or until garlic is lightly browned and onions are tender. Remove from heat, and stir in spinach until well blended; cool. Whisk together eggs, flour, salt, nutmeg and pepper in a large bowl. Whisk in milk and freshly grated parmesan cheese; stir in spinach mixture, and pour into a lightly greased 8-inch square baking dish. Bake at 350° for 33 to 35 minutes or until set. Let stand 5 minutes before serving. **Serves 4-6**

SPICY RICE & CASHEWS

3 tablespoons olive oil	2 teaspoons cumin seeds
1/4 teaspoon ground cloves	1 bay leaf
1/2 teaspoon chili powder	1 small onion, minced
2 garlic cloves, minced	1 cup uncooked wehani rice
1/3 cup roasted cashews, chopped	1/2 teaspoon sea salt

Heat oil in a large heavy saucepan with tight fitting lid. Add cumin seed, cloves and stir. Add chili powder, onion and garlic. Continue to cook, stirring until the onion is soft. Stir in wehani until coated thoroughly. Add 2¼ cups hot water and salt and bring to a boil. Reduce heat and simmer, covered for 45 minutes. Do not remove lid. Remove pan from heat and let sit, covered for 15 minutes. Stir in cashews and serve. **Serves 2-4**

RICE PRIMAVERA

3 cups hot cooked wehani rice	2 tablespoons olive oil
1/4 cup grated parmesan cheese	1 to 2 cloves garlic, minced
1/2 cup julienned sun dried tomatoes	1/2 cup sliced olives

Blend all ingredients together and serve immediately. **Serves 8-10**

SQUASH CASSEROLE

1 stick butter	2 cups milk
3 tablespoons unbleached flour	3 eggs, beaten
2 cups cooked squash	2 cups grated cheese
Buttered breadcrumbs	Sea salt & pepper to taste

Make white sauce with butter, flour and milk. Cook slowly until thick, add eggs. Add cheese; stir well until melted. Add squash. Pour into casserole dish and top with breadcrumbs. Cook uncovered at 350° for 45 minutes or until golden brown. **Serves 4-6**

SQUASH SOUFFLE

1½ pound sliced squash

1 tablespoon minced parsley

¼ cup milk

½ teaspoon sea salt

¼ cup finely chopped pecans

1 small onion, minced

1 egg, slightly beaten

½ cup cottage cheese

½ teaspoon pepper

1 teaspoon fructose

Parboil squash and mash. Add all ingredients except nuts. Place in greased 2-quart casserole; sprinkle pecans on top. Bake at 350° for about 25 minutes or until top is golden brown. **Serves 4-6**

BROCCOLI & BEAN CASSEROLE

1 package frozen baby lima beans

2 packages frozen chopped broccoli

Sea salt and pepper to taste

1 cup grated cheese

1 can mushroom soup

Breadcrumbs

Cook lima beans and broccoli until tender; pour off water. Layer in buttered baking dish with cheese in the middle of the layers. Top with soup and breadcrumbs. Bake for 30 minutes at 350°. **Serves 6-8**

GARLIC MASHED POTATOES

2 pounds baking potatoes, peeled
  and cut in quarters

2 tablespoons olive oil

½ teaspoon sea salt

½ teaspoon black pepper

3 medium cloves garlic, peeled

⅓ cup grated parmesan cheese

Cook potatoes and garlic in water to cover over medium heat for 20 to 25 minutes or until tender. Ladle off and reserve ⅔ cup cooking water. Drain potatoes and return to pot. Mash hot potatoes with potato masher or beat with hand-held mixer on medium-high speed, adding olive oil and reserved cooking water. Stir in cheese, salt and pepper. Spoon into serving bowl. Drizzle with a little olive oil and sprinkle with parsley. **Serves 8-10**

TURMERIC RICE PILAF

2 tablespoons butter

½ cup slivered almonds

1½ cups uncooked basmati rice

¼ teaspoon ground cinnamon

3 cups chicken broth

1 small onion, chopped

½ cup golden raisins

1½ teaspoon ground turmeric

½ teaspoon sea salt

Melt butter in a skillet over medium-high heat; add onion and almonds and sauté for 7 minutes or until onion is tender and almonds are golden. Stir in rice, raisins, turmeric, cinnamon and salt. Sauté for 2 minutes. Add broth and bring to a boil; cover, reduce heat and simmer 20 to 25 minutes or until rice is tender.
Serves 4-6

TUSCAN BEANS

3 cans cannelloni beans, rinsed

1½ pounds butternut squash, cut in 1-in chunks

1 medium onion, cut in thin half rounds

1 box frozen chopped spinach, thawed

½ teaspoon sea salt

¼ cup grated parmesan cheese

1 teaspoon dried thyme

1 cup chicken broth

1 tablespoon grated lemon peel

½ teaspoon sage

¼ cup shredded cheddar

Heat oven to 350°. Have a shallow baking dish ready. Mix beans, squash, onion, spinach, lemon peel, thyme, sage and salt in baking dish. Add broth; cover tightly. Bake 55 minutes or until squash is tender. Sprinkle with the cheeses; bake uncovered 5 to 10 minutes longer, until cheeses melt. **Serves 6-8**

ORANGE BEETS

4 medium beets

1 tablespoon brown sugar

1/4 teaspoon finely shredded orange peel

1 tablespoon butter

1 teaspoon cornstarch

1/4 cup orange juice

In a saucepan cook fresh whole beets, covered in boiling water for 40 to 50 minutes or until tender; drain. Cool slightly; slip off skins and slice. In a medium saucepan melt butter. Stir in brown sugar and cornstarch. Stir in orange peel and juice. Cook and stir until thickened and bubbly. Add sliced beets; cook and stir for 3 to 4 minutes or until heated through. **Serves 6-8**

BAKED BROCCOLI

6 cups fresh broccoli, chopped

1 can cream of mushroom soup

1/4 cup shredded American cheese

1 tablespoon mayonnaise

2 tablespoons milk

1 tablespoon chopped pimento

2 tablespoons crushed crackers

Cook broccoli, covered, in a small amount of water for 9 to 11 minutes or until tender-crisp; drain. Transfer to a 1½-quart casserole dish. Combine soup, cheese, milk, mayonnaise and pimento. Stir into broccoli. Top with crushed crackers. Bake at 350° for 30 minutes or until heated through. **Serves 6-8**

ORANGE GINGER BASMATI

1 large onion, diced

Peel of one orange, grated

1 tablespoon ginger, minced

1¾ cups water

1 tablespoon olive oil

1 garlic clove, minced

1 cup basmati rice

¾ teaspoon sea salt

In a medium saucepan heat oil over medium-low heat. Add onion and orange peel, stirring frequently, until onion is very tender, 15 to 20 minutes. Add garlic and ginger; cook 2 minutes. Add rice, stirring to coat. Add water and salt and bring to a boil. Reduce heat and simmer, covered, until rice is tender, about 20 to 30 minutes. **Serves 4**

CORN CASSEROLE

¼ cup chopped green pepper

2 tablespoons butter

1 can cream style corn

1 can whole kernel corn

Dash of pepper

¼ cup chopped onion

1 beaten egg

½ cup milk

½ cup crushed crackers

Cook onion and pepper in 1 tablespoon of the butter until tender. Combine egg, milk, ⅓ cup of the crackers and pepper. Stir in onion mixture and corn. Pour into buttered 1-quart casserole dish. Melt remaining butter; toss with remaining crumbs. Sprinkle crumb mixture on top of corn mixture. Bake at 350° for 35 minutes or until a knife inserted in the center comes out clean. **Serves 6-8**

TOMATO SCALLOP

3 slices bread, toasted

½ cup chopped celery

3 medium tomatoes, peeled and cut up

½ teaspoon fructose

2 tablespoons water

⅛ teaspoon pepper

2 tablespoons butter

½ cup chopped onion

1 tablespoon unbleached flour

½ teaspoon dried marjoram

¼ teaspoon sea salt

Spread toast with 1 tablespoon butter. Cut into cubes. Set aside. Cook celery and onion in remaining butter until tender-crisp. Add fresh tomatoes. Bring to boiling; reduce heat. Cover; simmer for 8 minutes. Combine flour, fructose, marjoram, water, salt and pepper. Stir into tomatoes. Cook and stir until bubbly. Stir ⅔ of the toast cubes into tomato mixture. Pour into a 1-quart casserole dish. Top tomato mixture with remaining toast cubes. If desired, sprinkle with grated parmesan cheese. Bake at 350° for 20 minutes or until bubbly. **Serves 4-6**

CHEESY CREAMED PEAS

2 cups shelled peas

1 tablespoon butter

½ cup shredded swiss cheese

½ teaspoon finely shredded lemon peel

¾ cup sliced green onion

1 tablespoon unbleached flour

⅛ teaspoon sea salt

¾ cup milk

Cook peas, covered, in a small amount of boiling water for 10 to 12 minutes or until tender-crisp. Meanwhile, for sauce, in a medium saucepan cook onion in butter until tender. Stir in flour and salt. Add milk all at once. Cook and stir until thickened and bubbly. Cook and stir 1 minute more. Add cheese and lemon peel, stirring until cheese melts. Stir in drained peas. If necessary, stir in additional milk to make of desired consistency. **Serves 4**

BLACKEYED PEAS & SPINACH

2 slices nitrate free turkey sausage, cut in cubes

4 tablespoons olive oil

3 cups frozen blackeyed peas, thawed

1 (10 ounce) package fresh spinach, torn

1 medium onion, diced

2½ cups water

½ teaspoon sea salt

½ teaspoon pepper

Sauté onion in olive oil until tender. Add peas and turkey sausage; bring to a boil. Reduce heat and simmer 30 minutes or until peas are tender; stir in salt and pepper. Stir in spinach; cook over medium heat 3 to 5 minutes or until spinach wilts. Drain and serve. **Serves 6-8**

CHICKEN COUSCOUS

2 cans chicken broth
3 cups uncooked couscous
½ cup pine nuts, toasted
¼ cup chopped fresh mint
1 tablespoon fresh lemon juice
¼ teaspoon sea salt
½ teaspoon ground red pepper
1 tablespoon olive oil

¼ cup butter, divided
½ cup currants
4 green onions, sliced
½ teaspoon grated lemon rind
2 tablespoons minced dill
¾ teaspoon curry powder
¼ teaspoon black pepper

Bring broth and 3 tablespoons butter to a boil in a saucepan over medium heat; remove from heat. Stir in couscous. Cover and let stand 5 minutes; fluff with a fork. Stir in currants, pine nuts, onions, mint, lemon grind, lemon juice and dill. Stir in salt, curry and red pepper. **Serves 6**

SOUTHWESTERN CABBAGE

2 tablespoons olive oil
1 green bell pepper, sliced
¾ cup chopped cilantro
1 teaspoon sea salt

½ red cabbage, sliced
1 small onion, sliced
1 tablespoon lime juice
½ teaspoon pepper

Heat oil in large skillet or wok at high heat 3 to 4 minutes. Add cabbage, bell pepper and onion and stir-fry 7 to 10 minutes or until crisp-tender or to desired° of doneness. Stir in cilantro and remaining ingredients. **Serves 4**

SAVORY GARLIC CABBAGE

1 small cabbage	6 garlic cloves, sliced
3 tablespoons olive oil	½ cup chicken broth
1 teaspoon sea salt	⅛ teaspoon pepper

Remove outside leaves and stalk from cabbage; cut into 4 wedges. Sauté garlic in hot oil in an ovenproof skillet over medium heat 1 to 2 minutes or until golden. Add cabbage to skillet, cut sides down; cook 5 minutes. Turn to other cut sides and cook 2 to 3 minutes. Stir in broth and sprinkle evenly with salt. Bake at 350° for 20 to 25 minutes or until crisp-tender. Sprinkle evenly with pepper. Serve immediately. **Serves 4**

FRIED TOMATOES

3 large tomatoes, sliced ¼ inch thick	¼ cup grape seed oil
1¼ cups yellow corn meal	2 large eggs
¼ cup unbleached flour	½ teaspoon sea salt

In a large shallow bowl, whisk eggs. Add tomatoes and coat completely. In another bowl, add corn meal, flour and salt. Heat oil in large cast iron skillet. Take several tomato slices from eggs and place in corn meal mixture, thoroughly coating each slice. Lay tomato slices in skillet and cook until golden brown, turning occasionally. Place on paper towels to absorb oil. **Serves 6-8**

FRIED OKRA

1 pound okra, trimmed & sliced $\frac{1}{2}$ inch thick
$1\frac{1}{4}$ cups yellow corn meal
$\frac{1}{4}$ cup grape seed oil
$\frac{1}{4}$ teaspoon pepper

2 large eggs
$\frac{1}{4}$ cup unbleached flour
$1\frac{1}{2}$ teaspoon sea salt

In a large shallow bowl, whisk together eggs. Add okra and toss to coat thoroughly. In another bowl, combine cornmeal, flour, salt and pepper. Lift half the okra from egg mixture, letting excess drain off; add to cornmeal mixture in one bowl, and toss to coat evenly. Repeat with remaining okra, adding it to second bowl. In a deep 12-inch cast iron skillet, heat oil. Carefully place the okra in oil. Gently flip with spatula. Cook until golden brown, 10 to 15 minutes; adjust heat as needed to keep oil temperature between 300° and 350°. With a slotted spoon, transfer okra to a paper-towel lined baking sheet to drain. **Serves 4-6**

CHEESY RICE CRISP

2 cups cooked white Arborio rice
$\frac{1}{2}$ cup grated parmesan cheese
$\frac{1}{2}$ cup seasoned dried breadcrumbs
Sea salt & pepper to taste

2 eggs
2 tablespoons chopped parsley
2 tablespoons olive oil

Beat eggs and mix with cooked rice, add grated cheese, mix well and add salt and pepper to taste. Heat 2 tablespoons oil in a non-stick 9-inch frying pan. Add rice mixture and pour breadcrumbs and parsley on top. Flatten mixture out evenly and cook until bottoms turn crispy. Put pan into heated 350° oven and bake until top is lightly browned. Remove from oven and slide the rice crisp into a serving dish and cut into serving pieces. **Serves 4-6**

The Dessert Tray

Cakes,
Pies,
and
Puddings

10

YUM YUM YUM PINEAPPLE CAKE

½ cup softened butter

½ cup light brown sugar

2 cups unbleached flour

2 teaspoon aluminum free baking soda

1 (20 ounce) can crushed pineapple, in its juices

½ cup chopped candied cherries

⅔ cup fructose

2 large eggs, beaten

½ teaspoon sea salt

1 cup light brown sugar

½ cup chopped pecans

½ cup flaked coconut

Preheat oven to 350°. Butter and lightly flour a 13-by-9-by-2-inch cake pan. Cream butter with ½ cup light brown sugar and fructose using an electric mixer on medium speed. Add the eggs one at a time, beating until mixture is smooth. Sift the flour, baking soda and salt together. Blend the flour mixture into the creamed mixture, beating on medium speed for 2 minutes. Stir the pineapple and all of the juice into the batter. Pour the batter into the prepared pan and sprinkle the pecans, coconut, cherries and 1 cup brown sugar evenly over the top. Place on middle oven rack and bake for 45 minutes or until cake tests done when a toothpick inserted in the middle comes out clean. Remove from oven and place on a wire rack to cool before cutting.

CINNAMON BREAD PUDDING

3 cups milk

2 cups soft cubed cinnamon bread

1½ tablespoons butter

½ teaspoon sea salt

5 tablespoons fructose

¼ cup light brown sugar

3 eggs, beaten

1 cup golden raisins

Preheat oven to 350°. Butter a glass 9-by-5-inch loaf pan. Heat the milk in a pot and stir in bread cubes and butter. Combine the eggs, raisins, fructose and brown sugar. Stir until well mixed. Blend the milk mixture into the egg mixture and pour into the prepared pan. Place in a larger pan and pour hot water into the larger pan until it is 1-inch deep all around. Bake uncovered for 60 to 70 minutes or until set. Remove from oven and place loaf pan on a rack to cool.

GONE BANANAS CAKE

Preheat oven to 350°. Butter and lightly flour 2 (9-inch) round cake pans.

Cake Recipe:

2 cups whole wheat flour	$\frac{1}{2}$ teaspoon sea salt
$\frac{1}{2}$ teaspoon aluminum free baking powder	$\frac{1}{2}$ cup fructose
$\frac{3}{4}$ teaspoon aluminum free baking soda	$\frac{1}{2}$ cup softened butter
$\frac{1}{4}$ cup light brown sugar, packed	2 large eggs, beaten
$\frac{1}{4}$ cup milk, mix in 2 teaspoon lemon juice	2 teaspoons vanilla extract
3 very ripe bananas, mashed	$\frac{1}{2}$ cup chopped pecans

Sift the flour, salt, baking powder and baking soda together and set aside. In a separate bowl, mix the butter, fructose, brown sugar, eggs and vanilla. Using an electric mixer, beat on medium speed about 2 minutes or until light and fluffy. Stir the bananas, milk and lemon juice together until well blended. Alternately add the flour mixture and the banana mixture to the butter mixture, being sure to begin and end with the flour mixture. Continue beating on medium high speed for 2 minutes. Stir in the pecans until well blended. Pour batter into the prepared cake pans and bake on middle oven rack for 30 minutes or until a toothpick comes out clean when inserted in the top of the cake. Cool for 10 minutes in the pans and then remove and place on wire racks to cool completely before frosting.

Frosting Recipe:

3 ounces low fat cream cheese, softened	$\frac{1}{3}$ cup softened butter
3 tablespoons fructose	$1\frac{1}{2}$ teaspoon vanilla extract
2 to 3 teaspoons milk	$\frac{1}{2}$ cup chopped pecans

Cream the butter and cream cheese with an electric mixer, beating on medium speed until light and fluffy. Beat the fructose in slowly until all of it has been added. Add the milk and continue beating until frosting is smooth and of a spreading consistency. Stir in the vanilla extract and frost the cake. Evenly sprinkle the pecans over the top of the frosted cake.

APPLE RAISIN WALNUT DELIGHT

Preheat oven to 350°. In a large bowl, combine the following ingredients until well mixed.

3½ pounds Granny Smith apples, peeled, cored & sliced	1 teaspoon vanilla extract
1 cup raisins	1 cup chopped walnuts
½ cup fresh honey or Agave nectar	3 tablespoons fresh lemon juice
1 tablespoon unbleached flour	2 teaspoons ground cinnamon

Pour mixture into a well buttered 2-quart glass baking dish and dot with 3 tablespoons butter and set aside while making the batter.

Batter Recipe:

¼ cup butter, melted & cooled	2 eggs
½ cup milk	1 teaspoon vanilla extract
Pinch of sea salt	½ teaspoon ground nutmeg
1½ cups unbleached flour	5 tablespoons fructose
1 teaspoon aluminum free baking powder	

Mix the fructose, baking powder, salt, nutmeg and flour in a bowl. In a small bowl, mix the butter, eggs, milk and vanilla extract. Beat on low speed until well blended. Gently stir the milk mixture into the flour mixture just until they are combined. ***Do not over mix!!!*** Spoon the batter evenly all over the fruit mixture in the glass baking dish, being sure to use all of the batter. Sprinkle the following mixture on top: 1 tablespoon fructose and ½ teaspoon ground cinnamon. Place baking dish on a cookie sheet and bake for 35 to 45 minutes or until crust is golden brown. Remove from oven and allow to set for 30 minutes before serving.

VERY BERRY COCONUT BREAKFAST CAKE

1 1/4 cups milk

1 1/2 teaspoons vanilla extract

3 cups unbleached flour

1/4 teaspoon aluminum free baking soda

7 tablespoons butter, cut in small pieces

1/4 cup honey or Agave nectar

2 cups fresh berries, your choice

3 eggs

1/4 cup fructose

1/2 cup flaked coconut

1 teaspoon lemon juice

1/2 teaspoon sea salt

1/2 teaspoon minced lemon peel

Preheat oven to 350°. Butter and flour a 9-by-5-inch loaf pan.

Combine the milk, eggs, honey and vanilla in a small bowl until well blended. Sift the flour, fructose, salt and baking soda in a large bowl. Drop the pieces of cold butter evenly over the flour mixture. Using a pastry blender, cut in until the mixture looks like pea size crumbs. Add the milk mixture to the flour mixture and stir just until combined. Gently stir the berries, lemon juice, lemon peel and coconut together. Fold into the batter. Pour the batter into the prepared loaf pan and bake for 75 to 90 minutes or until a toothpick inserted in the center comes out clean. Cool in the pan on a wire rack for 15 minutes. Carefully remove from pan and place right side up on the rack. Allow cake to cool for 1 hour, and drizzle with icing.

Icing recipe:

1/4 cup fructose

1/2 teaspoon minced lemon peel

1 tablespoon milk

1 tablespoon melted butter

1 teaspoon fresh lemon juice

Mix all of the ingredients together until well blended and smooth.

MAPLE NUT FROSTED HEAVENLY CHOCOLATE CAKE

Cake Recipe:

1 cup unsweetened cocoa powder	2 cups boiling water
2¾ cups unbleached flour, sifted	½ teaspoon sea salt
2 teaspoons aluminum free baking soda	4 large eggs
½ teaspoon aluminum free baking powder	1 cup olive oil
1 cup fructose	2 teaspoons vanilla extract

Preheat oven to 350°. Butter well and lightly flour 3-by-9-inch round cake pans.

In a medium size bowl, mix the cocoa and boiling water. Beat with a whisk until smooth. Allow cocoa mixture to cool completely. Sift the flour, baking soda, baking powder and salt together. In a large bowl, using high speed, beat oil, fructose, eggs and vanilla. Beat for 5 minutes, scraping the bowl occasionally or until the mixture is light and fluffy. At low speed, beat in the flour mixture alternately with the cocoa mixture, being sure to begin and end with the flour mixture. *Do not over-beat mixture!!!* Divide batter evenly into the pans and smooth the tops. Bake for 25 to 30 minutes or until cake springs back when gently pressed with your fingertip. Cool in pans for 10 minutes. Remove from pans and cool completely on racks before frosting.

Maple Nut Frosting:

1 cup fructose	¼ cup softened butter
¼ cup low fat cream cheese, softened	½ cup maple syrup
½ cup toasted pecans, chopped	

Beat the fructose, butter and cream cheese on low speed. Add the maple syrup and beat for 3 minutes or until smooth and of a spreading consistency. Stir the toasted pecans into the frosting. Fill and frost the three cake layers.

LEMON ORANGE CARROT CAKE

Preheat oven to 325°. Butter and flour 3-by-9-inch round cake pans.

Cake Recipe:

1¼ cups butter, melted & cooled	½ cup fructose
½ cup light brown sugar, packed	4 large eggs
2 cups unbleached flour	1 teaspoon sea salt
1 teaspoon aluminum free baking powder	1 teaspoon ground cinnamon
1 teaspoon aluminum free baking soda	½ teaspoon orange extract
3 cups shredded carrots	zest of 1 orange, minced
1 teaspoon minced lemon zest	½ teaspoon lemon extract

Beat the melted butter, fructose and brown sugar on medium speed until well blended. Add the eggs one at a time, beating well after each egg. Whisk the flour, baking powder, baking soda, salt and cinnamon, then gradually mix into the sugar mixture. Stir the carrots, orange zest, lemon zest, orange extract and lemon extract into the batter. Divide the batter evenly into the three prepared cake pans. Bake on middle oven rack for 35 minutes or until a toothpick comes out clean. Cool for 10 minutes, remove from pans and cool completely on wire racks before frosting. Frost with creamy orange lemon frosting.

Orange Lemon Frosting:

12 ounces low fat cream cheese, softened	¾ cup butter, softened
2 teaspoons grated orange zest	1 teaspoon grated lemon zest
½ teaspoon orange extract	½ teaspoon lemon extract
1 cup fructose	

Beat cream cheese, butter, orange zest and lemon zest on medium speed until smooth. Gradually add the fructose, beating on low speed until smooth and creamy. Add the orange extract and lemon extract and stir until well blended. Fill and frost the three cake layers.

COCONUT DREAM CAKE

Preheat oven to 350°. Butter and flour 3-by-9-inch round cake pans.

Cake Recipe:

1 cup butter, softened	¾ cup fructose
5 eggs, room temp, yolks & whites separated	1 cup buttermilk
1 teaspoon aluminum free baking soda	1½ teaspoon vanilla extract
2 cups unbleached flour	1⅔ cup grated coconut

Cream butter and fructose on medium speed until creamy. Beat egg yolks into butter mixture until fluffy. Add baking soda to buttermilk. Stir buttermilk and flour alternately into the egg mixture, beginning and ending with the flour. Beat the egg whites until stiff peaks form. Add the vanilla and fold into the cake batter. Fold the coconut into the cake batter and pour into prepared cake pans. Bake for 30 minutes or until a toothpick inserted in the top of the cake comes out clean. Allow cakes to cool in pans for 10 minutes. Remove from pans and cool completely on wire racks before frosting.

Frosting Recipe:

½ cup butter, softened	1½ teaspoon vanilla extract
8 ounces cream cheese, softened	1 cup shredded coconut
½ cup fructose	1 cup chopped pecans

Beat the butter and cream cheese on low speed until well blended. Gradually beat in the fructose until mixture is fluffy. Add the vanilla extract. Fold the coconut and pecans into the frosting. Fill and frost the cake and sprinkle with ¼ cup fresh coconut.

FRUITY PECAN UPSIDE DOWN CAKE

Fruity Pecan Topping:

1½ cups diced pineapple   1 cup diced mango

1 cup dried sweet cherries, cut in half   1½ cups chopped pecans

Stir the ingredients above together and set to the side.

Preheat oven to 375°.

Cake Batter:

1 cup softened butter   ½ cup fructose

4 large eggs, bring to room temperature   ¼ cup light brown sugar

Beat the butter on medium speed, slowly adding the fructose and brown sugar until light and fluffy. Add the eggs one at a time only until blended.

Sift together the following ingredients:

3 cups whole wheat flour   ½ teaspoon sea salt

2½ teaspoons aluminum free baking powder

Mix the following ingredients together in a small bowl:

1 cup milk   1 teaspoon vanilla extract

1 teaspoon grated lemon rind   ½ teaspoon almond extract

Being sure to begin and end with the flour mixture, add flour mixture and milk mixture to the butter/fructose mixture, beating on low until each addition is blended. Gently fold in 1 cup of grated coconut into the batter.

Place ½ cup butter in a sheet cake pan and place in oven until it melts completely. Remove cake pan from oven and sprinkle 1 cup light brown sugar evenly over butter. Pour fruit mixture evenly over butter and brown sugar. Pour cake batter over the fruit mixture. Bake on middle oven rack for 35 minutes or until toothpick inserted in middle comes out clean. Allow cake to cook for 10 minutes on a wire rack, then turn upside down onto a serving tray and remove pan. Cool completely before serving.

Brown Sugar Pound Cake with Fruit Sauce

Sauce Recipe:

1½ cups diced pineapple	1½ cups diced mango
1 cup sweet dark cherries, halved	1 cup chopped pecans
1 cup shredded coconut	½ cup orange juice
1 cup pineapple juice	1 cup cherry juice
¼ cup lemon juice	¼ cup lime juice
1 cup fructose	3 tablespoons corn starch

Put the fructose and cornstarch in a heavy pot. Slowly add all of the juices, stirring until well blended. Add the mangos, pineapple and cherries. Cook over low heat, stirring often, until sauce thickens. Remove from heat and stir in the coconut and pecans. Allow sauce to set for about 30 minutes. Put sauce in a glass container and cover tightly. Refrigerate until ready to use.

Preheat oven to 325°. Butter and flour a tube or bundt pan.

Lazy Day Blackberry Cobbler

Preheat oven to 350°.

6 cups fresh blackberries	1 cup fructose
2 cups whole wheat flour	½ teaspoon sea salt
2 teaspoons aluminum free baking powder	1 cup milk
1½ sticks melted butter	1 teaspoon vanilla extract

Mix ½ cup of the fructose and the 6 cups of blackberries in a heavy pan and bring to a slow boil, stirring constantly. Remove from heat and allow to stand while making the batter. Mix flour, salt, baking powder and the remaining fructose. Slowly stir in vanilla and milk until blended. Put melted butter in glass 13-by-9-by-2-inch baking dish. Pour the blackberry mixture in the dish on top of the melted butter. **Do not stir!!!** Drop dough mixture by spoonfuls on top of the blackberry mixture. Bake on middle oven rack for 35 to 40 minutes or until dough is done. Best when served warm with homemade ice cream.

BROWN SUGAR POUND CAKE

2 cups softened butter
¾ cup fructose
1 cup light brown sugar
6 large eggs, at room temperature
½ cup + 2 tablespoons milk

⅛ teaspoon sea salt
¼ teaspoon ground nutmeg
¼ teaspoon ground allspice
2 teaspoons vanilla extract
4 cups unbleached flour

Beat butter on medium speed until creamy. Slowly add fructose and brown sugar, beating for about 10 minutes. Add the eggs one at a time, beating only until each one is blended. Sift the flour, salt, nutmeg and allspice together in a bowl. Add the flour mixture alternately with the milk to the butter mixture. Be sure to begin and end with the flour, mixing on low speed after each addition only until blended. Stir in the vanilla. Spoon batter evenly into prepared pan and bake for 70 to 85 minutes or until a toothpick inserted in the middle comes out clean. Remove cake from oven and cool in pan for 15 minutes. Remove from pan and cool completely before slicing. Serve cake with fruit sauce on the side or poured over the top.

PINEAPPLE COCONUT PUDDING

¾ cup fructose
¼ cup + 1 tablespoon cornstarch
6 cups milk
2 cups diced pineapple

½ teaspoon sea salt
1 tablespoon vanilla extract
1½ cups flaked coconut

Use a large saucepan that has a thick bottom and with a wooden spoon, stir the fructose, cornstarch and salt together. Slowly stir in 2 cups of the milk until the mixture is smooth. Add the rest of the milk and cook over medium heat, stirring constantly. When pudding starts to thicken and bubble softly, lower heat and simmer for about 5 minutes. Remove from heat and stir in the vanilla extract, pineapple and coconut. Put pudding in a glass serving dish and allow to cool to the touch. Cover tightly and refrigerate until ready to eat.

GEORGIA PEACH DELIGHT

Preheat oven to 350°. Butter a 2-quart baking dish.

3 cups chopped peaches	½ teaspoon ground cinnamon
¼ cup butter, melted & cooled	1 tablespoon cold butter
½ cup light brown sugar	¼ teaspoon ground nutmeg
¼ teaspoon aluminum free baking soda	⅛ teaspoon sea salt
⅔ cup whole wheat flour	¼ teaspoon vanilla extract
⅔ cup rolled oats (do not use instant)	

Evenly spread the peaches in the baking dish. Sprinkle with half of the sugar and dot with the cold butter. Stir the melted butter and remaining sugar until well combined. Sift the baking soda, flour, salt and nutmeg together. Stir in the oats. Mix the butter mixture with the dry mixture. Add the vanilla extract. Using your hands, crumble the mixture well and spread over the peaches. ***Do not stir!!!*** Bake for 40 to 45 minutes or until the peaches are bubbly and topping is crispy and golden brown.

APPLE RICE PUDDING

3 cups milk	2 apples
1 teaspoon vanilla	⅛ teaspoon ground nutmeg
½ cup basmati rice	2 large egg yolks
1 cup sweetened condensed milk	

In medium saucepan, combine 1 cup milk, condensed milk and nutmeg. Bring to a boil; remove from heat; let stand, covered, 30 minutes. Stir in rice; cook, covered, over low heat, stirring occasionally, until liquid is mostly absorbed, about 40 minutes. Peel and core apples; grate on large holes of box grater. In a small bowl, whisk egg yolks with remaining 2 cups milk. Stir into rice mixture with grated apples, stirring constantly until thickened, 10 to 15 minutes. Add vanilla. Do not boil. Remove pudding from heat; transfer to bowl; let cool slightly. Transfer pudding to individual dishes. May be eaten warm, at room temperature, or chilled.

MAMA'S APPLESAUCE CAKE

Preheat oven to 325°. Butter and flour a tube pan.

2 cups whole wheat flour	½ cup fructose
1 teaspoon aluminum free baking soda	2 teaspoons cinnamon
½ teaspoon nutmeg	¼ teaspoon cloves
½ teaspoon sea salt	½ teaspoon allspice
1 tablespoon corn starch	1 stick butter
2 cups natural applesauce	1 cup raisins
1 cup chopped walnuts	1 tablespoon fructose

In a large bowl, mix together the flour, ¾ cup fructose, baking soda, nutmeg, cloves, salt, allspice, cornstarch and 1 teaspoon of the cinnamon. Place applesauce and butter in a pan and heat until butter is melted and sauce is warm, stirring constantly. Add the applesauce mixture to the dry mixture, stirring until well blended. Add the raisins and walnuts to the batter and stir until mixed thoroughly. Pour into the prepared pan and bake on middle oven rack for 55 to 65 minutes or until a toothpick inserted in the middle comes out clean. Cool on a wire rack for 15 minutes. Run a long flat knife all around the outside and inside edges. Turn cake out of the pan onto a wire rack. Cool cake completely and place on a serving dish right side up. Sift together the fructose and the remaining 1 teaspoon cinnamon. Sprinkle on top of completely cooled cake.

CHOCOLATE PECAN PIE

1 (9-inch) pre-made whole wheat pie crust	½ cup fructose
½ cup unbleached flour	½ cup butter, melted
2 eggs, slightly beaten	1 teaspoon vanilla
¾ cup semisweet chocolate chips	

Place pie crust in 9-inch pie plate. Stir together fructose, flour, butter and eggs until well blended. Stir in pecans and chocolate chips. Pour into pie crust. Bake at 350° on lowest rack in over for 30 minutes. Cool on wire rack.

AWESOME CHUNKY BROWNIES

Preheat oven to 350°. Lightly butter a 13-by-9-by-2-inch pan.

1 cup light brown sugar

2 large eggs, lightly beaten

2 teaspoons aluminum free baking powder

1½ cups chopped pecans

1 cup semisweet chocolate chips

1 cup olive oil

2 cups unbleached flour

1 teaspoon sea salt

1 teaspoon vanilla extract

Melt the brown sugar and oil together in a large pan over low heat. Allow the sugar/butter mixture to cool. Stir in the beaten eggs until well blended. Stir the vanilla extract into the egg mixture. Combine the flour, baking powder, salt and 1 cup of the chopped pecans and gradually stir into the sugar/egg mixture until well mixed. Stir ½ cup of the semisweet chocolate chips into the batter. Spread the batter evenly in the prepared pan. Bake for about 30 minutes or until set. Remove pan from oven and sprinkle with the remaining semisweet chocolate chips and pecans. Return pan to oven for 3 more minutes. Cool completely on wire rack before cutting.

PINEAPPLE ALMOND TRUFFLES

1 cup evaporated milk

12 ounces milk chocolate chips

12 ounces semisweet chocolate chips

¼ cup fructose

½ cup pineapple preserve

1½ cups toasted almonds, finely chopped

In a heavy bottomed saucepan, stir the milk and fructose together. Bring mixture to a full boil over medium heat. Stirring constantly, boil mixture for 4 minutes. Remove from heat and stir in both kinds of chocolate chips and the pineapple preserves until the mixture is smooth. Cover and place in the refrigerator for 1 hour. Roll spoonfuls of the mixture into 1-inch balls. Roll the balls in the toasted chopped almonds and place on the lined cookie sheets. Cover and chill until firm. Put well-chilled truffles in an airtight container and store in the refrigerator.

RICE PUDDING WITH PINEAPPLE SAUCE

2 cups water	1 teaspoon sea salt
1 cup brown rice	1/2 cup butter
1/2 cup fructose	1 teaspoon ground nutmeg
4 cups milk	4 large eggs, beaten

Preheat oven to 350°. Combine the water and salt in a medium saucepan. Bring to a boil over high heat. Stir the rice into the boiling salted water, reduce heat to low, and cook for 20 minutes. **Do not disturb rice while cooking!** Add the butter to the hot rice and stir until butter is melted and mixed in completely with the rice. Beat the fructose, nutmeg, milk and eggs until well blended. Stir the milk mixture into the rice and mix well. Pour the mixture into a lightly buttered 3-quart shallow baking dish and bake for 1 hour or until very lightly browned. Serve with pineapple sauce or if preferred, plain. This pudding is good served warm or cold.

Pineapple Sauce:

1/2 cup fructose	1/4 cup cornstarch
1 cup crushed pineapple, well drained	1 1/4 cups water

Stir the fructose and cornstarch together in small saucepan. Stir in the water and pineapple. Cook over low heat for 15 minutes or until thick, stirring often.

CREAMY MINTS

1/2 cup butter	1 cup fructose
1 egg white, stiffly beaten	2 tablespoons milk
8 drops peppermint oil	1/2 teaspoon sea salt
1/2 teaspoon vanilla extract	

Melt butter in double boiler; add sugar. Remove from heat; add beaten egg white and remaining ingredients; stir until a smooth cream. Drop by teaspoonfuls onto wax paper and allow to set.

APPLE PUDDING WITH CUSTARD SAUCE

Preheat oven to 350°. Butter a 9-by-5-by-3-inch loaf pan.

¼ cup fructose	¼ cup butter, softened
1 large egg, lightly beaten	½ teaspoon sea salt
2 cups apples, peeled & chopped	1 teaspoon ground cinnamon
1 cup unbleached flour, sifted	½ teaspoon ground nutmeg
1 teaspoon aluminum free baking soda	

Cream the fructose and butter until fluffy. Beat in the egg. In a separate bowl, sift the salt, flour, cinnamon, nutmeg and baking soda. Add the dry mixture to the butter mixture and stir until well blended. Stir the apples into the batter. The batter will be very stiff. Spoon the batter into the prepared loaf pan and bake for 25 to 35 minutes or until golden brown. Cool for 10 minutes and remove from pan. Cool completely before slicing. Serve with custard sauce.

Custard Sauce:

1 cup fresh milk	3 large egg yolks
1 vanilla bean, split lengthwise	⅛ cup fructose
2 teaspoons cornstarch	

In a quart size heavy saucepan, heat the milk over medium heat until very warm, but not boiling. Turn off the heat and add the vanilla bean. Cover pan and allow milk and vanilla bean to infuse for about 20 minutes. Whisk the egg yolks, fructose and cornstarch until well mixed and smooth. Remove vanilla bean from milk and whisk milk into egg yolk mixture until smooth. Pour mixture back into the saucepan and cook over low heat for 5 minutes, stirring constantly with a wooden spoon. Custard is done when it is smooth and it coats the back of the spoon. Custard will thicken as it cools.

FROZEN CHERRY PINEAPPLE COCONUT DESSERT

Line muffin pan with 12 paper baking cups.

8 ounces low fat cream cheese, softened

1 (15 ounce) can crushed pineapple, drained

1 (8 ounce) cartons low fat cherry yogurt

4 teaspoons chopped pecans

¼ cup fructose

¼ cup light brown sugar

1 cup grated coconut

Beat the cream cheese, fructose and brown sugar on low speed until fluffy. Add the drained pineapple, cherry yogurt and coconut and stir until well mixed. Divide the mixture evenly between the 12 paper lined muffin cups. Spoon pecans on top of the creamy mixture in the muffin cups. Wrap desserts well and place in the freezer. When ready to serve, remove frozen dessert from freezer and allow to set for 10 minutes before serving.

PEANUT BUTTER ICE CREAM

1 (18 ounce) jar creamy natural peanut butter

6 large eggs, lightly beaten

1 (14 ounce) can sweetened condensed milk

2 tablespoons unbleached flour

1½ quarts milk

1 tablespoon vanilla extract

¾ cup fructose

Combine the peanut butter, 2 cups of the milk and the eggs in a large heavy bottomed pan. Cook over medium low heat, whisking mixture constantly until candy thermometer reaches 160°. Remove pan from heat. Whisk in the last of the milk, condensed milk and vanilla extract. Mix the fructose and flour together and whisk into the hot mixture until all the sugar has melted. Pour the mixture into the freezer container of a 5-quart ice cream freezer. Freeze using the manufacturer's directions.

NOTE: If preferred, chunky peanut butter may be used.

VANILLA BEAN ICE MILK

15 cups milk

2 vanilla beans

1 cup fructose

¼ teaspoon sea salt

Place 5 cups of the milk and the fructose in a heavy pan. Split the vanilla beans lengthwise and scrape the seeds out. Add to the milk/fructose mixture along with the bean pods. Bring the mixture to the scalding point, stirring constantly. Remove mixture from the heat and allow to cool for 30 minutes at room temperature. Stir the mixture into the remaining 10 cups of milk and place in the refrigerator over night. Be sure to cover well. Remove from refrigerator and remove the bean pods and stir well. Place in an electric or hand cranked ice cream freezer and follow the manufacturer's directions.

AVOCADO CAKE

1 cup fructose

½ teaspoon aluminum free baking soda

8 chopped dates

½ teaspoon cinnamon

1 ¾ cups unbleached flour

½ cup raw chopped nuts

1 cup mashed avocado

½ cup buttermilk

½ cup butter

½ teaspoon nutmeg

½ teaspoon allspice

2 eggs

Cream the fructose and butter together. Mix the buttermilk and baking soda together in a separate bowl. Add the buttermilk mixture, eggs, avocado and spices to the fructose and butter. The batter will be stiff. Pour in 9-inch pan sprayed with olive oil and bake at 325° for 30 minutes or until golden brown.

YOGURT SUPREME

1½ cups cooked short grain brown rice

¾ cup crushed pineapple

8 ounces pineapple yogurt

2 bananas, diced

Combine all ingredients and chill well before serving.

PEACH PUDDING

3 cups cooked short grain brown rice

¼ cup fructose

¼ cup rice syrup

2 teaspoons fresh lemon juice

½ teaspoon ground nutmeg

2 cups fresh sliced peaches

3 cups milk

1 teaspoon vanilla

2 tablespoons butter

1 teaspoon grated lemon peel

⅛ teaspoon sea salt

Combine rice, milk and fructose in 3-quart saucepan. Cook over medium heat until thick and creamy, stirring often. Add vanilla. Pour into 4 -quart serving bowl. Heat syrup, margarine, lemon juice, lemon peel, nutmeg and salt. Stir in peaches, cook on low heat for 10 minutes. Spoon over rice pudding. Serve warm or cold.

RICE PUDDING

1½ cups cooked short grain brown rice

½ cup raisins or chopped dates

¼ teaspoon sea salt

3 cups milk

Finely chopped nuts (optional)

3 eggs

½ cup fructose

½ teaspoon vanilla extract

Nutmeg

Beat eggs, add sugar and beat until smooth. Add milk, salt and vanilla. Add rice and raisins. Pour into greased shallow baking dish. Sprinkle with nutmeg. Set in pan of hot water and bake at 350° for 90 minutes or until custard is set. After baking for approximately 30 minutes, gently stir custard to suspend rice. Serve warm or cold with milk or whipped cream.

APPLE CRISP

2 cups cooked short grain brown rice
1 cup fructose
½ teaspoon cinnamon
¾ cup rice flour
6 large apples, peeled & sliced, mixed
    with 1 cup fructose, 1 cup water and
    cooked for 10 minutes or until soft

1½ cups uncooked oats
1 tablespoon fresh lemon juice
¼ cup rice syrup
¼ teaspoon sea salt
6 tablespoons butter
½ cup chopped almonds

Combine the cooked rice, apples, lemon juice and rice syrup and pour into a 9-by-13-inch pan treated with olive oil spray or butter. Mix flour, oats, fructose, salt and cut in butter until crumbly. Sprinkle over rice-apple mixture. Bake at 350° for 30 minutes or until brown and bubbly.

CINNAMON RAISIN RICE PUDDING

2 cups milk
4 egg whites
4 cups cooked sweet brown rice
1 cup low-fat peach yogurt

½ cup honey
2 teaspoons vanilla extract
1 cup raisins
1 teaspoon cinnamon

Preheat oven to 350°. In a large bowl, whisk egg whites and stir in milk, honey and vanilla. Add rice and raisins. Stir well and transfer to greased 2-quart casserole dish. Cook for 40 minutes, stirring occasionally during cooking. Remove from oven and stir in peach yogurt and cinnamon. Serve immediately.

CHOCOLATE CRUNCHIES

6 ounces semisweet chocolate
1 cup crisp rice cereal
1 teaspoon vanilla extract

½ cup flaked coconut
½ cup chopped nuts

Melt chocolate in top of double boiler over hot water; remove from heat and stir in remaining ingredients; mix well. Drop by teaspoonfuls onto wax paper; chill until firm.

PINEAPPLE CARROT CAKE

1½ cups macadamia nut oil

1 cup fructose

2½ cups unbleached flour

2 teaspoons aluminum free baking soda

1 cup grated carrots

1 cup crushed pineapple, drained

3 eggs

1 teaspoon sea salt

2 teaspoons cinnamon

2 teaspoons vanilla extract

1 cup chopped nuts

1 cup coconut

Glaze:

½ cup fructose

1 teaspoon aluminum free baking soda

4 tablespoons butter

1 teaspoon vanilla extract

½ cup milk

Mix oil, eggs and fructose in large bowl. Stir in the flour, salt, soda and cinnamon and blend well. Add the vanilla, carrots, coconut, pineapple and nuts and blend well. Bake in a well greased and floured 9-by-13-inch pan. Bake at 350° for 45 to 50 minutes. While cake is cooking, prepare glaze by combining all ingredients and cooking over low heat for 5 minutes. When cake is done, pour glaze over hot cake.

ANGEL FOOD CAKE

2 cups egg whites

¾ teaspoon cream of tartar

1 teaspoon vanilla extract

6 ounces unbleached flour

1 teaspoon almond extract

½ teaspoon sea salt

½ cup fructose

Sift together fructose and flour. Beat egg whites, salt and cream of tartar on medium speed until soft peaks form. Slowly add vanilla and almond extracts. Beat until soft-medium shiny peaks are formed. Then fold ⅓ of the fructose/flour mixture into the whites. Continue to do this until all of the flour is in the egg white mixture. ***Do not over fold!*** Bake for 35 minutes at 375° in un-greased tube pan.

APPLE CAKE

1 cup fructose

2 cups whole wheat flour

4 cups diced apple

1 teaspoon aluminum free baking soda

½ cup macadamia nut oil

2 teaspoons cinnamon

2 eggs

1 teaspoon nutmeg

1 teaspoon sea salt

Combine fructose, oil, eggs and apples. Sift dry ingredients together and add to apple mixture. Pour into 9-by-13-inch greased pan. Bake for 1 hour in a 350 degree oven. Serve hot or cold, plain or with icing or whipped cream.

COUNTRY CUSTARD

2 tablespoons fructose

2 large egg yolks

1 teaspoon vanilla extract

2 tablespoons cornstarch

2 cups milk

Mix together the fructose and the cornstarch in a large saucepan. Add egg yolks and whisk to combine; then gradually whisk in the milk. Cook over medium-low heat, stirring constantly, until custard thickens to the consistency of thick cream, about 25 minutes. Transfer to a large bowl and add vanilla. Cover surface of custard with plastic wrap to prevent a skin from forming, and refrigerate until completely chilled, about 2 hours.

BREAD PUDDING

4 beaten eggs

¼ cup fructose

½ teaspoon vanilla

⅓ cup raisins

2 cups milk

½ teaspoon ground cinnamon

3 cups dry bread cubes

In a mixing bowl beat together eggs, milk, fructose, cinnamon and vanilla. Place dry bread cubes in an 8-inch round baking dish. Sprinkle raisins over bread cubes. Pour egg mixture over all. Bake at 325° for 35 to 40 minutes or until a knife inserted near the center comes out clean. Cool slightly.

HUMMINGBIRD CAKE

3 cups unbleached flour

1 teaspoon aluminum free baking soda

$\frac{1}{2}$ cup softened butter

1 cup grape seed oil

1 (8 ounce) can crushed pineapple

2 medium bananas, chopped

1 teaspoon sea salt

1 teaspoon cinnamon

1 cup fructose

3 eggs

1 teaspoon vanilla extract

1 cup chopped nuts

Sift flour, soda, salt, cinnamon and fructose together in large bowl. Stir in oil, butter, eggs and pineapple. Mix well by hand. Add bananas, nuts and vanilla; mix thoroughly. Bake in greased and floured tube pan at 350° for 1 hour and 5 minutes. Let cool before removing from pan.

Frosting Recipe:

$\frac{1}{2}$ cup butter, softened

8 ounces cream cheese, softened

$\frac{1}{2}$ cup fructose

$1\frac{1}{2}$ teaspoon vanilla extract

1 cup shredded coconut

1 cup chopped pecans

Beat the butter and cream cheese on low speed until well blended. Gradually beat in the fructose until mixture is fluffy. Add the vanilla extract. Fold the coconut and pecans into the frosting. Fill and frost the cake and sprinkle with $\frac{1}{4}$ cup fresh coconut.

KENTUCKY DERBY PIE

$\frac{1}{2}$ cup fructose

$\frac{1}{2}$ cup unbleached flour

2 eggs, slightly beaten

1 cup chocolate chips

1 unbaked 8-inch pie shell

1 stick butter

1 teaspoon vanilla extract

$\frac{1}{2}$ cup walnuts

$\frac{1}{2}$ cup pecans

Mix fructose and flour well with fork; add eggs and melted butter. Blend together well. Add coarsely chopped nuts, chocolate chips and vanilla; mix well. Pour into unbaked pie shell and bake at 350° for 40 to 45 minutes.

LANE CAKE

1 cup butter	¾ cup fructose
3¼ cups unbleached flour	¾ teaspoon sea salt
3½ teaspoon aluminum free baking powder	1 cup milk
8 egg whites	1 teaspoon vanilla extract

Filling:

8 egg yolks	½ cup fructose
1 stick butter	1 cup raisins
1 cup chopped pecans	1 cup grated coconut

Cream butter well; add fructose and beat gradually until light. Sift flour, baking powder and salt; add alternately with milk, beating until smooth. Beat egg whites stiff but not dry; add vanilla and fold in. Bake at 375° for 15 minutes in 3 to 4 layers. For filling, cook eggs, fructose and butter together in double boiler until thick. Remove from heat; add remaining ingredients. Spread between layers; frost top and sides with boiled white icing.

ORANGE COCONUT CAKE

⅔ cup butter	½ cup fructose
2 teaspoons orange zest	3 eggs
2½ cups unbleached flour	1 teaspoon sea salt
2½ teaspoons aluminum free baking powder	1 cup orange juice

Filling:

⅓ cup fructose	2 tablespoons butter
3 tablespoons unbleached flour	1 cup orange juice
2 egg yolks	

Cream butter, fructose and orange zest; add eggs one at a time, beating after each addition. Sift flour, salt and baking powder together; add alternately with orange juice, beating well after each addition. Bake in 3 layers at 350° until done. Cool completely before filling. Mix fructose and flour; add orange juice and egg yolks and cook over medium heat until thick. Add butter. Spread between layers. Frost top and sides with 7-minute frosting.

SWEET POTATO CAKE

1 cup fructose	3 eggs
1½ cups grape seed oil	2 teaspoons vanilla extract
3 cups unbleached flour	¾ cup coconut
1 small can crushed pineapple	4 egg whites
2 cups sweet potato, grated	

Icing:

1¼ cups evaporated milk	¾ cup fructose
4 egg yolks	1¼ stick butter
1¼ cups coconut	1 teaspoon vanilla extract

Mix oil and fructose; add eggs, flour, vanilla, pineapple and juice, coconut and potatoes; beat well. Beat egg whites left over from icing; add to batter last. Pour into 3 layer cake pans, greased and floured lightly. Bake at 350° about 45 minutes or until a knife comes out clean. For icing, put milk, fructose, eggs and butter in a double boiler and cook for 15 minutes or until thick. Remove from heat; add coconut and vanilla. Frost when cake is cool.

BUTTERMILK CAKE

¾ cup fructose	2 sticks butter
3 eggs or 6 whites	1 teaspoon vanilla extract
3 cups unbleached flour	1½ cups buttermilk
1½ teaspoon aluminum free baking soda	

Yellow Coconut Filling:

1 teaspoon vanilla extract	2 cups coconut
12 egg yolks	2 cups milk
2 tablespoons cornstarch	1 cup fructose

Cream butter and fructose; add eggs one at a time. Mix soda in milk; add flour and milk alternately, beating well after each addition. Add vanilla; mix well. Bake in 3 layers at 325° until golden brown. For filling, cook egg yolks, cornstarch, milk and fructose until thick; add 1½ cups coconut and vanilla. Frost cake; sprinkle remaining coconut on top and sides of cake.

SWEET POTATO PIE

⅓ cup milk	1 teaspoon cinnamon
2 medium sweet potatoes	½ teaspoon nutmeg
⅔ cup brown rice syrup	3 eggs
1 stick butter	1 tablespoon vanilla extract
1 unbaked 8-inch pie shell	

Boil potatoes until well done; drain. Add all ingredients and beat well. Bake in pie shell for 35 to 40 minutes at 350°.

CHOCOLATE SOUFFLE

2 tablespoons butter	3 tablespoons unbleached flour
¾ cup milk	4 beaten egg yolks
½ cup semisweet chocolate pieces	4 egg whites
½ teaspoon vanilla	⅛ cup fructose

Butter the sides of a 2-quart soufflé dish. Sprinkle sides with a little fructose. Set aside. In a small saucepan melt butter. Stir in flour. Add milk all at once. Cook and stir until thickened and bubbly. Add chocolate; stir until melted. Remove from heat. Gradually stir chocolate mixture into beaten egg yolks; set aside. Beat egg whites and vanilla until soft peaks form. Gradually add the ⅛ cup fructose, beating until stiff peaks form. Fold about 1 cup beaten egg whites into chocolate mixture. Then fold chocolate mixture into remaining beaten egg whites. Transfer to prepared dish. Bake at 350° for 35 to 40 minutes or until a knife inserted in the center comes out clean. Serve at once with whipped cream.

CLASSIC CHEESECAKE

1¾ cups finely crushed graham crackers

¼ cup finely chopped walnuts

3 (8 ounce) packages cream cheese, softened

2 tablespoons unbleached flour

½ teaspoon finely shredded lemon peel

1 egg yolk

½ teaspoon ground cinnamon

½ cup butter, melted

½ cup fructose

1 teaspoon vanilla

2 eggs

¼ cup milk

For crust, combine crushed crackers, nuts and cinnamon. Stir in butter. Reserve ¼ cup of the crumb mixture for topping, if desired. Press remaining onto bottom and about 2 inches up sides of an 8-inch springform pan. In a mixer bowl combine cream cheese, fructose, flour, vanilla and lemon peel. Beat with an electric mixer until fluffy. Add eggs and yolk all at once, beating on low speed just until combined. Stir in milk. Pour into crust-lined pan. Sprinkle with reserved crumbs. Place on a shallow baking pan in over. Bake at 375° for 45 to 50 minutes or until center appears nearly set when shaken. Cool for 15 minutes. Loosen crust from sides of pan. Cool for 30 minutes more; remove sides of pan. Cool completely. Chill at least 4 hours.

STRAWBERRY SHORTCAKE

6 cups sliced strawberries

2 cups unbleached flour

2 teaspoons aluminum free baking powder

⅔ cup milk

¼ cup fructose

½ cup butter

1 beaten egg

Whipped cream

Stir together berries and half of the fructose; set aside. Stir together remaining fructose, flour and baking powder. Cut in butter until mixture resembles coarse crumbs. Combine egg and milk; add all at once to dry ingredients. Stir just to moisten. Spread into a buttered 8-inch round baking pan, building up edge slightly. Bake at 450° for 15 to 18 minutes or until a toothpick inserted in the center comes out clean. Cool in pan for 10 minutes. Remove from pan. Split into 2 layers. Spoon fruit and whipped cream between layers and over the top. Serve immediately.

BROWNIE PUDDING CAKE

½ cup unbleached flour	⅛ cup fructose
3 tablespoons unsweetened cocoa powder	¼ cup milk
¾ teaspoon aluminum free baking powder	1 tablespoon olive oil
½ teaspoon vanilla	¼ cup chopped walnuts
¼ cup fructose	¾ cup boiling water

Stir together flour, the ⅛ cup fructose, 1 tablespoon of the cocoa powder and the baking powder. Add milk, oil and vanilla. Stir until smooth. Stir in nuts. Transfer batter to a 1-quart casserole dish. Combine the ¼ cup fructose and remaining cocoa powder. Gradually stir in boiling water. Pour evenly over batter. Bake at 350° for 30 minutes or until a toothpick inserted in the center comes out clean. Serve warm.

3-LAYER GERMAN CHOCOLATE CAKE (TED'S FAVORITE CAKE)

2 boxes organic chocolate cake mix	6 eggs
⅔ cup macadamia nut oil	2 cups sour cream

Beat cake mix with remaining ingredients with an electric mixer on low speed until moistened. Beat at medium speed for 2 minutes. Pour evenly into 3 oiled and floured round cake pans. Bake at 350° for 25 to 35 minutes or until a toothpick inserted in the center comes out clean. Do not overcook. Cool cakes on wire racks. While cakes are cooling, prepare icing.

Coconut Pecan Icing:

1 (14 ounce) can evaporated milk	2 eggs
⅓ cup fructose	¼ cup butter
2 cups shredded coconut	1 cup chopped pecans

In a large saucepan, slightly beat eggs. Stir in the milk, fructose and butter. Cook and stir over medium heat for 6 to 8 minutes or until thickened and bubbly. Remove from heat. Stir in coconut and pecans. Spread over each layer of cake. Stack layers and spread icing over top and sides of cake.

PEAR & APPLE STREUSEL PIE

3 cups thinly sliced, peeled apples
3 cups thinly sliced, peeled pears
¾ cup brown sugar, divided
¼ cup butter
Pre-made pie crust

2 tablespoons tapioca
½ cup unbleached flour
¾ teaspoon ground cinnamon
½ cup chopped walnuts

Preheat oven to 400°. Mix apples and pears with ½ cup of the brown sugar, tapioca and cinnamon in a large bowl. Let stand 15 minutes. Mix flour and remaining brown sugar in medium bowl. Cut in butter until mixture resembles coarse crumbs. Stir in walnuts; set aside. Prepare pie crust in 9-inch pie plate as directed on package. Fill with fruit mixture; top with crumb mixture. Bake 45 to 50 minutes.

PEACH SKILLET CAKE

½ cup butter, softened
3 large eggs
1¼ cups unbleached flour
¼ teaspoon aluminum free baking powder
4 cups diced, peeled peaches

¼ cup + 1 tablespoon fructose
1 teaspoon vanilla extract
½ teaspoon sea salt
½ teaspoon ground cinnamon
⅓ cup sliced almonds

Preheat oven to 350°. Butter a 10-inch cast iron skillet. In a large bowl, cream butter and the ¼ cup fructose with an electric mixer until fluffy. Add eggs, one at a time, and vanilla; beat to combine. In a medium bowl, whisk together flour, baking powder and salt. With mixer on low speed, gradually add flour mixture to butter mixture; beat until incorporated. Fold in peaches. Spread batter in prepared skillet. In a small bowl, mix together remaining 1 tablespoon fructose, cinnamon and almonds. Sprinkle mixture over top; bake until a toothpick inserted in center comes out clean and topping is golden, 45 to 50 minutes. Let cool 20 minutes before serving.

APPLE ENCHILADAS

4 granny smith apples, peeled & chopped	4 tablespoons butter
6 (8-inch) tortillas	1 teaspoon cinnamon
½ cup brown rice syrup	⅓ cup butter

Sauté apples in 4 tablespoon butter until tender. Spoon fruit filling evenly down the center of each tortilla; sprinkle evenly with cinnamon. Roll up, and place, seam side down, in a lightly greased 2-quart baking dish. Bring ⅓ cup butter, brown rice syrup and cinnamon to a boil in medium saucepan; reduce heat, and simmer, stirring constantly, 3 minutes. Pour over enchiladas; let stand 30 minutes. Bake at 350° for 20 minutes.

SOUTHERN BANANA PUDDING

2 boxes vanilla wafers	6 to 8 sliced bananas
3 large containers Kozy Shack vanilla pudding (ready made)	

In medium oblong casserole dish, cover bottom with one layer of wafers. Spoon out enough pudding to cover wafers about ¼ inch thick. Slice bananas and place on top of pudding. Repeat layers until all ingredients are used, but leave at least ½ inch to top of dish for meringue.

Meringue:

3 egg whites	3 tablespoons fructose
½ teaspoon vanilla extract	

In stainless steel bowl, mix egg whites and vanilla on high with an electric mixer. When meringue starts to peak, slowly add fructose. Beat for 2 more minutes. Spread over banana pudding. Bake at 325° until meringue starts to lightly brown.

MINT WAFERS

8 ounces softened cream cheese
4½ cups fructose
½ cup semisweet chocolate chips

1 teaspoon peppermint extract
1 cup milk chocolate chips
3 tablespoons softened butter

Line cookie sheet with parchment paper.

In a large bowl, beat the cream cheese and peppermint on medium speed until smooth. Slowly add the fructose, beating until well blended. Shape mixture into 1-inch balls and place on lined cookie sheets. Flatten the balls into wafer shapes. Wrap cookie sheets with plastic wrap and refrigerate until well chilled. Mix the milk chocolate chips, semisweet chocolate chips and butter together in a bowl. Place bowl in microwave on high heat and melt the chips. This usually takes 1 to 2 minutes. Stir mixture until smooth and allow to cool slightly. Dip chilled wafers in melted chocolate and place back on cookie sheets until firm. Keep wafers stored in an airtight container in the refrigerator.

PEANUT BUTTER DROPS

1 cup natural creamy peanut butter
4½ cups fructose
1½ cups milk chocolate chips

1 teaspoon vanilla extract
3 tablespoons butter

Line cookie sheets with parchment paper.

In a large bowl, beat the peanut butter and vanilla extract until smooth. Gradually add the fructose to the peanut butter, beating until well mixed. Drop by teaspoonfuls onto lined cookie sheets. Wrap cookie sheets with plastic wrap and refrigerate until well chilled. Mix the chips and butter in a bowl and place in microwave. Using high heat, melt the chips and butter. Stir mixture until smooth and cool slightly. Dip the chilled peanut butter mounds into the chocolate, allowing excess to drip back into the bowl. Place dipped mounds back on cookie sheets until firm. Keep candy well covered and store in the refrigerator.

PECAN PRALINES

1 cup fructose
1 teaspoon aluminum free baking soda
1 teaspoon vanilla extract

1 cup buttermilk
1 tablespoon butter
1½ cups chopped pecans

Line cookie sheets with parchment paper.

In a heavy bottomed 3-quart saucepan, mix the fructose, buttermilk and baking soda. Cook over medium heat, stirring constantly until a candy thermometer reaches 210°. Stir the butter and pecans into the fructose mixture. Cook mixture until the candy thermometer reaches 230°. Remove pan from heat and add the vanilla. Beat the candy mixture briskly with a wooden spoon until it loses its gloss and starts to set. Working quickly, drop mixture by teaspoons onto the lined cookie sheets. Cool completely and store in an airtight container.

SUGARPLUM INTRIGUES

1 (15 ounce) package. golden raisins
6 ounces dried pitted cherries
6 ounces dried pineapple
1½ cups chopped toasted pecans

6 ounces pitted prunes
6 ounces pitted figs
1 cup flaked coconut
¾ cup fructose

Line cookie sheets with parchment paper.

Using a food processor, coarsely chop the raisins, prunes, figs, pineapple, cherries and pecans. Put fruit mixture in a large bowl and stir in the coconut. Mix until well blended. Roll the mixture into 1-inch balls and roll in the fructose. Place fructose-coated fruit balls on the lined cookie sheets. Allow the fruit balls to stand at room temperature for about 6 hours. Roll in the sugar again and store in an airtight container.

TOFFEE BUTTER CRUNCH

½ cup coarsely chopped toasted almonds
¾ cup semisweet chocolate chips
½ cup finely chopped toasted almonds
3 tablespoons water

1 cup butter
½ cup fructose
1 tablespoon light corn syrup

Line a baking pan with parchment paper, extending the paper over the edges of the pan. Sprinkle the ½ cup coarsely chopped almonds in pan. Butter sides of a heavy 2-quart saucepan. In saucepan melt butter. Add fructose, corn syrup and water. Cook and stir over medium-high heat to boiling. Clip candy thermometer to pan. Cook and stir over medium heat to 290°, soft-crack stage (about 15 minutes). Watch carefully after 280° to prevent scorching. Remove saucepan from heat; remove thermometer. Pour mixture into prepared pan. Let stand 5 minutes or until firm; sprinkle with chocolate chips. Let stand 1 to 2 minutes. When softened, spread chocolate over mixture. Sprinkle with the ½ cup finely chopped almonds. Chill until firm. Lift out of pan; break into pieces. Store tightly covered.

NOTES

The Cookie Cutter

Cookies,
Bars
and Tarts

11

BOMB BARS

Preheat oven to 375°.

½ cup softened butter	1 cup whole wheat flour
2 tablespoons fructose	1 teaspoon sea salt

Mix all of the ingredients above until well blended and press into the bottom of a buttered 8-inch square cake pan. Place on middle oven rack and bake for 12 minutes. Make the second layer while the first is baking.

2 large eggs, beaten	1 teaspoon vanilla extract
2 tablespoons whole wheat flour	½ cup chopped pecans
¾ cup light brown sugar	1 cup coconut

Stir all of the above ingredients together, mixing well. Pour the egg mixture over the warm baked layer, spreading evenly. Return pan to the oven and bake for 25 minutes. Remove from oven and allow to cool completely before cutting.

TOASTY COCONUT MOUNDS

3 large egg whites, at room temperature	½ teaspoon vanilla extract
½ cup fructose	½ teaspoon nutmeg
1 cup shredded coconut	

Preheat oven to 350°. Line 2 cookie sheets with parchment paper.

Beat egg whites in a large bowl on high speed until soft peaks form. Slowly add the fructose until stiff peaks form. Add vanilla and nutmeg and beat until blended. Fold in the coconut. Drop by tablespoons about one inch apart on the cookie sheets. Bake only one cookie sheet at a time on middle oven rack. Bake for 20 minutes or until cookies are set and light golden brown in color. Cool on cookie sheet for 2 minutes then transfer to a wire rack and cool completely.

NICE AND SPICY FIG COOKIES

½ cup melted butter	1 cup light brown sugar
½ cup low fat sour cream	1 egg, lightly beaten
1 teaspoon vanilla extract	2 cups whole wheat flour
¼ teaspoon aluminum free baking soda	½ teaspoon sea salt
1 teaspoon ground cinnamon	¼ teaspoon nutmeg
¼ teaspoon ground cloves	1 cup chopped figs
½ cup toasted walnuts, finely chopped	

Preheat oven to 350°. Evenly butter a jelly roll pan (15-by-9-by-1-inch).

In a large bowl, mix the melted butter and brown sugar with a wooden spoon until well combined. Add the sour cream, egg and vanilla and beat until very smooth. Sift the spices, flour, salt, and baking soda together. Add the flour mixture to the sour cream mixture and stir until thoroughly combined. Stir the figs and nuts into the dough. Spread the dough evenly into the prepared pan. Bake on middle oven rack for 30 minutes or until top springs back when touched lightly with your finger. Place pan on wire rack to cool completely before cutting.

BIG BATCH PEANUT BUTTER COOKIES

Preheat oven to 375°.

¼ cup + 1 tablespoon milk	2 tablespoons vanilla extract
1½ cups natural peanut butter	2 large eggs, beaten
2 cups light brown sugar	1½ teaspoons sea salt
3½ cups whole wheat flour	1 cup softened butter
1½ teaspoons aluminum free baking soda	

Combine the peanut butter, butter, sugar, milk and vanilla in a large bowl and beat on medium speed until well blended. Add eggs, beating just until combined. Sift the flour, salt, and baking soda together. Add the flour mixture to the creamy mixture and beat on low speed just until blended. Drop by heaping teaspoons onto un-greasers cookie sheets, 2 inches apart. Dip a fork in light brown sugar and press down on top of each cookie. Bake for 8 minutes or until set and light brown.

NOT JUST OATMEAL COOKIES

½ cup softened butter
½ cup orange blossom honey
¾ cup unbleached flour
½ teaspoon aluminum free baking soda
1 medium apple, peeled & chopped

1 large egg, beaten
1 teaspoon vanilla extract
1 teaspoon cinnamon
1½ cups rolled oats
½ cup chopped walnuts

Preheat oven to 375°.

In a bowl, beat the butter, honey, egg and vanilla until well blended. Using a separate bowl, stir the flour, baking soda and cinnamon together. Add the flour mixture to the egg mixture. Add the apples and walnuts, mixing well. Stir in the oats and drop by teaspoons onto a lightly greased cookie sheet. Bake for 10 to 12 minutes. Cool on sheet for 2 minutes before transferring to a cooling rack.

SNOWY PECAN MOUNTAINS

2 cups unbleached flour
2 cups chopped pecans
¼ teaspoon ground nutmeg
½ teaspoon vanilla extract
2 sticks softened butter

½ cup fructose
½ teaspoon sea salt
¼ teaspoon ground cinnamon
Extra fructose to roll
  baked cookies in

Put butter in a large bowl and beat until fluffy. Add salt, nutmeg, cinnamon, vanilla extract and the 1 cup fructose and beat mixture until smooth. Put mixer on low speed and add the flour and chopped pecans a little at a time. Beat mixture only until well mixed. Completely wrap bowl in plastic wrap and place in the refrigerator until the dough is firm.

Preheat oven to 350°.

Roll the pieces of chilled dough into 1-inch balls. Roll in the chopped pecans. Place on an un-greased cookie sheet and bake on middle oven rack for 13 minutes or until the cookies are set. Transfer cookies to a wire rack to cool. Cookies are tender, so handle very gently. When cookies are cooled, roll them in the extra fructose. Store in airtight containers at room temperature.

CHOCOLATE CHIP BAR COOKIES

½ cup fructose	¾ cup melted butter
2¾ cups unbleached flour	3 large eggs, beaten
2½ teaspoons aluminum free baking powder	½ teaspoon sea salt
12 ounces mini semisweet chocolate chips	1 teaspoon vanilla extract

Preheat oven to 350°.

Butter and flour a 13-by-9-by-2-inch baking pan.

Stir the fructose and butter together in a large bowl until well blended. Add the eggs one at a time, stirring well after each egg. Combine the flour, baking powder and salt together. Stir the flour mixture into the fructose mixture until well blended. Add the chocolate chips and vanilla and stir well. Place batter in the prepared pan, spreading evenly. Bake for 35 to 40 minutes or until toothpick inserted in middle comes out clean. Cool in pan on wire rack before cutting.

CANDIED FRUIT AND NUT COOKIES

½ cup softened butter	½ cup fructose
1 large egg, lightly beaten	1 teaspoon vanilla extract
1 cup unbleached flour, sifted	1½ cups chopped pecans
½ teaspoon aluminum free baking soda	1 cup golden raisins
½ cup chopped pineapple, drained	1 cup dark raisins
½ cup chopped cherries, drained	

Cream the butter and fructose, beating on low speed until fluffy. Add the egg, and vanilla extract and beat until well blended. Sift the flour and baking soda together. Add flour mixture to creamed mixture and beat until well mixed. Stir in all of the fruit and nuts. Cover bowl and refrigerate until well chilled.

Preheat oven to 325°.

Drop dough by tablespoons onto a lightly greased cookie sheet. Bake for 15 minutes. Transfer to a wire rack to cool. When cookies are cool, sprinkle with ¼ cup powdered sugar mixed with 1 teaspoon cinnamon.

HONEY OF A COOKIE

2 cups unbleached flour

⅛ teaspoon ground cloves

¼ teaspoon ground nutmeg

¼ teaspoon aluminum free baking soda

⅓ cup light brown sugar

1 large egg, lightly beaten

½ teaspoon ground cinnamon

⅛ teaspoon ground ginger

½ teaspoon sea salt

½ cup softened butter

⅓ cup honey

Cream the butter, honey and brown sugar on medium speed. Add the egg and beat until light and fluffy. Sift the flour, cinnamon, cloves, ginger, nutmeg, baking soda and salt together. Stir the flour mixture into the creamed mixture until well blended and a soft dough is formed. Divide the dough in 2 to 3 portions, wrap well in plastic wrap and refrigerate 2 to 3 hours.

Preheat oven to 375°.

Roll a portion of the dough to ⅛ inch thick on well floured surface. Using a cookie cutter or sharp knife, cut desired shapes. Place the cut out cookies on an ungreased baking sheet. Bake for 6 to 9 minutes or until cookies are golden brown. Cool on a wire rack before eating.

CHOCOLATE CHIP COOKIES

1 cup brown sugar

4½ sticks butter

1 teaspoon vanilla extract

1 teaspoon aluminum free baking soda

2½ cups chocolate chips

¾ cup fructose

4 large eggs

1½ teaspoons sea salt

4 cups unbleached flour

Cream together the brown sugar, fructose and butter. Add eggs and mix well. Add vanilla, salt, baking soda, flour and chocolate chips and mix well. Drop by rounded tablespoons onto a buttered cookie sheet. Bake at 350° until light golden brown, about 8 to 10 minutes. If desired, you may also spread dough into the cookie sheet and bake until done; cool for 5 minutes and cut into squares. Makes 4 dozen. Cut in half for smaller batches.

BANANA NUT COOKIES
WITH ORANGE GLAZE

Preheat oven to 375°. Line baking sheets with parchment paper.

2 cups unbleached flour	½ teaspoon sea salt
¼ teaspoon aluminum free baking soda	½ cup fructose
1½ sticks softened butter	½ teaspoon vanilla extract
1 cup bananas, mashed	½ cup chopped pecans

Sift flour, salt and baking soda together into a small bowl. On medium speed, beat the butter and fructose until fluffy. Add the mashed bananas and vanilla extract and beat until well blended. With the mixer on low speed, slowly add the flour mixture and beat until well mixed. Stir in the pecans. Using a tablespoon, drop dough 2 inches apart on the parchment lined pan. Bake about 8 minutes or until set and cookies are getting brown around the edges. Leave cookies on baking sheet for 2 minutes and then transfer to a wire rack to cool completely. Glaze cooled cookies with following glaze, if desired.

Orange Glaze Recipe:

½ cup Agave nectar	4 teaspoons fresh orange juice
¼ teaspoon vanilla extract	½ cup chopped pecans
½ teaspoon grated orange peel	

Place chopped pecans in a mini grinder and grind into a paste. Put all of the ingredients above in a small mixing bowl. Using an electric mixer on low speed, beat the mixture until smooth. Add more fructose or juice if needed in order to have the right consistency.

LEMON LIME PIE BARS

2 cups whole wheat flour, sifted

½ cup fructose

4 large eggs

3 tablespoons lime juice

6 tablespoons unbleached flour, sifted

1 cup butter

½ teaspoon sea salt

3 tablespoons lemon juice

¾ cup fructose

2 tablespoons grated lemon zest

Preheat oven to 350°.

Mix the butter, 2 cups flour, salt and ½ cup fructose with your hands. Pat the mixture onto and up the sides of a cookie sheet. Place in preheated oven and bake for 20 minutes. Mix the eggs, lemon juice, lime juice, the 6 tablespoons flour and ¾ cup fructose, beating until well blended. Pour at once on top of baked crust. Place back in oven for 25 minutes. Remove from oven and cool completely. Top with grated lemon zest. Cut into squares just before serving.

CHERRY PASTRY SQUARES

½ cup butter

2 egg whites, beaten till stiff peaks form

1½ cups unbleached flour, sifted

Pinch of aluminum free baking soda

1½ cups cherry preserves

½ cup fructose

1 teaspoon vanilla extract

Pinch of sea salt

1½ cup chopped nuts

2 egg yolks

Preheat oven to 350°. Butter a 12-by-9-inch pan.

Cream the butter and fructose. Add egg yolks and beat until fluffy. Add the vanilla, flour, salt and baking soda, mixing well. Pat into the buttered pan. Spread the preserves over the dough. Sprinkle with ¾ cup of the nuts. Spread the beaten egg whites evenly over the nuts. Sprinkle with the remaining nuts. Bake for 30 minutes. Allow to cool completely before cutting.

NOTE: You may use any type of preserves you prefer in place of the cherry.

VANILLA CUT OUT COOKIES

Place oven rack in the top position. Preheat oven to 400°.

½ cup softened butter	½ cup fructose
2 teaspoons aluminum free baking powder	1 teaspoon vanilla extract
2¾ cups unbleached flour	2 large eggs, beaten

In a large bowl, cream the butter and fructose on medium speed. Add the eggs and vanilla to the creamed mixture and continue beating until light and fluffy. Sift the flour and baking powder together. Add the flour mixture to the creamed mixture, beating after each addition. Stir the last ½ cup of flour into the mixture by hand. The dough will be very stiff. Do not chill the finished cookie dough!!! Divide cookie dough into 2 portions. On a clean, floured surface, roll 1 portion of dough at a time. Roll into about a 12-inch round and about ⅛ inch thick. Cut out cookies with a cookie cutter dipped in flour between each cookie. Place cookies on un-greased cookie sheets and bake for 6 to 8 minutes or until lightly browned. Remove cookies from sheet immediately and place on rack to cool. When cookies are completely cool, you may ice or decorate if desired.

SPICED SHORTBREAD

1¼ cups unbleached flour	3 tablespoons brown sugar
½ cup butter	½ teaspoon ground cinnamon
¼ teaspoon ground ginger	⅛ teaspoon ground cloves

In a mixing bowl combine flour and brown sugar. Add cinnamon, ginger and cloves. Cut in butter until mixture resembles fine crumbs and starts to cling. Form the mixture into a ball and knead until smooth. To make wedges, on a buttered cookie sheet, pat or roll the dough into an 8 inch circle. Using your fingers, press to make a scalloped edge. With a knife, cut circle into 16 pie shape wedges. Leave wedges in the circle shape. Bake at 325° for 25 to 30 minutes or until bottom just starts to brown and center is set. Cut circle into wedges again while warm. Cool on the cookie sheet for 5 minutes. Remove from cookie sheet; cool on a wire rack.

BUTTER COOKIES

Preheat oven to 350°.

1 cup softened butter	1 cup unbleached flour
⅔ cup cornstarch	⅓ cup fructose
1 teaspoon vanilla extract	

Beat the butter on medium speed until fluffy. Stir the flour, cornstarch and fructose together and gradually add to the butter, beating until combined. Stir in the vanilla. Drop dough by teaspoons onto un-greased cookie sheet. Bake for 8 minutes or until light golden tan in color. Transfer to a wire rack to cool completely before glazing.

Glaze Recipe:

¾ cup fructose	2 teaspoons softened butter
3 to 4 tablespoons fresh juice, your choice	

Stir the butter and powdered sugar together and add the juice a little at a time, stirring well until the glaze is smooth and can be drizzled by a spoon over the tops of the cookies. Allow glaze to set before serving the cookies.

MERINGUE COOKIES

Preheat oven to 250°. Line cookie sheets with parchment paper.

3 large eggs whites	⅛ teaspoon sea salt
¾ cup fructose	1 tablespoon white vinegar
8 teaspoons any flavor gelatin powder	½ cup grated coconut
1 cup miniature white chocolate chips	

Beat egg whites and salt until foamy. Stir the fructose and gelatin powder together and gradually add to the egg whites, beating until fructose has dissolved and stiff peaks form. Beat in the vinegar. Gently fold in the coconut and miniature chips. Drop by teaspoons onto cookie sheets and bake for 25 minutes. Turn oven off and leave meringues in oven for 20 more minutes. Transfer to wire rack to cool.

Sweet Sesame Seed Cookie Crisps

1 cup sesame seeds, toasted	1 cup softened butter
¾ cup fructose	1 large egg, beaten
1¾ cups unbleached flour	2 teaspoons vanilla extract
2 teaspoons aluminum free baking powder	⅛ cup light brown sugar
1 teaspoon aluminum free baking soda	1 teaspoon sea salt

Cream the butter on medium speed until fluffy. Gradually add the fructose to the butter and beat well. Stir in the egg, sesame seeds and vanilla extract. Stir the flour, baking powder, baking soda and salt together. Add the flour mixture to the butter mixture and mix until well combined. Cover bowl of dough well and refrigerate for 3 hours.

Preheat oven to 325°. Lightly butter cookie sheets.

Shape dough into ½-inch balls and place on cookie sheets. Dip a flat-bottomed glass in flour and flatten each ball of dough to about ¹⁄₁₆-inch thick. Bake for 10 minutes or until a light golden brown. Remove from cookie sheet and place on wire rack.

Soft Mincemeat Cookies

¼ cup softened butter	½ cup fructose
2 large eggs, lightly beaten	¾ cup mincemeat
1½ cups unbleached flour	½ teaspoon ground cinnamon
1½ teaspoon aluminum free baking soda	¼ teaspoon ground nutmeg
1½ cups white chocolate chips	¼ teaspoon sea salt

Preheat oven to 350°. Line cookie sheets with parchment paper. Cream the butter and fructose until fluffy. Add the eggs and mincemeat, mixing until well combined. Stir the flour, baking soda, cinnamon, nutmeg and salt together and add to the creamed mixture, stirring until well mixed. Fold the white chocolate chips into the dough. Drop dough by tablespoons about 2-inch apart on lined cookie sheets. Bake for 12 minutes or until golden brown. Transfer to wire racks to cool.

BROWNIE DELIGHTS

Cookie Dough:

⅔ cup softened butter

1 cup light brown sugar

2 large eggs, lightly beaten

1½ cups unbleached flour

¼ teaspoon aluminum free baking soda

1 tablespoon buttermilk

1 teaspoon vanilla extract

½ teaspoon sea salt

⅓ cup cocoa powder

2 cups chocolate chips

Preheat oven to 375°. Line cookie sheets with parchment paper.

In a large mixing bowl, cream the butter, sugar, buttermilk and vanilla extract. Beat in the eggs on at a time. Combine the flour, cocoa powder, salt and baking soda. Add to the creamed mixture, gradually beating just until blended. Stir in the chocolate chips and drop dough by rounded teaspoons about 2-inch apart on lined cookie sheets. Bake for 8 minutes. Remove cookies from oven and allow to cool for 2 minutes on cookie sheet. Press your thumb gently into the top of each cookie and transfer to wire racks to cool completely. When cookies are cool, fill the hollows on top with cream cheese filling and top with half of a candied cherry.

Cream Cheese Filling:

4 ounces softened cream cheese

¾ cup fructose

1 teaspoon vanilla extract

Combine all of the ingredients above in a small bowl. Beat on medium speed until creamy and smooth.

BROWN RICE COOKIES

2 cups cooked short grain brown rice
1½ teaspoons aluminum free baking powder
¾ cup fructose
1 egg, beaten
1 cup unbleached flour, sifted
1 cup pecans or walnuts, finely chopped

½ cup butter
¾ cup coconut
2 teaspoons cinnamon
1 tablespoon fructose
1 teaspoon vanilla

Cream together the butter and fructose. Add beaten egg and vanilla and mix well. Add sifted dry ingredients. Fold in cooked rice and coconut. In another bowl, mix together 1 tablespoon fructose, cinnamon and nut meats. Drop cookie dough by teaspoons on un-greased cookie sheet. Sprinkle top of each cookie with cinnamon-nut mixture. Bake in 350° oven for 20 to 25 minutes or until cookies are golden brown in color.

CHOCOLATE DIPPED MACAROONS

4 large egg whites
½ cup fructose
¼ cup unbleached flour
3½ cups packed sweetened dry coconut

1½ teaspoons vanilla
2 tablespoons butter
4 ounces semisweet chocolate

Beat egg whites until frothy. Beat in vanilla, fructose and flour until well blended. Add coconut and mix well. Drop tablespoon of dough 2 inches apart on parchment lined cookie sheet. Bake at 325° until lightly browned. Cool. Melt chocolate and butter together in double boiler. Dip cookies halfway in chocolate mix and let cool.

OATMEAL COOKIES

¾ cup butter, softened	¾ cup light brown sugar
¼ cup fructose	1 egg
1 teaspoon vanilla	1 teaspoon sea salt
1 cup unbleached sifted flour	3 cups uncooked oatmeal
½ teaspoon aluminum free baking soda	1 cup raisins

Cream butter and sugar until light and fluffy. Add vanilla and egg, mixing well. Add dry ingredients. Mix well. Add oatmeal and raisins. Drop by teaspoonfuls onto ungreased cookie sheet. Bake at 350° for 10 to 12 minutes. Cool on wire rack.

GINGER SNAPS

2 cups unbleached flour	1 tablespoon ginger
1 teaspoon cinnamon	¾ cup butter
2 teaspoons aluminum free baking soda	½ cup fructose
¼ cup molasses	½ teaspoon sea salt
1 egg	

Cream butter and fructose. Beat in egg and molasses. Stir in dry ingredients. Blend well. Form teaspoonfuls of dough into balls. Roll in extra fructose and place on cookie sheet. Bake at 350° for 12 to 15 minutes, until tops are slightly cracked. Let sit in a tightly covered container for a couple of days for better flavor.

SCOTTISH SHORTBREAD

1¼ cups whole wheat flour	3 tablespoons cornstarch
½ cup butter, cut in small pieces	⅛ cup fructose

Mix flour, fructose and cornstarch with your hands. Crumble butter into flour mixture. Press into an 8 or 9-inch spring form pan. With tines of fork, around the edge of dough, prick surface evenly. Bake at 325° for about 40 minutes. Remove from oven and cut into 8 or 12 squares. Sprinkle fructose on top.

CRUNCHY COOKIES

1 cup butter	1/2 cup fructose
2 eggs	2 teaspoons vanilla
2 1/2 cups unbleached flour	1/2 teaspoon sea salt
1 teaspoon aluminum free baking soda	4 cups rice cereal
1 1/2 cups chocolate chips	

Cream butter and fructose. Blend in eggs and vanilla. Sift and add flour, baking soda and salt. Stir in cereal and chocolate chips. Drop by level tablespoonfuls onto greased cookie sheet. Bake at 350° for 10 minutes.

DREAM BARS

1/3 cup softened butter	1 teaspoon vanilla
1 teaspoon aluminum free baking powder	1/2 cup brown sugar
1 1/2 cups shredded coconut	2 eggs
1 cup + 1 tablespoon unbleached flour	1 cup chopped nuts
1/2 teaspoon sea salt	1/2 cup fructose

Beat butter and 1/2 cup of the brown sugar. With fork, blend in 1 cup flour until crumbly. Press mixture into greased 9-by-13-inch baking pan. Bake at 375° for 10 minutes. Place eggs in a bowl, beating until lemony colored; then beat in 1/2 cup of the fructose. Beat in vanilla and remaining 2 tablespoons flour, salt and baking powder. Stir in the nuts and coconut. Pour coconut mixture over baked crust. Return to oven for 20 minutes. Let cool in pan for 15 minutes. Prepare frosting (optional). Frost, then cut into serving pieces (in pan).

Orange Butter Frosting:

4 tablespoons butter	1 teaspoon vanilla
1/2 cup fructose	2 tablespoons orange juice
1 teaspoon grated orange zest	

Beat butter and fructose until creamy. Add vanilla and orange zest. Add orange juice a little at a time to make a good spreading consistency.

PERSIMMON COOKIES

½ cup butter

1 egg

2 cups unbleached flour

½ teaspoon cloves

1 cup nuts

1 cup persimmon pulp + 1 teaspoon
  aluminum free baking soda
  (mixed together to prevent curdling)

½ cup fructose

½ teaspoon ginger

½ teaspoon cinnamon

1 cup raisins

Cream butter and fructose. Add remaining ingredients except nuts and raisins. Mix well. Add nuts and raisins. Drop by spoonfuls on cookie sheet. Bake at 350° for 15 minutes.

PEANUT BUTTER COOKIES

1½ cups whole wheat flour

1 teaspoon vanilla

1 cup natural chunky peanut butter

½ teaspoon aluminum free baking soda

1 egg

¼ cup brown sugar

¼ cup fructose

½ cup butter

Preheat oven to 375°. Beat butter and peanut butter until creamy. Add fructose and brown sugar; beat until fluffy. Beat in egg and vanilla until blended. With mixer on low speed, add flour and baking soda. Roll teaspoons of dough into balls and place on cookie sheet. With a fork, make a criss-cross design on the top of each ball. Bake for 10 to 12 minutes. Store in a tightly covered container.

DATE PINWHEELS

1½ cups pitted whole dates, snipped	½ cup water
¼ cup fructose	2 tablespoons fresh lemon juice
1½ teaspoon vanilla	½ cup butter
½ cup macadamia nut oil	3 cups whole wheat flour
½ cup packed brown sugar	1 egg
3 tablespoons milk	¼ teaspoon sea salt
½ teaspoon aluminum free baking soda	

For filling, in a medium saucepan combine dates, water and ¼ cup of the fructose. Bring to boiling; reduce heat. Cook and stir about 2 minutes or until thick. Stir in lemon juice and ½ teaspoon vanilla; cool. In a mixing bowl beat butter and oil on medium to high speed for 30 seconds. Add about half of the flour, the remaining ¼ cup fructose, brown sugar, egg, milk, the remaining 1 teaspoon vanilla, soda and salt. Beat until thoroughly combined. Beat in remaining flour. Cover and chill for 1 hour or until easy to handle. Divide dough in half. Roll half of the dough between waxed paper into a 12-by-10-inch rectangle. Spread half of the filling over the dough. Roll up from one of the long sides. Moisten and pinch edges to seal. Wrap in waxed paper or clear plastic wrap. Repeat with remaining dough and filling. Chill 2 to 24 hours. Cut into ¼ inch slices. Place 1 inch apart on a buttered cookie sheet. Bake at 375° for 10 to 12 minutes or until edges are lightly browned. Cool cookies on a wire rack.

CHOCOLATE COCONUT GRAHAMS

1 stick butter	1 cup shredded coconut
1 cup graham cracker crumbs	1 cup broken pecans
1 can sweetened condensed milk	1 cup chocolate chips

Preheat oven to 350°; melt butter in 9-by-9-inch pan. Sprinkle crumbs over butter and stir. Sprinkle coconut over this. Add chocolate chips and sprinkle with pecans. Pour milk on top. **Do not stir!!!** Bake for 30 minutes, cool and cut into squares.

HAYSTACKS

6 egg whites, lightly beaten
3¼ cups flaked coconut
½ cup chopped nuts
¾ teaspoon vanilla

½ cup fructose
¾ cup chopped dates
¼ teaspoon sea salt

Combine egg whites and fructose. Cook in top of a double boiler over simmering water until mixture reaches 120° or feels hot to the touch. Stir constantly. In a large mixing bowl, combine the remaining ingredients and add the hot fructose mixture. Blend well. Form dough into balls and place on a lightly greased parchment covered cookie sheet. Bake for 20 minutes at 350° or until golden brown.

BILLY GOATS

1 cup butter
½ cup packed brown sugar
¼ cup cocoa powder
½ teaspoon aluminum free baking soda
8 ounces diced dates

1 egg
1 teaspoon vanilla
2 cups unbleached flour
1 cup shredded coconut
1 cup crisp rice cereal

Cream butter and sugar; add eggs and vanilla and beat well. Add cocoa powder gradually; mix well until blended. Sift flour and soda in and beat well. Blend in dates, coconut and crisp rice cereal; mix until all are coated and well distributed. Drop batter by spoonfuls onto un-greased baking sheet. Bake at 350° for 13 to 15 minutes.

The Herb Garden

12

Tea,
Broth,
Salad
and More

Herbs and Spices

Basil—Has a sweet, warm flavor and an aromatic odor. Can be used whole or ground with fish, lamb, stews, soups, beef dishes, vegetables, dressings and egg dishes.

Bay Leaves—Pungent flavor. Use whole leaf or crushed but remember to remove whole leaves before serving. Good in stews, pickles, vegetable dishes, seafood and Italian dishes.

Caraway—Has an aromatic smell and a spicy, nutty flavor. Use in cabbage dishes, soups, cheese and cheese dishes, cakes and breads.

Cilantro—Use fresh in salads, rice, beans, fish, chicken and Mexican dishes.

Curry Powder—Spices are combined in proper proportions to add distinct flavor to meat, rice, vegetables, poultry and fish.

Chives—Sweet, mild onion flavor. Excellent in salads, soups, fish and seafood dishes, potatoes, dressings, sauces and dips.

Cinnamon—Has a subtle, spicy sweet and slightly warm flavor. Ground cinnamon is often used to flavor puddings, pies, cakes, cookies, fruits, teas, breads and curries. Sticks are used to infuse flavor into syrups, milk, sugars, custards, mulled wines and mulled ciders.

Cloves—Very aromatic and has a sweet flavor. Whole cloves are excellent to both flavor and decorate onions, oranges and apples. Use ground cloves to flavor desserts, fruits, breads and oils.

Dill—Seeds and leaves are useful and very flavorful. Used as a garnish or cooked with rice, beans, egg dishes, fish, soups, dressings, potatoes and to flavor pickles.

Fennel—Has a sweet, hot flavor. Both the leaves and the seeds may be used. Use in small amounts in baked goods and fish.

Ginger—Pungent root and is very aromatic. Sold fresh, ground and dried. May be used in soups, meat dishes, poultry dishes, teas, cakes, cookies, fish dishes, preserves and sauces.

Marjoram—May be used fresh or dried to flavor stews, lamb, fish, poultry, egg dishes, stuffing and vegetable juices.

Mint—Has a cool flavor and is very aromatic. Very good used in beverages, fish, lamb, cheese, sweet peas, carrots, cookies, candies and fruit desserts.

Oregano—Has a strong aromatic taste and smell. May be used fresh or dried. May be used whole but is used ground most of the time. Often used to flavor sauces, vegetable juices, stews, soups, vegetables, egg dishes, chili, gravies, poultry, fish, pizza and Italian dishes.

Paprika—A bright red pepper, this spice is ground into a powder and is used in meat, vegetables and soups and as a garnish for potatoes, salads, egg dishes, poultry dishes and casseroles.

Parsley—Fresh is best, but dried can be used. Excellent when used to season as well as a garnish for fish, egg dishes, soups, stews, dressings, salads, meats, poultry, stuffing, vegetables, potatoes and casseroles.

Rosemary—Fresh rosemary has a pungent, spicy yet refreshing flavor. Dried rosemary is much milder. Good in marinades, dressings, lamb, chicken, potatoes, Italian dishes and breads.

Sage—Use fresh or dried. Often used in tomato juice, fish, beef, omelets, poultry, stuffing, cheese dishes and breads.

Tarragon—Leaves have a pungent, slightly hot taste. Often used to flavor salads, sauces, dressings, green beans, fish, carrots, eggs, cooking oils, relishes, tomatoes and poultry.

Thyme—Has a distinctive and pleasant flavor. Use to flavor lamb, beef, poultry, stuffing, egg dishes, sauces, dressings, pastas, tomatoes and cheese dishes.

NOTE: Remember, when using fresh herbs to use 2 to 3 times more than dried herbs. Crush dried herbs and snip fresh herbs. Add all herbs in small amounts and adjust to taste. Always remember, it is easier to add more if needed than to remove too much.

Bonus Herbal Recipes

LICORICE SPICE TEA

1 tablespoon dried licorice root

1 tablespoon dried orange zest

1 teaspoon whole cloves

¼ teaspoon ginger powder

1 tablespoon dried fennel seed

1 tablespoon dried lemon zest

1 teaspoon anise seed

Blend all of the above ingredients together in a glass jar and cover tightly. To make tea, use one teaspoon to one cup of boiling water. Allow to steep for 15 minutes. May be sweetened to taste by adding fructose or honey. This tea is excellent for sore throats, colds and flu symptoms.

HERB AND CHICKEN BROTH

1 small chicken (2 to 3 pounds)

2 cloves garlic, finely diced

1 red onion, finely diced

2 stalks celery, finely diced

1 teaspoon ground black pepper

4 quarts water

1 teaspoon rosemary

1 teaspoon thyme

1 teaspoon salt

Boil chicken in 3-quarts of the water until tender. Remove chicken from the pot and clean the meat from the bones. Dice the chicken and return back to the broth. Add the remaining quart of water and all of the other ingredients. Bring back to a boil and then lower to a simmer and cover. Simmer over low heat for 30 minutes. Remove from heat and keep covered. Allow broth to set for 15 minutes before serving.

MINTY SUGAR SNAP PEAS

3 pounds fresh sugar snap peas
4 sprigs fresh mint
Salt and pepper to taste

1 teaspoon honey
1 tablespoon butter

Place sugar snap peas in boiling water with the honey and fresh mint. Boil gently for about 10 minutes or until tender. Drain and add butter, salt and pepper.

HERB AND SPINACH OVEN OMELETTE

Preheat oven to 350°. Butter a baking dish.

2 cups fresh spinach, chopped
4 ounces grated mozzarella cheese
1 tablespoon chopped parsley
1 tablespoon chopped tarragon
1 tablespoon extra light olive oil

8 large eggs
1 red onion, diced
1 teaspoon chopped chives
¼ cup milk

In a large bowl, beat eggs. Add spinach and remaining ingredients. Mix well and pour into the buttered baking dish. Cover and bake for 30 to 35 minutes. Remove cover and sprinkle with additional grated cheese and return to oven long enough to melt cheese. You can also make this into a quiche by baking in a piecrust.

ROSEMARY AND BAY LEAF OVEN POTATOES

6 baking potatoes, quartered lengthwise
12 sprigs fresh rosemary

6 bay leaves
6 tablespoons butter

Place potatoes in a shallow casserole dish. Top with the bay leaves, rosemary, and pats of butter. Cover and bake for 45 minutes. Remove bay leaves before serving.

DILLY BAKED POTATO SALAD

6 medium baked potatoes, peeled & diced

1 small red onion, chopped

1 green pepper, diced

1 red pepper, diced

1 cucumber, peeled & chopped

1 tablespoon dill weed, chopped

½ cup red wine vinegar

¼ cup water

¼ cup fructose

1 teaspoon celery seed

1 clove garlic, minced

Salt and pepper to taste

Toss all of the vegetables together in a large bowl. Whisk the remaining ingredients together until well blended and pour over vegetable mixture. Toss well and cover tightly. Refrigerate for several hours before serving.

Appendix

Weights and Measures
Roasting Chart
Fun Cooking Hints
Tips for Creating a Warm Workable Kitchen
More Exciting Books and Video Tapes

Weights and Measures

3 teaspoons = 1 tablespoon

4 tablespoons = ¼ cup

5 ⅓ tablespoons = ⅓ cup

8 tablespoons = ½ cup

16 tablespoons = 1 cup

1 tablespoon = ½ fluid ounce

1 cup = 8 fluid ounces

1 cup = ½ pint

2 cups = 1 pint

4 cups = 1 quart

4 quarts = 1 gallon

1 pound = 453.59 grams

1 ounce = 28.35 grams

Roasting Chart

Meats	Weight	Time	Temperature
Chicken	3 to 3 ½ pounds	12 minutes/pound	350 °
	4 to 7 pounds	20 minutes/pound	400 °
Turkey	16 to 24 pounds	15 minutes/pound	325 °
Ribeye	3 pounds	12 minutes/pound	350 °
Beef Brisket	5 to 6 pounds	30 minutes/pound	375 °
Beef Rib	4 to 6 pounds	25 minutes/pound	300 °
Tenderloin	3 to 3 ½ pounds	12 minutes/pound	350 °

All cooking times for the cuts of beef listed are for rare. Simply add more time for a less rare piece of meat. When stuffing any poultry, add 10 minutes per pound to the total cooking time.

Fun Cooking Hints

 Add two tablespoons of fructose to the boiling water when cooking fresh corn to plump up and sweeten the kernels.

When cooking rice, use broth or vegetable juice instead of water for added taste.

 When cooking oatmeal, use apple juice instead of water. Add a little honey and butter for a real taste treat.

When making pancakes or waffles, try using fruit juice instead of milk or water in the batter.

 Scrambled eggs are extra fluffy and soft if you add ½ tsp. low fat organic mayonnaise per egg used and then whisk until well blended.

 A can of cream of mushroom with roasted garlic soup will liven up your macaroni and cheese.

Add 2 chopped hard-boiled eggs to a pot of chicken and dumplings just before serving.

 Poaching eggs in broth eliminates the need for butter .

When making pineapple upside down cake, try using canned coconut milk for the liquid called for in the recipe.

Use orange juice as the liquid in a pound cake.

When making a yellow layer cake, use your favorite jam or preserves between the layers and on top. Use frosting on the sides or leave them plain.

Add 1 cup of salsa for every 3 cups of beans used when making baked beans.

Simmer fresh lima beans in milk instead of water.

Tips for Creating a Warm, Workable Kitchen

Since Ted and I have decided to give you the best recipes available for making exciting transitions to a more healthy lifestyle, we have also decided to give you our suggestions on how to build and or remodel to achieve an awesome gourmet healthy cooking kitchen.

1. Choice of stove—There is only one choice, Wolf. These gas stoves are simply the best available at any price. We recommend the gas top with griddle and grill along with the double gas convection oven. The oven is incredible, always cooking perfectly. The griddle and grill are so fast and convenient. All of the gas burners have a simmer feature which keeps food at a perfect temperature.

2. Refrigerator—Sub Zero period! The dual compressors, one for the refrigerator and one for the freezer, stop all transfer of food odors. The temperature remains perfect. The unit is so quiet you don't hear it running.

3. Sub Zero refrigerator drawers—A must for salad and fresh vegetable preparation. If you can build them next to your vegetable sink, it is incredibly convenient.

4. Asko Dishwasher—So quiet, around 35 D.B., the noise of a whisper.

If you need additional information on these incredible appliances please give the Westye Group a call at 1-800-782-0013.

5. Flooring—We decided to go with hardwood in our kitchen which is risky with water, but beautiful and easy to keep clean. We used Bast Hardwoods in Central Florida. Give them a call at 1-800-664-2278. Ask for Gary.

6. Cabinets—An excellent company throughout Florida is Busby. Their number is 1-800-654-7090. Ask for Dave Stanley.

7. Pantry—Closet Master is the key to an incredibly efficient and beautiful pantry. Every space is utilized. No one does a better, more professional production and installation line. Call 1-407-876-1344. Ask for Wayne.

We hope these suggestions will give you some great ideas. When Ted and I remodeled last year it was indeed an adventure, especially living here during the remodeling and experiencing 3 hurricanes in that time period. But, we must admit it was worth the wait. I can honestly say I love my kitchen and I love sharing it with my family and friends and some good healthy country cooking.

Eat, Drink, and Be Healthy Program

BY TED AND SHARON BROER

Our Six Week Program to Optimal Health and Energy!

Tape 1: The Top Ten Foods Never to Eat

Tape 2: Forever Slim (Do's and Don'ts of Weight Loss)

Tape 3: Winning Choices for Your Health

Tape 4: Double Your Energy, Double Your Output

Tape 5: Simplifying the Supermarket Safari

Tape 6: Foods That Heal

Tape 7: Food Choices: Facts & Myths

Plus reports on: ADD, Hypertension, Cancer, Diabetes, Depression, and Prostate Problems.

FOREVER FIT: at 20, 30, 40, and Beyond Program

BY TED BROER

Lose Weight* Feel Great* Fitness/Health Series

Our Latest, Up-to-Date Series on Health, Nutrition, Sports Medicine, and exercise!

Tape 1: Fat Loss, Not Weight Loss—The Key to Looking Great! Hormones and How They Control the Body

Tape 2: Exercise—Its Role in Burning Fat/Lean Muscle Mass—What Types & How much

Tape 3: Trace Minerals, Vitamin Supplements, Fatty Acids/Joint Repair and Arthritis

Tape 4: Artificial Sweeteners/Chemicals and Foods in Our Environment to Avoid

Tape 5: Chronic Fatigue Syndrome, Yeast Infection, Hypoglycemia, and Your Immune System

Tape 6: Constipation, the Colon, and Your Health

Tape 7: Fasting: The Physical & Spiritual Benefits

Tape 8: Water: Use a Filter or Be a Filter/Why You Absorb As Many Toxins in One Hot Shower as If You Had Drunk 8 Glasses of Contaminated Water

Plus reports on:
Nutrasweet, Constipation, Eating for Body Fat Loss, Yeast Infections, Epstein-Barr, and Chronic Fatigue Syndrome

248

THE MAXIMUM ENERGY
Health & Fitness Program

BY TED AND SHARON BROER

Feel Twenty Years Younger, Increase Your Energy Levels, and Greatly Improve Your General Health in 30 Days

- Staying Heart Disease and Cancer Free
- Which Supplements Really Work to Reverse the Aging Process
- 10 Key Secrets to Looking and Feeling 20 Years Younger
- Stress Free Living Made Simple
- The Wisdom of the Ages
- Top Ten Foods Not to Eat
- Top 5 Ways to Burn Body Fat
- Breaking Food Addictions
- Bypass the Bypass

MAXIMUM SUCCESS
A Three Dimensional Lifestyle Program for Unlimited Increase in all the Areas of Your Life

BY TED BROER

Learn How to Live Disease Free, Debt Free and Worry Free

Tape 1: Healthy Choices for Maximum Energy and Vitality, Living the Balanced Life

Tape 2: Top 35 Reasons Why You're Not Prospering

Tape 3: 34 Key Leadership Strategies to Becoming Super Successful

Tape 4: Personal Development — Becoming All You Were Meant to Be

Tape 5: Stress Management — How to Stop Worrying and Start Living!

Tape 6: 28 Secrets of Starting a Successful Business with Little Or No Money

BONUS TAPES

Tape 7: Trace Mineral Supplementation

Tape 8: Toxic Personal Care Products and How to Find Out If You Have Vitamin and Mineral Deficiencies

TO ORDER: 1-800-726-1834 • 1-800-592-4325 • www.healthmasters.com

Maximum Energy book

BY TED BROER

- The Top Ten Foods Never to Eat!
- The Top Ten Health Strategies for Maximum Energy!
- Double Your Energy in 30 Days with the Right Choices in this Insightful Book!

Maximum Energy Cookbook

BY TED AND SHARON BROER

A Health Guide to Survive!

This book is an ideal gift for loved ones.

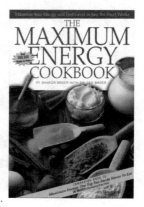

It includes:
- Back to Basics Recipes
- Infant, toddler, & children's diet
- Holiday Recipes
- Drinks, Shakes, and Coolers
- Fruit, Vegetables, Grains, and Meat Recipes
- Stress Avoidance, Exercise, Water, Goat's Milk, and More . . .

Train Up Your Children in the Way They Should Eat

BY SHARON BROER

The Ultimate Childrens' Program!
A Must for Every Concerned Parent

- Ensure the Good Health of Your Unborn Baby
- Nourish the Infant and Toddler So they Can Thrive
- Protect and Enhance the All-Important Immune Systems of Your Children
- Fuel Active Minds and Bodies for Complete Physical and Mental Growth
- Learn What Your Pediatrician Won't Tell You about Nutrition and Your Child's Health
- Stop Serving the Beverage That's More Toxic Than Lead!
- No Ritalin
- No Ear Infections
- No Allergies

Maximum Solutions for ADD, Learning Disabilities and Autism

BY TED BROER

• Top Five Foods Never to Feed a Hyperactive Child
• Truth About Measles, Immunization and Autism
• Natural Treatments for ADD, ADHD and Autism

Maximum Fat Loss

BY TED BROER

Finally, a Super Easy and Permanent Way to Lose Weight

• The Alarming Truth About Protein Diets
• The 12 Step Program to Lose Body Fat, Not Muscle
• What Weight Loss Products You Should Never Use!
• 3 Easy Steps to Stop the Obese Child Epidemic
• The Key to Permanently Speeding Up Your Metabolism
• Discover 5 Secret Supplements that Melt Body Fat and Cellulite
• Why You Should Never Drink Diet Sodas

Maximum Fat Loss Workbook

BY TED BROER

Lose Fat One Change at a Time

• Master the 12 Step Program for Losing Body Fat, Not Muscle
• Learn How to Permanently Speed up Your Metabolism
• Discover the 5 Secret Supplements that Melt Body Fat
• Follow 3 Easy Steps to Free Your Kids from the Obese Child Epidemic
• Identify Weight Loss Products You Should Never Use!
• Uncover the Truths about High Protein Diets
• Understand Why You Should Never Consume Diet Sodas or Anything with Artificial Sweeteners

251

Maximum Age Reversal

BY TED BROER

Feel Twenty Years Younger,
Increase Your Energy Levels, and Greatly Improve
Your General Health in 30 Days

- Staying Heart Disease and Cancer Free
- Which Supplements Really Work to Reverse the Aging Process
- 10 Key Secrets to Looking and Feeling 20 Years Younger
- Stress Free Living Made Simple
- Hormone Replacement Therapy
- Cutting Edge Age Reversal Therapies

Maximum Memory

BY TED BROER

See a Significant Improvement in
Your Memory and General Health in Only 30 Days,
No Matter How You Currently Feel

- The 10 Most Powerful Nutrients to Enhance Memory
- Alzheimer's Therapies that Really Work
- How to Boost Test Scores
- Stroke Prevention and Recovery
- Key Memory Building Exercises
- 4 Key Strategies for Stopping Senile Dementia
- 3 Products that Actually Poison the Brain
- "Smart" Foods and Herbs

Eat, Drink and be Healthy exercise videos

BY TED BROER

A scientific Approach to Athletic Conditioning and Proper Nutrition.

It Includes:
- Non Impact Training
- Lean Muscle Growth & Fat Loss in 6 Weeks
- For Men and Women of all ages
- Three tape series for Men or Women — 6 total tapes
- Lifetime warranty on videos

Understanding God's Dietary Principles tape series

This one answers all the Biblical Nutrition Questions

BY TED BROER

Tape 1: How God's Dietary Principles Relate to Us

Tape 2: In Depth Scriptural Overview

Tape 3: How to Break the Dietary Curses of Degenerative Disease

Hypoglycemia: A Sensible Approach tape series

BY TED BROER

Tape 1: Sugar & Controlling Hypoglycemia

Tape 2: Sugar and the American Sweet Tooth

Tape 3: What has Happened to Our Health?

If you have it, you need this series.

Nutrition and Your Healthy Heart tape series

BY TED BROER

Tape 1: Preventing Heart Disease

Tape 2: Exercising the Smart Way

Tape 3: Stress and Your Health

Learn how to keep this critical organ in top shape.

Natural Cooking for the Holidays tape series

BY SHARON BROER

Tape 1: Using Meat Replacements and Grains

Tape 2: Holiday Meal Planning

Tape 3: Sugar Replacements and Holiday Desserts

For those who ask: "Where do I start?"

Breaking the Dietary Curses of Cancer tape series

BY TED BROER

Tape 1: Cancer Prevention

Tape 2: The Benefits of Fasting

Tape 3: Fiber and a Healthy Colon

Tape 4: God's Dietary Principles

Tape 5: Clean & Unclean Foods

The nation's 2nd largest killer can be prevented.

Helping Your Family Make Dietary Changes tape series

BY TED AND SHARON BROER

Tape 1: Fiber & Food Preparation

Tape 2: Healthy Food Substitutes

Tape 3: Attitudes on Nutrition

This one makes it easy!

Preventing Arthritis and Osteoporosis tape series

BY TED BROER

Tape 1: Arthritis and Osteoporosis

Tape 2: The Importance of Calcium

Tape 3: Is Supplementation Necessary?

It's easier to prevent!

Train Up a Child in the Way He Should Eat tape series

BY SHARON BROER

Tape 1: Prenatal Nutrition

Tape 2: Infant & Toddler Nutrition

253

INDEX

A

Agave Nectar 10
Almond
    Butter 7
    Pineapple Truffles 192
    Stix 233
Angel Hair Pasta 7
Apples
    and Sweet Bell Pepper Skillet 162
    Apple Cake 198
    Brown Rice Apple Crisps 198
    Chicken & Apple Kebabs 48
    Enchiladas 208
    French Toast 17
    Oatmeal Bread 75
    Pear and Apple Streusel Pie 207
    Pudding with Custard Sauce 194
    Raisin Breakfast Muffins 69
    Raisin Walnut Delight 182
    Rice Pudding 190
    Stuffed 25
    Sweet Potato and Apple Bake 148
    Turkey Sausage Coffee Cake 27
Asparagus
    Casserole 19
    Rice Salad .83
    Risotto 166
Artichoke
    Chicken 139
Avocado
    Cake 196
    Pitas 42

B

Baking Mix 7
Balls
    Festive Cheese Balls 43
    Orange 45
Banana
    Berry Banana Walnut Bread 74
    Breakfast Banana Splits 26
    Gone Bananas Cake 181
    Nut Bread 72
    Nut Cookies with Orange Glaze . . . 219
    Nut Muffins 72
    Southern Banana Pudding 208
Bars
    Bomb Bars 214
    Dream Bars 227
    Granola Bars 231
    Lemon Lime Pie Bars 220
Bean
    Black Bean Salad 88
    Broccoli & Bean Casserole 171
    Salad 81
Beans
    Deluxe Baked Beans with
      Smoked Turkey 158
    Lazy Day Spicy Bean Soup 52
    Tuscan 172
Beef
    and Spinach Shells 138
    Barbecued Steak 106
    Broiled Sirloin Steak 129
    Burrito Casserole 142
    Classic Meatloaf 134
    Favorite Barbecue 102
    Hobo Beef Stew 104
    Mom's Day Off Oven Stew 109

Oven Beef Roast 107
Roast with Potato Special 108
Shepherds Pie 135
Short Ribs. 99
Stew 51
Stir Fry 102
Stroganoff. 127
Beets
Orange 173
Biscotti
Easy. 62
Biscuits
Cheddar, Garlic, Parsley 67
Cheesy 67
Pecan Swirls 25
Simply Delicious 62
Black Beans
Corn & Black Bean Cheddar
Salsa. 34
Fiesta Black Bean & Cheese
Spread 34
Salad 88
Soup 60
Blackberry
Lazy Days Cobbler 188
Bok Choy
Ramen Salad 94
Black-Eye Peas
and Spinach 175
Bread
Almost a Meal Bread. 63
Apple Oatmeal Bread 75
Autumn Bread 70
Banana Nut Bread 72
Berry Banana Walnut Bread 74
Cheesy Twists. 44

Cinnamon Bread Pudding 181
Country Style Cornbread 71
Fruity Nut Bread 64
Golden Raisin Breakfast Bread. 66
Grandma's Cornbread. 66
Molasses Rye Round
Bread Loaves. 65
Nutty Citrus Bread. 70
Nutty Sticky Buns 24
Pecan Biscuit Swirls. 25
Popeye's Bread 65
Pudding 200
Pumpkin Bread 73
Raisin Bread 63
Soda Bread 74
Strawberry Bread 75
Sweet Pepper and Onion
Spoon Bread 64
Sweet Potato Nut Bread 69
Zucchini Bread. 73
Breakfast
Banana Split. 26
Parfait 27
Puffs 21
Rice Burrito. 16
Very Berry Coconut
Breakfast Cake 183
Broccoli
and Bean Casserole 171
Baked 173
Cheesy Broccoli and Rice
Casserole. 123
Cream of Broccoli Soup 53
Brownie
Awesome Chunky 192
Delights 224

Pudding Cake 206
Brown Rice (see also Rice)
    and Mushroom Soup 56
    Apple Crisp 198
    Apple Rice Pudding. 190
    Arborio Rice 7
    Baked Rice 163
    Basic Risotto. 165
    Basmati Rice. 7
    Black Japonica 154
    Cheesy Asparagus Risotto 166
    Cheesy Rice Crisp 178
    Chicken Rice Soup 56
    Cinnamon Raisin Rice
      Pudding. 198
    Cookies. 225
    Curried Rice 160
    Holiday Risotto 165
    Italian Basmati 168
    Japonica Rice 7
    Jasmine Rice. 7
    Lemon Pesto 153
    Long Grain Rice. 7
    Mexican Rice 167
    Orange Ginger Basmati 173
    Pilaf. 167
    Pilaf with Blue Cheese, Pears and
      Pecans 164
    Primavera 170
    Pudding 197
    Pudding with Pineapple Sauce 193
    Raisin Brown Rice Muffins 71
    Regal Basmati. 167
    Short Grain Rice 7
    Spicy Rice with Cashews 170
    Sushi Rice 8

Wehani Rice 8
Wild Mushroom Risotto 168
Wild Rice Dressing 169
Yogurt Supreme 197
Brown Sugar 10
Brown Rice Syrup 10
Brussels Sprouts
    and Onions 163
Buns
    Nutty Sticky 24
Butter
    Pecan Butter 30
    Cookies. 222
Buttermilk
    Cake 203

C

Cabbage
    Cranberry Cabbage Slaw 95
    South Western 176
    Savory Garlic 177
Cake
    Apple Cake. 200
    Angle Food Cake. 199
    Avocado Cake 196
    Brownie Pudding Cake 206
    Brown Sugar Pound Cake with
      Fruit Sauce 188
    Buttermilk Cake. 203
    Classic Cheesecake 205
    Coconut Dream Cake 186
    Fruit Coffee Cake. 22
    Fruity Pecan Upside Down
      Cake. 187
    Gone Bananas Cake 181
    Hummingbird Cake. 201

Lane Cake 202
Lemon Orange Carrot Cake. 185
Mama's Applesauce Cake. 191
Maple Nut Frosted Heavenly
    Chocolate Cake 184
Orange Coconut Cake 202
Peach Skillet Cake 207
Peanut Butter Coffee Cake 23
Pineapple Carrot Cake 199
Strawberry Shortcake 205
Sweet Potato Cake. 203
3-Layer German
    Chocolate Cake 206
Very Berry Coconut
    Breakfast Cake 181
Yum Yum Yum Pineapple Cake 180
Cake Mixes. 8
Carrot
    Citrus and Honey Glazed. 159
    Lemon Orange Carrot Cake. 185
    Pineapple Carrot Cake 199
    Salad. 93
Casserole
    Asparagus. 19
    Beef Burrito 142
    Broccoli and Bean 171
    Cheesy Broccoli & Rice. 123
    Corn 174
    Deluxe Salmon. 113
    Eggy Vegetable Casserole with
        Cheesy Mushroom Sauce 161
    Grandpa's Favorite 104
    Oatmeal 16
    Scrambled Eggs 19
    Squash 170
    Squash and Chicken 127

Sweet Potato & Pecan. 157
Tuna and Rice. 126
Zucchini Rice 127
Catsup. 8
Celery
    Stuffed 35
Cereal 8
Cheese
    Cheesy Pecan Bites. 37
    Soup 58
    Spicy Cheese Wafers 39
    Twists 44
Cheesecake
    Classic. 205
Cherry
    Frozen Pineapple Coconut
        Dessert 195
    Pastry Squares 220
Chicken
    and Apple Kebabs 48
    and Dumplings 117
    and Rice Soup 56
    and Spinach Pizza 145
    Angel Hair Chicken. 128
    Artichoke Chicken. 139
    Apricot Roll-ups 137
    Baked Fried Chicken 141
    Barbecue Wings 47
    Best Ever Salad 85
    Broth. 50
    Company Chicken Salad 93
    Couscous 176
    Couscous Chicken Salad. 82
    Cucumber Spread 46
    Destiny. 38
    Dijon Chicken Rice 116

Easy Gourmet Chicken Breast 115

Fajitas 145

Family Reunion Chicken. 121

Fingers 40

Fried Rice 142

Grilled Chicken & Apple Kebabs. . . . 48

Grilled Chicken with

    Pineapple 131

Gumbo 60

Holiday Chicken and Rice 110

Herb Chicken Broth 240

Honey Chicken Salad 96

Honey Dijon Chicken 130

In Black Bean Sauce 144

Island Chicken and Pineapple 115

Italian Stuffed Chicken 119

Japonica Chicken Stir-fry 118

Lemon-Herb Chicken 135

Mama Mia Chicken with

    Italian Turkey Sausage 122

Orange Honey Chicken 136

Parmesan Crusted Chicken 140

Peanut Butter Chicken 132

Phyllo Chicken. 140

Preachers Coming Roasted

    Chicken. 118

Raisin Couscous Chicken 144

Roast Chicken, Classic 130

Roasted Chicken

    Mushroom Soup 54

Smoked Chicken Risotto 122

Squash and Chicken

    Casserole. 127

Spread. 43

Surprise Oven Chicken. 116

Sweet and Sour Chicken 134

Tettrazini. 138

Tomato Basil Chicken 141

Wild Rice Chicken Salad. 90

With Fresh Vegetables and Basil. . . . 119

Chili

    Bobby's chili with Creamy

        Vegetable Sauce 55

Chocolate

    Awesome Chunky Brownies 192

    Brownie Delights. 224

    Brownie Pudding Cake 206

    Chip Bar Cookies. 217

    Chip Cookies 218

    Coconut Grahams 129

    Crinkles. 233

    Crunchies 198

    Dipped Macaroons 225

    Fudge Ecstasies. 232

    Maple-Nut Frosted Heavenly

        Chocolate Cake 184

    Pecan Pie 191

    Soufflé. 204

    Three Layer German

        Chocolate Cake 206

Chocolate Chips 8

Cobbler

    Lazy Day Blackberry 188

Coconut

    Dream Cake. 186

    Frozen Cherry Pineapple

        Coconut Desert. 195

    Lemon Coconut Tarts 234

    Milk. 2, 9

    Orange Coconut Cake 202

    Pecan Oatmeal. 31

    Pineapple Coconut Pudding. 189

Toasty Coconut Mounds.........214
Very Berry Coconut Breakfast
  Cake.......................181
Coffee Cake
  Apple – Turkey Sausage
    Coffee Cake 27
  Fruit Coffee Cake...............22
  Peanut Butter Coffee Cake 23
Coffee Substitutes 8
Condensed Milk 9
Condiments 8
Cookies
  Almond Stix.................233
  Banana Nut Cookies with
    Orange Glaze 219
  Banana Spice 232
  Big Batch Peanut Butter 215
  Billy Goats 230
  Bomb Bars 214
  Brownie Delight................224
  Brown Rice Cookies 225
  Butter 222
  Candied Fruit & Nut............217
  Cherry Pastry Squares 220
  Chocolate Chip Bar 217
  Chocolate Chip................218
  Chocolate Coconut Grahams 229
  Chocolate Crinkles 233
  Chocolate Dipped Macaroons......225
  Crunchy 227
  Date Pinwheels 229
  Dream Bars...................227
  Fudge Ecstasies 232
  Ginger Snaps 226
  Granola Bars 231
  Haystacks 230

Honey of a Cookie..............218
Jam Fingerprints 235
Lemon Coconut Tarts 234
Macadamia Lime Snowflakes......231
Meringue 222
Nice & Spicy Fig 215
Not Just Oatmeal...............216
Oatmeal......................226
Peanut Butter 228
Persimmon 228
Scottish Shortbread 226
Snickerdoodles.................234
Snowy Pecan Mountains.........216
Soft Mincemeat 223
Spiced Shortbread 221
Sweet Sesame Seed 223
Toasty Coconut Mounds 214
Vanilla Cut Out 221
Corn
  Casserole 174
  Chowder.....................58
  Creamy Fried 149
Cornbread
  Grandma's Cornbread...........66
  Country Style Cornbread 71
  Pot Pie.......................103
Cornbread Mix.....................7
Cornish Hens
  Stuffed 120
Couscous
  Chicken Couscous..............176
  Raisin and Chicken 144
Crackers
  Pecan Cheese..................46
Cranberry
  Sauce.........................45

Cucumbers

Chicken Cucumber Spread 46

Creamy 92

Tomato Salad 96

Custard

Country 200

D

Dates

Pinwheels 229

Dip

Artichoke 41

Cheese 41

Creamy Salmon 36

Eight Layer 44

Guacamole 40

Sour Cream Fruit 47

E

Easter Coins 148

Eggs

Cheesy Poached 18

Eggy Vegetable Casserole with

Cheesy Mushroom Sauce 161

Over Easy 15

Pepper Omelet 26

Salmon Stuffed Eggs 81

Scrambled Egg Casserole 19

Southern Scrambled 15

South of the Border 24

Tex – Mex Soft Scrambled 29

Evaporated Milk 9

F

Figs

Nice and Spicy Fig Cookies 215

Stuffed 35

Fish

Baked Grouper with Sauce 106

Baked Haddock with

Vegetables 114

Baked Red Snapper 128

Baked Salmon with

Fruit Salsa 130

Deluxe Salmon Casserole 113

Garlic Lime Salmon 136

Lemon Garlic Salmon Kebabs 48

Pan Seared Grouper with

Lemon Garlic 112

Poached Salmon with Lemon

Herbed Butter 111

Salmon and Zucchini Teriyaki 129

Salmon Stuffed Eggs 81

Salmon with Herbed Rice 143

Truly a Meal Tuna Salad 85

Tuna and Rice Casserole 126

Walnut Crusted Salmon 139

Flour 9

French Toast

Apple 17

Coconut 29

Fructose 10

Fruit

Cinnamon Fruit Salad 95

Galore Salad 78

G

Granola
Orange Compote. 27
Bars 231
Grape Seed Oil 9
Gravy
Turkey Sausage 15
Green Beans
and Onions with
Mustard Sauce 160
Company Style. 152
Deluxe. 156
Grits
Cheese 26
Grannies. 14

H

Haddock
Baked with Vegetables. 114
Homogenized Milk 2
Huevos
Rancheros. 21

I

Ice Cream
Peanut Butter 195
Ice Milk
Vanilla Bean 196

K

Kebabs
Grilled Chicken 48
Lemon Garlic Salmon. 48

L

Lamb Chops
Baked Apple. 133
Lasagna
Classic. 133
Lemon
Coconut Tarts 234
Lime Pie Bars 220
Lima Beans
and Tomato Skillet. 149

M

Macadamia
Nut Oil. 9
Lime Snowflakes 231
Macaroni
Garden Salad 82
Mayonnaise. 8
Meatballs
Hearty 98
Tangy. 45
Meat Loaf
Spinach Stuffed 100
Surprise. 101
Mints
Creamy. 193
Wafers. 209
Molasses. 10
Muffins
Apple Raisin Breakfast 69
Banana Nut 72
Breakfast Puff. 21
Orange Marmalade 28
Raisin Brown Rice 71

Mushrooms
  Brown Rice and Mushroom
    Soup 56
  Roasted Chicken Mushroom
    Soup 55
  Stuffed Deluxe 35

N

Nuts
  Chili. 41
  Goat Cheese, Dried Fruit and
    Nut Log 37
  Spicy Mixed 39

O

Oatmeal
  Apple Oatmeal Bread. 75
  Baked 23
  Casserole 16
  Coconut Pecan 31
  Cookies. 226
  Not Just Oatmeal Cookies 216
Okra
  Fried 178
Olive Oil. 9
Omelets
  Veggie French. 20
  Pepper. 26
Orange
  Coconut Cake 202
  Spinach Salad. 92
Organic Dairy. 2

P

Pancakes
  Buckwheat 22
  Pecan. 17
  Strawberry Buttermilk. 30
  Sweet Potato 28
Parfait
  Breakfast. 27
Peach
  Georgia Delight 190
  Pudding 197
  Skillet Cake 207
Peanut Butter
  Big Batch Peanut Butter
    Cookies 215
  Chicken. 132
  Coffee Cake 23
  Cookies. 228
  Drops 209
  Ice Cream 195
Pear
  and Apple Streusel Pie 207
Peas
  Cheesy Creamed 175
  My Favorite 158
  Minty Sugar Snap Peas 241
  Salad. 93
Pecan
  Butter 30
  Chocolate Pecan Pie 191
  Coconut Pecan Oatmeal 31
  Pancakes. 17

Pralines. 210
Snowy Pecan Mountains. 216
Persimmons
Cookies. 228
Pies
Chocolate Pecan Pie 191
Kentucky Derby Pie. 201
Lemon Lime Pie Bars. 220
Pear and Apple Streusel Pie. 207
Pot Pie, Cornbread. 103
Sweet Potato Pie 204
Turkey Sausage and
Vegetable Pie. 123
Pineapple
Almond Truffles 192
Cake 180
Carrot Cake 199
Coconut Pudding. 188
Frozen Cherry Pineapple
Coconut Dessert. 195
Pizza
Chicken and Spinach. 145
Turkey Rice 126
Popcorn
Italian 47
Potato
Baked Potato Skins 46
Dilly Baked Potato Salad. 242
Garlic Mashed Potatoes 171
Granny's Sunday Potatoes 151
Hearty Mashed Potatoes. 156
Kentucky Potato Salad 79
Mashed Potatoes Supreme. 150
Nellie's Potato Soup 54
Rosemary & Bay Leaf
Oven Potatoes. 241

Sky Fries. 150
Smoked Turkey Sausage and
Potato Soup 51
Pot Pie
Cornbread Pot Pie 103
Pudding
Apple Pudding with
Custard Sauce. 194
Apple Rice 190
Bread. 200
Brownie Pudding Cake. 206
Cinnamon Bread 180
Cinnamon Raisin Rice. 198
Peach. 197
Pineapple Coconut 189
Rice 197
Rice Pudding with
Pineapple Sauce. 193
Southern Banana. 208
Pumpkin
Bread. 73

R

Raisin
Apple Walnut Delight 182
Brown Rice Muffins. 71
Cinnamon Rice Pudding. 198
Golden Raisin Breakfast Bread 66
Rapadura Sweetener. 10
Raw Cows Milk 2
Red Snapper
Baked 128
Ribs
Beef Short. 99
Rice (see also Brown Rice)

Asparagus Rice Salad 83
Apple Rice Pudding. 190
Baked Rice 163
Best Ever Rice. 105
Breakfast Burrito 16
Brown Rice Yogurt Supreme 197
Cheesy Broccoli and
   Rice Casserole. 123
Chicken Fried Rice. 142
Cinnamon Raisin
   Rice Pudding. 198
Country Wild Rice Salad 89
Dijon Chicken and Rice 116
Fresh Sweet Pea and Rice Salad. 79
Garden Rice Salad 87
Holiday Chicken and Rice 110
Italian Basmati 168
Japonica Chicken Stir-Fry 118
Japonica Rice Ravioli 125
Lemon Pesto Rice 153
Mexican Rice 167
Raisin Brown Rice Muffins 71
Regal Basmati. 167
Rice Pilaf. 167
Rice Pilaf with Blue Cheese,
   Pears and Pecans 164
Rice Primavera 170
Rice Pudding 197
Rice Pudding with
   Pineapple Sauce 193
Salmon, Walnut Crusted with
   Herbed Rice 139
Smoked Turkey and Rice Loaf with
   Tomato Salsa 124
Smokey Rice Round 120
Spicy Rice and Cashews 170

Tuna and Rice Casserole 126
Turkey Sausage Pizza 126
Turmeric Rice Pilaf. 172
Vegetable Rice Bake. 157
Wild Rice Chicken Salad. 90
Wild Rice Pecan Salad 87
Wild Rice Salad with
   Cheesy Bruschetta. 86
Zucchini Rice Casserole 127
Risotto
   Asparagus. 166
   Curried with Sour Cherries 164
   Fresh Vegetable & Mushroom 154
   Holiday 165
   Smoked Chicken 122
Rolled Oats. 9
Rolls
   Quick 68
Roll-ups
   Apricot Chicken. 137
   Cheesy 20

S

Salad
   Asparagus Rice. 83
   Bean Salad 81
   Berry Spinach. 80
   Best Ever Chicken 85
   Black Bean 88
   Carrot 92
   Carrot Slaw. 80
   Chicken Couscous. 82
   Cinnamon Fruit 95
   Company Chicken Salad 93
   Country Wild Rice
      Chicken Salad. 90

Cranberry Cabbage Slaw 95
Creamy Cucumbers. 92
Festival 89
Fiesta Layered 90
Fresh Sweet Pea and Rice 79
Fruit Galore 78
Fruity Slaw 81
Garden Macaroni. 82
Garden Rice 87
Hawaiian 89
Honey Chicken 96
Jubilee. 86
Kentucky Potato. 79
Macaroni, Garden 82
Macaroni. 94
Mediterranean 88
Navy Bean and Turkey 84
Nine Day Cole Slaw 91
Pea. 93
Ramen Bok Choy. 94
Sauerkraut 91
Southwestern. 78
Spinach Orange. 92
Spring. 90
Summer 84
Tomato-Cucumber. 96
Truly a Meal Tuna. 85
Wild Rice 91
Wild Rice Pecan 87
Wild Rice Salad with
    Cheesy Bruschetta 86
Salmon
    and Zucchini Teriyaki 129
    Baked Salmon with
        Fruit Salsa 130
    Broiled Lemon Salmon 132

Creamy Dip 36
Deluxe Salmon Casserole 113
Garlic Lime Salmon 136
Lemon Garlic Salmon Kebabs 48
Poached Salmon with
    Lemon Herb Butter 111
Salmon Stuffed Eggs. 81
Walnut Crusted Salmon with
    Herbed Rice 139
    with Herbed Rice. 143
Salsa
    Corn, Black Bean and Cheddar 34
Sauce
    Tangy Cranberry 45
Sauerkraut
    Salad. 91
Scones
    Triple Fruit Almond. 68
Short Bread
    Scottish. 226
    Spiced. 221
Shortcake
    Strawberry 205
Slaw
    Cranberry Cabbage 96
    Fruity. 81
    · Nine-Day Cole. 91
Soufflé
    Chocolate 204
    Squash 166
Soup
    Beef Stew 51
    Black Bean 60
    Bobby's Chili with Creamy
        Vegetable Sauce 55
    Brown Rice and Mushroom. 56